C.S. Lewis vs t

C.S. Lewis vs the New Atheists

Peter S. Williams

Paternoster:
thinking faith

First published 2013 by Paternoster
Paternoster is an imprint of Authentic Media Limited
52 Presley Way, Crownhill, Milton Keynes, MK8 0ES
www.authenticmedia.co.uk

British Library Cataloguing in Publication Data

A catalogue record for this book is available from the
British Library

ISBN 978-1-84227-770-6

Cover design by David McNeill (www.revocreative.co.uk)

This book is dedicated to Dr Peter May

Contents

Good philosophy must exist, if for no other reason,
because bad philosophy needs to be answered.

C.S. *Lewis*, 'The Weight of Glory'

Foreword

This book shows the breadth, depth, and durability of Lewis's Christian apologetics. In his extraordinary body of work, Lewis gives an account of Christianity which is ethical, aesthetic, and rational – or, in other words, he argues that the faith once given to the saints is Good, Beautiful, and True. And he defends these qualities not because he believes in 'hypostatised abstract nouns', but because he believes that God is himself the source of all goodness, beauty, and truth, and, correlatively, because he believes that human beings, having been made in God's image, naturally want to share in those divine attributes. All of us, whether Christian or non-Christian, find in ourselves an urge (which is both a desire and a need) to be happy, attractive, and right. The very existence of this urge reveals how God meets us before we meet him. He is our Beginning and our End.

Apologetics is the explicating – or unfolding – of these matters in ways which have traction with unbelievers. But of course one cannot go on unfolding forever. Eventually, one will arrive at that which is simple, without folds. At the end of the day, to use Lewis's own terms, one will no longer be speaking a language made up of *master's metaphors* which can be rearranged to suit one's intellectual preferences, but will be speaking *pupil's metaphors*, living humbly and contentedly within the linguistic paradigm given by the One who is Ultimate Reality, the Master of all masters.

The distinction Lewis draws between magistral and pupillary metaphors is found in an extremely important but much overlooked article, entitled 'Bluspels and Flalansferes: A Semantic Nightmare' (in *Selected Literary Essays*). It is here also that he gives his clearest definition of those slippery terms 'reason' and 'imagination'. Reason, he says, is 'the natural organ of truth', imagination is 'the organ of meaning', and meaning itself is 'the antecedent condition both of truth and falsehood'. For Lewis, then, reason is necessarily imaginative because reason *cannot* operate without (imaginatively discerned) meaning. And imagination *ought not* to operate without reason because without reason imagination's products will be merely 'imaginary', containing no insights into truth or falsehood. Reason and imagination are mutually, if asymmetrically, informing.

It would therefore be a mistake to divide Lewis's various titles into two groups labelled on the one hand 'rational' and on the other hand 'imaginative'. In his view, a purely rational product is impossible and a purely imaginative product is undesirable. The division we should make is rather one between works that are 'less story-like' and works that are 'more story-like'. The less story-like works include *Mere Christianity*, *Miracles*, and *The Problem of Pain*: these are relatively impersonal, abstract, argumentative, propositional. The *more* story-like works are obviously titles such as *The Chronicles of Narnia*, *The Great Divorce*, and *The Ransom Trilogy*, which are personal, concrete, narrative, dramatic.

Although Lewis clearly values both the less story-like approach and the more story-like approach, he ranks them. The more story-like approach is the better way of trying to understand reality, he thinks, because Reality itself is more like a story than it is like an argument. History has a narrative shape and God himself is the supremely concrete Being, a Being who is not a proposition but a Person, indeed a dance or drama of Persons in that original and final simplicity which is the mystery of the Holy Trinity.

It is with this mystery, or a version thereof, that Lewis ends what he regarded as his best work, *Till We Have Faces*. The heroine of the story, Queen Orual, in the climactic scene, meets 'the god of the mountain', the One who has perplexed, tantalised and haunted her throughout the tale. Orual takes off her veil and as she does so finds that the god will at last meet her face to face. Orual says: 'I know now, Lord, why you utter no answer. You are yourself the answer. Before your face questions die away. What other answer would suffice? Only words, words; to be led out to battle against other words.'

It is good to pit words against other words, to battle out ideas and arguments in a keen encounter of wits. That is the right and proper task of apologetics, and it is demonstrated thoroughly and helpfully in this excellent volume. However, as Peter Williams reminds us at the end of the book, God is more than the conclusion of a syllogism; and philosophical analysis, though it may be necessary, is certainly not sufficient to the life of faith, hope and love.

When all is said and done, we want not analysis (things loosened into fragments and explained in other terms) but religion (things tied together into a Unity so perfect that it is self-explanatory). The babble of analytical words will fall silent before the Word himself as he brings peace to our moral action, peace to our aesthetic sense, peace to our intellectual understanding.

Dr Michael Ward, Senior Research Fellow, Blackfriards Hall,
Oxford

Author's Preface

Many thanks to commissioning editor Dr Mike Parsons for inviting me to rediscover C.S. Lewis, a formative influence originally introduced to me by my parents. Thank you, Mum and Dad, for reading the Narnia books to me as a child and lending me some of his apologetic writings as a teenager. Through Lewis you stoked the fires of both imagination and reason within me. Thanks are also due to copy editor Mollie Barker and production manager Peter Little, to Dr Mike Strickland for acting as a sounding board at the start of this pro-ject and to all those who have supported and encouraged me during the writing process. Finally, my gratitude goes to Revd Dr Michael Ward, author of *Planet Narnia: The Seven Heavens in the Imagination of C.S. Lewis* (Oxford University Press, 2008) – cf. www.planetnarnia.com/ – for honouring me with a foreword.

This book is about the most influential twentieth-century defender of the Christian faith, but it is dedicated to a friend whose ministry in 'persuasive evangelism' straddles the centuries: Dr Peter May (MRCS, LRCP, MRCGP). Dr May (1945-) studied medicine at The Royal Free Hospital in London, was a lay member of the General Synod of the Church of England from 1985 to 2010 and chaired the Universities and Colleges Christian Fellowship (www.uccf.org.uk/) from 2003 to 2010 (having been a staff worker in the mid 1970s). Since 2008 Dr May has partnered with Professor Keith Fox and myself in running the 'Reasonable Faith?' course at Highfield Church, Southampton (www.high field.org.uk/church/index.php?id=184). Soon after retiring from general practice (and while undergoing chemotherapy) Dr May chaired the committee, of which I was a member, organizing William Lane Craig's October 2011 Reasonable Faith Tour of

England (cf. www.bethinking.org/who-are-you-god/introduct-ory/audio-video-from-the-reasonable-faith-tour.htm). I'd like to take this opportunity to thank Dr May for the inspiration, fellowship, encouragement and opportunities he has given me, and to draw attention to some of his work in apologetics:

Audio

- Christian Persuader's Interview
  www.uccf.org.uk/download/cp-podcast-peter-may
- Peter May and John W. Loftus in Conversation, Part 1
  www.premierradio.org.uk/listen/ondemand.aspx?medi-aid={ED9F643A-3DBD-4A5F-8628-7F00E7624ED5} and Part II
  www.premierradio.org.uk/listen/ondemand.aspx?medi-aid={1CD5DAB8-2F2B-4176-9828-A54A430A36E7}
- Peter May and William Lane Craig – Tour Preview with Q&A
  www.premierradio.org.uk/listen/ondemand.aspx?medi-aid={BBBB39AC-EDFF-4991-8B12-DDD46E0CEED5}
- 'Reasonable Faith?' Course Audio Archive
  www.highfield.org.uk/church/index.php?id=469

Online papers

- 'The Atheist's Problem with Suffering' www.faithinterface
  .com.au/apologetics/the-atheist's-problem-with-suffering
- 'Avoiding the Circular Argument'
  www.faithinterface.com.au/apologetics/avoiding-the-circu-lar-argument
- Bethinking Papers
  www.bethinking.org/search/author/Peter%20May
- Christian Medical Fellowship Papers
  www.cmf.org.uk/publications/authors/?id=173&index=0
- 'Fine-Tuning the Multiverse Theory'
  www.faithinterface.com.au/science-christianity/fine-tuning-the-multiverse-theory
- 'Hawking Strikes Again'
  www.faithinterface.com.au/apologetics/hawking-strikes-again-dr-peter-may
- 'Responding to Goldilocks'
  www.faithinterface.com.au/science-christianity/responding-to-goldilocks

Printed works

- 'Claimed Contemporary Miracles', *Medico-Legal Journal* 71:4 (2003)
- *Dialogue in Evangelism* (Cambridge: Grove, 1990)
- 'The Faith Healing Claims of Morris Cerullo', *Free Inquiry* 14:1, Winter 1993/1994
- 'Focusing on the Eternal', in *Signs, Wonders and Healing: When Christians Disagree* (ed. John Goldingay; Leicester: IVP, 1989)
- (With Revd Dr Ernest Lucas) 'The Significance of Jesus' Healing Ministry', in *Christian Healing: What Can We Believe?* (ed. Ernest Lucas; London: Lynx, 1997)
- 'Something to Shout About?', Skeptic magazine, October 1991

Peter S. Williams
Southampton, January 2012

1.

Old-Time Atheism

Being an atheist is what's cool now.
Frank Skinner[1]

God's obituary appeared in *The Economist* magazine's millennium edition:

> After a lengthy career, the Almighty recently passed into history. Or did he?[2]

He didn't. Millennial rumours concerning the waning of belief in God were 'greatly exaggerated' (as Mark Twain said of the *New York Journal's* premature publication of *his* obituary). Indeed, in *God Is Back: How the Global Rise of Faith Is Changing the World* (Allen Lane, 2009), *Economist* editor John Micklethwait and Washington bureau chief Adrian Wooldridge acknowledged that 'God is returning to intellectual life.'[3] Dinesh D'Souza observes:

> The world is witnessing a huge explosion of religious conversion and growth, and Christianity is growing faster than any other religion. Nietzsche's proclamation 'God is Dead' is now proven false. Nietzsche is dead. The ranks of the unbelievers are shrinking as a proportion of the world's population . . . God is very much alive, and His future prospects look to be excellent. This is the biggest comeback story of the twenty-first century.[4]

Timothy Keller recalls: 'When I was in college . . . people looked at Europe and said, "See how secular Europe is getting, how unreligious people are? That's where all of humanity's going."

Except it's not working that way at all.'[5] As the *New Statesman* observed in 2010: 'A century ago, many progressives believed that religion was in steep decline. "Secularisation", they thought, was irreversible. Today, the situation looks rather different.'[6] Theologian Alister McGrath talks about the subsequent 'crisis of confidence which is gripping atheism'[7] at the moment. Likewise, David Fergusson observes that 'much modern atheism is . . . not merely dismissive of religion but angry and frustrated by its re-emergence as a powerful social force.'[8]

One can see this frustration in English philosopher A.C. Grayling's lament: 'One would have thought that by now the intellectual dinosaurs of superstition would have slunk away to die of their own absurdity.'[9] 'Never more than today,' complains French philosopher Michel Onfray, 'has there been such evidence of vitality in . . . religious thinking, proof that God is not dead but that he was merely and briefly dozing . . . The trend has escalated to such an extent that we are now obliged to take up old defensive positions.'[10] As D'Souza comments: 'The atheists thought they were winning, but now they realize that, far from dying quietly, religion is on the global upswing. So the atheists are striking back, using all the resources they can command.'[11]

Hence today's lively public conversation about God was, somewhat ironically, inaugurated by a loose confederacy of atheist writers who characteristically believe that 'religion is not only wrong; it's evil.'[12] These so-called 'new' or 'neo' atheists, members of what C.S. Lewis (1898-1963) once described as the 'bitter, truculant, sceptical, debunking, and cynical *intelligentsia'*,[13] display 'an enthusiastic advocation of atheism and a scathing criticism of both religious belief and cultural respect for religion.'[14] As Oxford philosopher Keith Ward observes:

> In the early twenty-first century atheism seems to have taken on a new lease of life. Buses in London carry the slogan: 'There's probably no God. Now stop worrying and enjoy your life.' A recent Christmas billboard in New York read 'You know it's a myth. This season, celebrate reason!' In the United States and in Britain there seems to be a concerted campaign to persuade people that atheism is the only reasonable form of belief. It is propagated by a group [whose] best-known evangelists are Richard Dawkins,

Christopher Hitchens, Sam Harris, and Daniel Dennett, though there are many others too.[15]

C.S. Lewis wouldn't have been at all surprised by the rise of 'the new atheism'. In a 1946 paper entitled 'The Decline of Religion' he declared:

> The present Christian movement may, or may not, have a long run ahead of it. But sooner or later it must lose the public ear . . . This mutability is the fate of all movements, fashions, intellectual climates and the like. But a Christian movement is also up against something sterner than the mere fickleness of taste. We have not yet had (at least in junior Oxford) any really bitter opposition. But if we have many more successes, this will certainly appear. The enemy has not yet thought it worth while to fling his whole weight against us. But he soon will. This happens in the history of every Christian movement, beginning with the Ministry of Christ Himself. At first it is welcome to all who have no special reason for opposing it: at this stage he who is not against it is for it. What men notice is its difference from those aspects of the World which they already dislike. But later on, as the real meaning of the Christian claim becomes apparent, its demand for total surrender, the sheer chasm between Nature and Supernature, men are increasingly 'offended'. Dislike, terror, and finally hatred succeed: none who will not give it what it asks (and it asks all) can endure it: all who are not with it are against it. This is why we must cherish no picture of the present intellectual movement simply growing and spreading and finally reclaiming millions by sweet reasonableness. Long before it became as important as that the real opposition would have begun . . . .[16]

An Oxford-Centric Debate

As Christopher Jervis (recipient of a Senior Farmington Fellowship at Oxford University) observes:

> Oxford has . . . been the focus for huge debates and controversies, often of a theological and religious nature . . . From 1942–1954 [C.S.]

Lewis . . . was President of the Oxford Socratic Club. There, each Monday evening of the term time, he would defend the Christian faith in the midst of those challenges presented by agnostics and atheists. Recently, those with a more atheistic agenda, quite overt – people like the chemist Professor Peter Atkins, the biologist Professor Richard Dawkins – have been very successful and vigorous in their campaign to support the creed of atheism. Equally, there are many leading academics here in Oxford who do believe in God, people who have argued persuasively and passionately for God's existence and the truth of the Christian faith.[17]

Oxford sits at the heart of contemporary debates about religion and irreligion because it is *the* academic powerhouse of the new atheism:

- Professor Peter Atkins is a Fellow and Professor of Chemistry at Lincoln College.
- Professor Richard Dawkins studied zoology at Balliol College and is an Emeritus Fellow of New College.
- Professor Daniel C. Dennett received his DPhil from Hertford College (under Gilbert Ryle).
- Professor A.C. Grayling received his DPhil from C.S. Lewis's old college, Magdalen (under the supervision of P.F. Strawson and A.J. Ayer). He remains a Supernumerary Fellow of St Anne's College.
- Christopher Hitchens (1949–2011) graduated from Balliol, where he obtained a third in PPE (Philosophy, Politics and Economics),[18] having 'utterly neglected the studies I was being subsidized by the taxpayers to pursue . . .'[19]

Indeed, among leading English-speaking neo-atheists, only American neuroscientist Sam Harris and American physicist Victor J. Stenger didn't study at Oxford (although Stenger has held two visiting positions on the faculty). On the other hand, as Jervis observes, several contemporary Christian critics of neo-atheism are likewise Oxford academics:

- Professor John C. Lennox – author of *God's Undertaker: Has Science Buried God?* (Lion, 2007); *God and Stephen Hawking:*

Whose Design Is It Anyway? (Lion, 2011) and *Gunning for God: A Critique of the New Atheism* (Lion, 2011) – is Fellow in Mathematics and the Philosophy of Science at Green Templeton College. Lennox received his first doctorate from Cambridge, where he attended C.S. Lewis's last lectures.

- Professor Alister E. McGrath – author of *Dawkins' God: Genes, Memes, and the Meaning of Life* (Blackwell, 2005); *The Dawkins Delusion* (SPCK, 2007) and *Why God Won't Go Away: Engaging with the New Atheism* (SPCK, 2011) – holds both a DPhil (in molecular biophysics) and a Doctor of Divinity degree from Oxford. A former president of Wycliffe Hall, McGrath is currently President of the Oxford Centre for Christian Apologetics.
- Professor Richard Swinburne – author of books including *The Existence of God* (Clarendon, 2004) and *Was Jesus God?* (Oxford University Press, 2008) – is Emeritus Nolloth Professor of the Philosophy of the Christian Religion, and Emeritus Fellow of Oriel College.
- Professor Keith Ward – author of *God, Chance and Necessity* (OneWorld, 1996); *Why There Almost Certainly Is a God: Doubting Dawkins* (Lion, 2008) and *The God Conclusion: God and the Western Philosophical Tradition* (Darton Longman and Todd, 2009) – holds a DD from Cambridge and a DD from Oxford (under Gilbert Ryle), where he was Regius Professor of Divinity (1991–2003).

Keith Ward consequently refers to 'the Oxford God debate.'[20]

Bitter Opposition

Let's consider another Oxford graduate, an atheist and one-time colleague of Professor Dawkins;[21] a man of letters who published as Clive Hamilton,[22] but whose friends knew him as 'Jack'. In his autobiography Jack recalls that, as a child, he 'was taught the usual things and made to say my prayers and in due time taken to church. I naturally accepted what I was told but I cannot remember feeling much interest in it.'[23] However, despite (or perhaps in part due to) his Protestant roots during 'the troubles' in Ireland, one of Jack's friends from prep school called him a 'foul

mouthed' and 'riotously amusing atheist.'[24] Indeed, Jack's brother felt that they both suffered from 'a deep-seated spiritual
illness of long standing – an illness that had its origins in our
childhood, in the dry husks of religion offered by the semi-polit-
ical church-going of Ulster.'[25] Jack's maternal grandfather, the
Revd Thomas Hamilton, would use sermons to accuse Catholics
of consorting with the devil![26] Jack called the Anglican Church he
was obliged to attend while at boarding school in England an
abode of 'Roman hypocrites and English liars.'[27]

Jack's childhood experience of religion is summarized by the following passage from his first, semi-autographical novel (Jack was,
like Richard Dawkins, a Fellow of the Royal Society of Literature):

> The Steward then took down from a peg a big card with small
> print all over it, and said, 'Here is a list of all the things the
> Landlord says you must not do. You'd better look at it.' So John
> took the card: but half the rules seemed to forbid things he had
> never heard of, and the other half forbade things he was doing
> every day and could not imagine not doing: and the number of
> rules was so enormous that he felt he could never remember them
> all. 'I hope,' said the Steward, 'that you have not already broken
> any of the rules?' John's heart began to thump, and his eyes
> bulged more and more, and he was at his wit's end when the
> Steward took the mask off and looked at John with his real face
> and said, 'Better tell a lie, old chap, better tell a lie. Easiest for all
> concerned,' and popped the mask on his face all in a flash. John
> gulped and said quickly, 'Oh, no, sir.' 'That is just as well,' said the
> Steward through the mask. 'Because, you know, if you do break
> any of them and the Landlord got to know of it . . . He'd take you
> and shut you up for ever and ever in a black hole full of snakes
> and scorpions as large as lobsters – for ever and ever. And besides
> that, he is such a kind, good man, so very, very kind, that I am sure
> you would never *want* to displease him.'[28]

Another nail in the coffin of his childhood faith was undoubtedly the death of his mother:

> There came a night when I was ill and crying both with a headache
> and toothache and distressed because my mother did not come to me.

That was because she was ill too; and what was odd was that there were several doctors in her room, and voices, and comings and goings all over the house and doors shutting and opening. It seemed to last for hours. And then my father, in tears, came into my room and began to try to convey to my terrified mind things it had never conceived before. It was in fact cancer . . . My father never fully recovered from this loss . . . With my mother's death all settled happiness, all that was tranquil and reliable, disappeared from my life . . . It was sea and islands now; the great continent had sunk like Atlantis.[29]

Jack's prayers for his mother went unanswered:

When her case was pronounced helpless I remembered what I had been taught; that prayers offered in faith would be granted. I accordingly set myself to produce by will-power a firm belief that my prayers for her recovery would be successful; and, as I thought, I achieved it. When nevertheless she died I shifted my ground and worked myself into a belief that there was to be a miracle. The interesting thing is that my disappointment produced no results beyond itself. The thing hadn't worked, but I was used to things not working, and I thought no more about it.[30]

Jack continued to struggle with prayer into his teens:

I had been told as a child that one must not only say one's prayers but think about what one was saying . . . I tried to put this into practice. At first it seemed plain sailing. But soon the false conscience . . . came into play. One had no sooner reached 'Amen' than it whispered, 'Yes. But are you sure you were really thinking about what you said?'; then, more subtly, 'Were you, for example, thinking about it as well as you did last night?' The answer . . . was nearly always No. 'Very well,' said the voice, 'hadn't you, then, better try it over again?' And one obeyed it; but of course with no assurance that the second attempt would be any better.[31]

Jack had set himself a standard whereby:

No clause of my prayer was to be allowed to pass muster unless it was accompanied by . . . a certain vividness of the imagination and the affections. My nightly task was to produce by sheer will-power a phenomenon which will-power could never produce, which was so ill-defined that I could never say with absolute confidence whether it had occurred . . . This was a burden from which I longed with soul and body to escape. It had already brought me to such a pass that the nightly torment projected its gloom over the whole evening, and I dreaded bedtime.[32]

He would later observe: 'the trouble about God is that he is like a person who never acknowledges one's letters and so, in time, one comes to the conclusion either that he does not exist or that you have got the address wrong.'[33]

Before going to Oxford, Jack spent three years under the tutelage of former school headmaster William T. Kirkpatrick, 'a staunch rationalist and atheist'.[34] Jack recounts that 'if ever a man came near to being a purely logical entity, that man was Kirk. Born a little later, he would have been a Logical Positivist . . . he had been a Presbyterian and was now an Atheist . . . a "rationalist" of the old, high and dry nineteenth-century type.'[35] Partly due to Kirk's influence, Jack added additional reasons to his experiential motives for unbelief, noting to a religious friend: 'You take too many things for granted. You can't start with God. *I don't accept God!*'[36] As biographer David C. Downing reports:

> Jack's adolescent atheism was further reinforced by his reading of the natural and social sciences. From the former he gained a sense that life on earth was just a random occurrence in a vast, empty universe, that all of human history is no more than a teardrop on the vast ocean of eternity. From the latter he concluded that all the world's religions, including Christianity, could be best explained not as claims to truth, but as expressions of psychological needs and cultural values.[37]

Jack explained:

> my early reading . . . had lodged very firmly in my imagination the vastness and cold of space, the littleness of Man. It is not strange that I should feel the universe to be a menacing and unfriendly

place. Several years before I read Lucretius I felt the force of his argument (and it is surely the strongest of all) for atheism . . .

> *Had God designed the world, it would not be*
> *A world so frail and faulty as we see*

. . . And so, little by little, with fluctuations which I cannot now trace, I became an apostate, dropping my faith with no sense of loss but with the greatest relief.[38]

Jack wrote in a letter to a friend:

> You ask me about my religious views: you know, I think, that I believe in no religion. There is absolutely no proof for any of them, and from a philosophical standpoint Christianity is not even the best. All religions, that is, all mythologies to give them their proper name, are merely man's own invention – Christ as much as Loki. Primitive man found himself surrounded by all sorts of terrible things he didn't understand – thunder, pestilence, snakes etc: what more natural than to suppose that these were animated by evil spirits trying to torture him. These he kept off by cringing to them, singing songs and making sacrifices etc. Gradually from being mere nature-spirits these supposed being[s] were elevated into more elaborate ideas, such as the old gods: and when man became more refined he pretended that these spirits were good as well as powerful.[39]

He extended this evolutionary explanation to Christianity: 'after the death of a Hebrew philosopher Yeshua (whose name we have corrupted into Jesus) he became regarded as a god, a cult sprang up, which was afterwards connected with the ancient Hebrew Jahweh-worship, and so Christianity came into being – one mythology among many, but the one we happen to have been brought up in . . .'[40]

By the time he arrived at Oxford Jack had adopted an atheistic outlook of 'Stoical Monism'[41] influenced by his reading of thinkers such as Lucretius, James Frazer, David Hume, Bertrand Russell, Arthur Schopenhauer and H.G. Wells. Having seen active service in the British army, Jack proudly observed that he 'never sank so low as to pray'[42] during combat. With a turn of phrase reminiscent of Christopher Hitchens, Jack affirmed: 'I am

quite content to live without believing in a bogey who is prepared to torture me forever and ever if I should fail in coming to
an almost impossible ideal.'[43]

Surprised by Jack

Jack endorsed many of the anti-religious complaints one hears
today from the so-called 'new atheists' *even though he died in 1963.*
Jack's personal experience of church was of a hypocritical, dead
religious institution embroiled in politics and connected to verbal
abuse and physical violence. His personal experience of religion
was pragmatically fruitless and psychologically oppressive. He
finally broke free from his childhood indoctrination by reading
the natural and social sciences, as well as the work of sceptical
philosophers: 'I then began Hume: and greatly enjoyed the perfect clarity, ease, humanity and quietness of his manner. This is
the proper way to write philosophy.'[44] For Jack, the natural sciences explained away the obvious appearance of design in the
world, revealing that life was in fact the unintended result of
physical laws and chance acting over time: 'a meaningless dance
of atoms.'[45] Hence Jack wrote of a female acquaintance: 'Valerie is
prettier than ever: but the knowledge of this fact is rapidly spoil-
ing her . . . she has adopted . . . all those provocative little
mannerisms which underline the fact that *blind nature made her for
one purpose.*'[46] As Richard Dawkins says: 'We are machines for
propagating DNA . . . It is every living object's sole reason for living.'[47] Jack recounts the following conversation about evolution:
'Maureen . . . asked me if the evolutionary theory meant that we
had come from monkeys. I explained what it really meant. She
asked me where Adam and Eve came in. I explained that the
Biblical and scientific accounts were alternatives. She asked me
which I believed. I said the scientific.'[48]

While the natural sciences did away with divine design to
Jack's satisfaction, the social sciences explained away religion as
the product of primitive psychology and social evolution. In a
phrase typical of the new atheism Jack defined religious beliefs as
mythologies that have 'absolutely no proof',[49] and which spring
from wishful thinking prompted by primitive fears of natural

forces that can now be understood through science. Christianity arose when divinity was foisted upon a Jewish philosopher long after the fact, a cultic variation upon a common evolutionary theme with no more rational justification than any other religious tradition into which one might happen to be born:

> The accepted position seemed to be that religions were normally a mere farrago of nonsense, though our own, by a fortunate exception, was exactly true . . . the impression I got was that religion in general, though utterly false, was a natural growth, a kind of endemic nonsense into which humanity tended to blunder. In the midst of a thousand such religions stood our own, the thousand and first, labeled True. But on what grounds could I believe in this exception? It obviously was in some general sense the same kind of thing as all the rest. Why was it so differently treated? Need I, at any rate, continue to treat it differently?[50]

Hence, as (classical) atheist Richard Norman comments, it would appear that 'the "New Atheism" is not really new. Its distinctive themes – religion as the enemy of science, of progress and of an enlightened morality – are in a direct line of descent from the 18th-century enlightenment and 19th-century rationalism. The "new" movement is better seen as a revival . . .'[51] Hence Rabbi Moshe Averick's cheeky response to the new atheism: 'Wouldn't it have been simpler to reprint Bertrand Russell's succinct essay, "Why I Am Not A [Christian]," and have been done with it?'[52]

As well as being someone whose atheistic views prefigured much that characterizes the new atheism, *Jack is one and the same person as C.S. Lewis*, 'without doubt the most popular Christian apologist internationally in the twentieth century.'[53] Best known for his literary Planets suite for children, *The Chronicles of Narnia*,[54] Lewis is also the author of many books and essays advocating 'mere' Christianity. In 1947 a *Time* magazine cover story hailed Lewis as 'one of the most influential spokesmen for Christianity in the English-speaking world.'[55] Lewis's influence has only grown in the intervening years. Biographer A.N. Wilson recalls:

> One old don, a fellow of Magdalen in those days, once advanced to me the preposterous notion that Lewis was 'the most evil man

he had ever met'. On further inquiry, it transpired that what this man meant was that he could not share Lewis's religious opinions. 'Using his cleverness to corrupt the young', he called it – a criticism which, it occurred to me, had been levelled at Socrates.[56]

Backhanded Compliments

Perhaps because he understands their frustrations with religion from the inside out, today's 'new atheists' can't help paying backhanded compliments to C.S. Lewis, even as they attempt to smother his legacy. For example, Lewis is name-checked by Richard Dawkins in the preface to the paperback edition of *The God Delusion*: '"I *used* to be an atheist, BUT . . ." That is one of the oldest tricks in the book, much favoured by religious apologists from C.S. Lewis to the present day. It serves to establish some sort of street cred up front, and it is amazing how often it works. Look out for it.'[57]

Dawkins says the phrase 'I used to be an atheist, BUT . . .' is a trick, but he doesn't say what the trick is supposed to be (or why Dawkins isn't pulling the same trick when he describes his own mid-teens de-conversion). One presumes Dawkins isn't saying that everyone who self-describes as an atheist-turned-Christian (e.g. Mortimer J. Adler,[58] Charles Colson,[59] Francis S. Collins,[60] William Lane Craig,[61] C.E.M. Joad,[62] Christopher Hitchens' brother Peter Hitchens,[63] Peter Van Inwagen,[64] Alister McGrath,[65] Anne Rice,[66] Lee Strobel,[67] Fay Weldon[68] or A.N. Wilson[69]) is lying! It is clear from Lewis's private and public writings, as well as the testimony of friends and family, that he was indeed an atheist who became first a theist and then a Christian. But what else could Dawkins mean?

The testimony of someone who says 'I used to be an atheist, BUT . . .' certainly gains a certain rhetorical force (it bolsters their *ethos*); but isn't this because we are right to set more store by the testimony of someone who has been convinced of something *against their prior inclinations*? Dawkins complains that 'dyed-in-the-wool faith-heads are immune to argument, their resistance built up over years of childhood indoctrination using methods [such as issuing] a dire warning to avoid even opening a book like [*The God Delusion*], which is surely a work of Satan.'[70] Hence, anyone who can honestly claim 'I used to be an atheist, BUT . . .' sidesteps Dawkins' trick of caricaturing religious believers as 'faith-heads' whose rational faculties have been overwhelmed by their 'childhood indoctrination'. Moreover, in Dawkins' view, anyone who is 'open-minded', whose 'childhood indoctrination was not too insidious . . . or whose native intelligence is strong enough to overcome it', will 'need only a little encouragement to break free of the vice of religion altogether.'[71] Hence C.S. Lewis transcends Dawkins' 'faith-head' stereotype twice over. Having been raised in a Christian home, Lewis abandoned his childhood beliefs at school. Dawkins would presumably conclude that Lewis's childhood indoctrination 'was not too insidious', or else that his 'native intelligence' was strong enough to overcome it. In either case, Lewis's adult conversion to theism (in 1929) and his subsequent conversion to Christianity (in 1931) naturally gain a measure of testimonial kudos. The trick doesn't lie with those who can report 'I used to be an atheist, BUT . . .' Rather, it lies with those (like Dawkins) who attempt to 'poison the well' against anyone who can say 'I used to be an atheist, BUT . . .'! Indeed, as Dawkins once said during an interview with Alister McGrath: 'Alister, for an apologist for religion to be able to say that you once were an atheist gives you a certain amount of street cred that not everybody can boast.'[72]

Not Some Weak-Tea Christian

> He was that hateful anomaly, the wrong sort of scientist.
> *C.S. Lewis*, That Hideous Strength[73]

In the course of discussing the career-ending remarks of one noted scientist, neo-atheist Sam Harris launches an astonishing attack upon another:

> James Watson, the co-discoverer of the structure of DNA, a Nobel laureate, and the original head of the Human Genome Project, recently [asserted] in an interview that people of African descent appear to be innately less intelligent than white Europeans. A few

sentences, spoken off the cuff, resulted in academic defenestration
. . . Watson's opinions on race are disturbing, but his underlying
point was not, in principle, unscientific . . . there is, at least, a *possible* scientific basis for his views. While Watson's statement was
obnoxious, one cannot say that his views are utterly irrational or
that, by merely giving voice to them, he has repudiated the scientific worldview and declared himself immune to its further discoveries. Such a distinction would have to be reserved for
Watson's successor at the Human Genome Project, Dr. Francis
Collins.[74]

Professor Henry F. Schaefer (five-time Nobel Prize nominee and
recipient of the Centenary Medal) writes that 'Francis Collins is
one of the most outstanding research biologists of our generation',[75] while Nobel laureate William D. Phillips calls Collins 'one
of the world's most distinguished scientists.'[76] Indeed, Sam
Harris writes: 'Collins is currently the director of the National
Institute of Health, having been appointed to the post by
President Obama. One must admit that his credentials were
impeccable: he is a physical chemist, a medical geneticist, and the
former head of the Human Genome Project.'[77] However, Collins
is also an adult convert to Christianity; and Harris is deeply disturbed to see *a scientist who believes that Christianity is true* (what
is the world coming to?!) set loose to run the NIH. Harris's distress comes across very clearly in an interview with *New
Statesman*:

> Why, if atheism is the world-view that best accords with the scientific evidence, do so many intelligent people persist in faith?
> For Harris, this can be explained only as a 'failure of intellectual
> honesty'. He is particularly scathing about Collins. 'There's
> something repugnant about the fact that he [is a Christian] and
> one of the most prominent and influential representatives of science in the United States,' he says. 'And he's not some weak-tea Christian – he thinks the dead will walk again and will be
> remade out of new matter. And not only that, he doesn't keep
> those crazy convictions private. He publishes on the mutually
> reinforcing character of those two world-views [science and religion].'[78]

Thus the implication of Harris's comparison of Collins with Watson becomes crystal clear: *Christianity is an intellectually substandard opinion when compared to racism!*

In *The Language of God: A Scientist Presents Evidence for Belief* (Free Press, 2006) Francis Collins describes how he was prompted to investigate the God question by the faith of patients he met as a medical student: 'I was confident that a full investigation of the rational basis for faith would deny the merits of belief, and reaffirm my atheism. But I determined to have a look at the facts, no matter what the outcome.'[79] Harris notes the prominent role in Collins' conversion played by C.S. Lewis: 'Collins' uncertainty about the identity of God could not survive a collision with C.S. Lewis.'[80] Collins explains that, having worked his way through an investigation of various major religions, he:

> doubted that there was any rational basis for spiritual belief undergirding any of these faiths. However, that soon changed. I went to visit a Methodist minister . . . to ask him whether faith made any logical sense. He listened patiently to my confused (and probably blasphemous) ramblings, and then took a small book off his shelf and suggested I read it. The book was *Mere Christianity* by C.S. Lewis.[81]

Collins recalls:

> in the next few days, as I turned its pages, struggling to absorb the breadth and depth of the intellectual arguments laid down by this legendary Oxford scholar, I realized that all of my own constructs against the plausibility of faith were those of a schoolboy . . . Lewis seemed to know all of my objections, sometimes even before I had quite formulated them. He invariably addressed them within a page or two.[82]

He reflects: 'When I learned subsequently that Lewis had himself been an atheist, who had set out to disprove faith on the basis of logical argument, I recognized how he could be so insightful about my path. It had been his path as well.'[83] Collins was particularly impressed by Lewis's defence of the moral argument for God, a topic to which we will return in a later chapter.

Like Sam Harris, neo-atheist Victor J. Stenger laments that 'Collins himself . . . tells us that his conversion from atheism to Christianity came from essentially one source – the writings of C.S. Lewis.'[84] Stenger goes on to suggest that Collins 'would have done better to refer to the latest literature on cosmology and evolutionary psychology, and to consult theological sources besides an author of children's literature. While a favourite among evangelical Christians, Lewis is not highly regarded today by either theologians or philosophers.'[85]

This characterization of Lewis as 'an author of children's literature' is of course a fact carefully selected and presented out of context in order to undermine both Lewis and Collins. While we can't dismiss the possibility that good grounds for theism might be given by 'an author of children's literature', it would appear that anyone who forms their metaphysical beliefs wholly on the basis of reading 'an author of children's literature' is casting their net in shallower metaphysical waters than wisdom dictates. So, are Collins' metaphysical beliefs analogous to those of an atheist who has only read the anti-religious works of a chemist (e.g. Peter Atkins), or a zoologist (e.g. Richard Dawkins), or a journalist (e.g. Christopher Hitchens), rather than of someone schooled in the philosophy of religion? Not at all, as becomes apparent when we ask why Stenger thinks it matters that 'an author of children's literature' is 'not highly regarded' by theologians and philosophers. After all, I dare say many theologians and philosophers aren't highly regarded by writers of children's literature! The subtext here is of course that Lewis was *not merely* 'an author of children's literature'. Rather, he was an Oxbridge don (Lewis ended his career teaching at Cambridge) who combined his day-job with a career as the twentieth-century's most influential intellectual advocate of Christian belief. Lewis was 'one of only a handful of people ever to earn three Firsts at Oxford . . .'[86] Oxford gave Lewis 'a liberal arts education, including the study of the classics, philosophy [including logic], history, and English language and literature.'[87] As Oxford philosopher Basil Mitchell observes: 'He'd read Greats, he'd taught philosophy for a while [lecturing on moral philosophy], he was well acquainted with the philosophical classics . . .'[88] Lewis continued to tutor philosophy students as a professor at Magdalen College: 'Lewis had to be always ready to "fill in" with a philosophy tutorial or lecture if required. Of the sixteen pupils Lewis had in 1926 only five were reading English.[89] In the mid 1920s Lewis regularly attended the University Philosophical Society, where he held his own among distinguished philosophical colleagues including E.F. Carritt, A.C. Ewing and W.D. Ross. Lewis can hardly be dismissed as merely 'an author of children's literature'!

Lewis in the Limelight

Stenger's dismissal of Lewis as 'a favourite among evangelical Christians' but 'not highly regarded today by either theologians or philosophers'[90] denies the existence of evangelical Christians *who are theologians and philosophers*! Noted philosopher Thomas V. Morris testifies: 'I for one became a philosopher in part because of the influence of C.S. Lewis. He was a vivid role model and a potent stimulus that set me out on the very first steps of a great adventure.'[91] Likewise, C. Stephen Layman 'read most of the works of C.S. Lewis' at college and comments: 'I think this experience is one of the deep roots of my love of philosophy.'[92] My own interest in philosophy was greatly stimulated by reading Lewis as a teenager.

Lewis isn't necessarily a 'favourite' of evangelical scholars. Philosopher Norman L. Geisler describes Lewis as 'arguably the most influential twentieth-century Christian theist and apologist' who 'so expressed profound truths in simple language that he reached into the hearts of millions'[93] and whose 'insight into the essentials of theism made him a significant apologist and communicator.'[94] Nevertheless, as an evangelical from the more 'conservative' end of the spectrum, Geisler criticizes Lewis for denying the literal occurrence of certain Old Testament miracles, for accepting certain ideas of higher biblical criticism, and for not publically rejecting evolution. The noted Oxford philosopher Basil Mitchell (1917–2011) said that Lewis:

> had the sort of mind which, had he addressed himself to the questions that engrossed philosophers of the time [i.e. linguistic analysis], would have made him into a good philosopher by

professional standards – but he simply wasn't 'one of the club', so to speak . . . I mean, he produced some good searching arguments and clearly had a feeling for what was philosophically interesting and what wasn't, but he didn't go into questions with the kind of meticulous care that was particularly characteristic of the philosophers of that period . . .[95]

Victor Reppert's assessment of Lewis takes a similar line:

Lewis was a thinker with what I believe to be outstanding philosophical instincts. And if he was in error in his thinking, there was usually a little more method in his madness than what would appear to someone who just gives a 'refutation' to the error and leaves it at that. And this, I think, is the real test of a great thinker. But while Lewis' arguments are suggestive, interesting and in my view often sound, he does not answer every question that a critic might ask . . . And it would be rather surprising if a popular apologist with philosophical training from the 1920's could do this for the benefit of people living [today].[96]

In his monumental study of Lewis's philosophical thoughts Adam Barkman concludes that 'while acknowledging some of Lewis' imprecisions as a philosopher . . . I would not hesitate to call Lewis a noteworthy philosopher and one well worth studying.'[97] Thus, while many evangelicals respect Lewis, those who are also members of the scholarly community (of whom there are many) don't appear to favour him in an uncritical manner (I myself, it should be noted, sometimes disagree with Lewis).

Moreover, *The Cambridge Companion to C.S. Lewis* (Cambridge University Press, 2010) notes that 'those who regard his thought as valuable and interesting can be found across the theological spectrum, including British and North American Anglicans, Roman Catholics and Eastern Orthodox.'[98] Lewis himself reported receiving letters 'from Jesuits, monks, nuns, and also from Quakers and Welsh Dissenters, and so on.'[99] As Richard Harris writes: 'people see in Lewis what must, on any historical view, be called mainstream Christianity. He is read equally by Roman Catholics and Evangelicals, Anglicans and Presbyterians, Methodists and Lutherans. Christians of all persuasions see in him the central tenets of historic Christianity.'[100] Thus Catholic philosopher Richard Purtill writes: 'I find both Lewis and his case for the Christian faith worthy of respect.'[101] Catholic philosopher Peter Van Inwagen recalls that as an atheist graduate student:

> I began to read the apologetic work of C.S. Lewis . . . I recognized him as a master of expository prose and thought – rightly – that I could learn a great deal from him about the art of expressing a line of argument in English. Like many other people, I first discovered what Christianity *was* from reading Lewis . . . I saw that Christianity was a serious thing and intellectually at a very high level. (I was thinking, of course, in terms of propositions and distinctions and arguments.)[102]

Not that the only intellectuals to take Lewis seriously are Christians. British moral philosopher Mary Midgely (who became acquainted with Lewis while studying at Oxford in the late 1930s and early 1940s) states: 'I am very fond of C.S. Lewis . . . Lewis doesn't get out of date. Like a good wine, he improves with time . . . I constantly find him relevant & useful.'[103] In 1997 Midgely declared that she 'very much liked *The Abolition of Man'*, praising Lewis's 1943 Riddell Lectures attacking subjectivism as 'first-rate – I wish I'd known about it earlier . . . I never expected the clear, balanced answer to current mistakes that it actually contains.'[104] In the course of accounting for his own conversion to Christianity the Oxford philosopher C.E.M. Joad noted: 'There is a book by C.S. Lewis, *The Abolition of Man*, which played no small part in preparing my change of view and in precipitating the new outlook which it involved . . .'[105] *The Abolition of Man* was voted the seventh most important work of non-fiction of the past century in a *National Review* poll (Lewis's *Mere Christianity* also appeared, in twenty-sixth place).[106]

Terry L. Miethe notes that what George Sayer called Lewis's 'most philosophical and most carefully considered'[107] work, *Miracles*, 'has become a classic in our time and is still considered one of the finest on the subject, even by some agnostic philosophers.'[108] Jerry L. Walls notes that Lewis's 'popular works were engaged by academic philosophers looking for Christian dialogue partners. For instance, in the landmark volume *New Essays in Philosophical Theology*, published in 1955, it is Lewis whom Antony Flew takes as one of his targets.[109] Flew (1923–2010), 'a legendary British philosopher and atheist [who was] an icon and champion for unbelievers for decades',[110] described Lewis as 'a distinguished apologist'[111] in his classic 1966 work *God and Philosophy*.

Flew publically renounced atheism after concluding in 2004 that 'the case for an Aristotelian God who has the characteristics of power, and also intelligence, is now much stronger than it ever was before.'[112] In *There Is a God* (HarperOne, 2007) Flew recollects being 'a regular participant' in the Oxford Socratic Club, of which Lewis was the 'redoubtable president from 1942 to 1954'.[113] Flew describes the club as 'a lively forum for debates between atheists and Christians'[114] and recalls how 'many of the leading atheists at Oxford locked horns with Lewis and his fellow Christians.'[115] Indeed, many notable figures presented or responded to papers at the Socratic Club, including: G.E.M. Anscombe, J.L. Austin, A.J. Ayer, F.C. Copleston, I.M. Crombie, A.C. Ewing, Austin Farrer, J.B.S. Haldane, R.M. Hare, C.E.M. Joad, H.D. Lewis, Gabriel Marcel, E.L. Mascall, Basil Mitchell, Iris Murdoch, Michael Polanyi, H.H. Price, Gilbert Ryle, Dorothy L. Sayers, Bernard Williams and John Wisdom. As Walls comments: 'it is particularly significant that several speakers at the Socratic Club were prominent philosophers, including some notable atheists. As president, Lewis was typically expected to provide a rejoinder to the main speaker, and it was in this role that he gained a reputation as a formidable debater.'[116] Flew notes that 'the first and only paper I ever read to the Socratic club' was his famous paper on 'Theology and Falsification'.[117] He states: 'I thought that Lewis was a fine man . . . Lewis's contributions would always be relevant and to the point. He was a first class thinker.'[118] Flew also pays Lewis the following compliment:

> Lewis was the most effective Christian apologist for certainly the latter part of the twentieth century. When the BBC recently asked if I had absolutely refuted Lewis's Christian apologetic, I replied: 'No. I just didn't believe there was sufficient reason for believing it. But of course when I later came to think about theological things, it seemed to me that the case for the Christian

revelation is a very strong one, if you believe in any revelation at all.'[119]

Stenger's breezy dismissal of Lewis as 'an author of children's literature' is economical with the truth.

Conclusion

As Thomas D. Williams writes: 'Though their arguments are not new, the neo-atheists require a reasoned response. If nothing else, their very popularity means that many people are exposed to the objections they raise, without necessarily hearing the other side of the story.'[120] C.S. Lewis is an obvious intellectual counterfoil to the 'new atheism'. For one thing, it's partly under the influence of professors with whom Lewis rubbed shoulders (e.g. A.J. Ayer, Gilbert Ryle, P.F. Strawson) that today's Oxford-centric 'new atheists' continue to espouse many views that Lewis held when he was himself an atheist. For another, although Lewis only just scrapes into Daniel Dennett's *Breaking the Spell* (in the form of a quotation from *Mere Christianity* that introduces chapter seven), the 'new atheist' movement as a whole clearly acknowledges Lewis as an influential Christian voice of continuing relevance. In *God Is Not Great* (Atlantic Books, 2007) Christopher Hitchens goes so far as to dub Lewis 'the main chosen propaganda vehicle for Christianity in our time.'[121] As Midgely says: 'Lewis doesn't get out of date. Like a good wine, he improves with time . . .'[122]

Lewis gradually moved away from a brand of anti-theism not unlike the 'new atheism', eventually rediscovering the Christian faith of his childhood, albeit in a far from childish (or straightforward) manner: 'my own progress has been from "popular realism" [i.e. materialism] to Philosophical Idealism; from Idealism to Pantheism; from Pantheism to Theism; and from Theism to Christianity.'[123] In literary company with Lewis, this book will place the central arguments that led him from atheism to Christ into a contemporary dialogue with the new atheists. For as Philip Vander Elst writes, the life and work of C.S. Lewis is 'the perfect antidote to the spirit of "scientific" rationalism and humanism which has so dominated the twentieth century and which is incarnated in the works of men like Bertrand Russell, H.G. Wells, and their successors today.'[124]

* * *

Recommended Resources

By C.S. Lewis:
The Pilgrim's Regress (London: Fount, 3rd edn, 1977)
Surprised by Joy (London: Fount, 1998)

Video

Berlinski, David. 'The Devil's Delusion: Atheism and Its Scientific Pretensions'
http://booktv.org/Watch/9256/The+Devils+Delusion+Atheism+And+Its+Scientific+Pretensions.aspx.
Craig, William Lane. 'Is God a Delusion?' www.reasonable-faith.org/site/News2?page=NewsArticle&id=9183.
(DVD) Jervis, Christopher, John Lennox, Alister McGrath and Keith Ward. *Philosophy, Science and the God Debate* (The Nationwide Christian Trust, 2011).
Ward, Keith. 'Philosophy and the New Atheism'
https://publicchristianity.org/library/atheism-philosophy-science-and-belief.
Williams, Peter S. 'Five Flaws in the Thinking of New Atheists'
www.highfieldschurch.org.uk/media/high-five/new-atheists.

Audio

Craig, William Lane. 'The Arguments for God's Existence and Critique of the New Atheists'
www.rfmedia.org/av/audio/gracepoint-gods-existence-and-critique-of-new-atheists/.
—'Response to Richard Dawkins' Book *The God Delusion*'
www.rfmedia.org/RF_audio_video/Other_clips/UF-

Responding-to-Dawkins-The-God-Delusion/UF_Bill_Craig_s_Response_to_The_God_Delusion.mp3.
— 'Thoughts on Sam Harris' Claims'
www.rfmedia.org/RF_audio_video/Other_clips/Thoughts-on-Sam-Harris-claims.mp3.
Williams, Peter S. 'A Sceptic's Guide to the New Atheism' (King's Community Church, 2011) www.damaris.org/cm/podcasts/578.
— 'The New Atheism' (Belgrade University, 2012) www.damaris.org/ cm/podcasts/763.

Online papers

Hazen, Craig J. 'My Pilgrimage from Atheism to Theism: An Exclusive Interview with Former British Atheist Professor Antony Flew' www.biola.edu/antonyflew/.
Plantinga, Alvin. 'The Dawkins Confusion' www.christianitytoday.com/bc/2007/002/1.21.html.
Roberts, Mark. '*God Is Not Great* by Christopher Hitchens: A Response' www.markdroberts.com/htmfiles/resources/godisnotgreat.htm.
Swinburne, Richard. 'Response to Dawkins' *The God Delusion*' http://users.ox.ac.uk/~orie0087/pdf_files/Responses%20to%20Controversies/Response%20to%20Dawkins%27%20The%20God%20Delusion%20(revised)_copy(1).pdf.
Williams, Peter S. 'A.C. Grayling's *The Good Book: A Secular Bible*' www.bethinking.org/right-wrong/intermediate/a-c-graylings-the-good-book-a-secular-bible.htm.
– 'The Big Bad Wolf, Theism and the Foundations of Intelligent Design Theory' http://epsociety.org/library/articles.asp?pid=53.
— 'A Change of Mind for Antony Flew' www.bethinking.org/science-christianity/intermediate/a-change-of-mind-for-antony-flew.htm.
— 'A Christian Response to *Against All Gods*. Part One: Intellectual Respectability' www.bethinking.org/resource.php?ID=385.
— 'A Christian Response to *Against All Gods*. Part Two: Ethical Respectability' www.bethinking.org/resource.php?ID=392.
— 'Darwin's Rottweiler and the Public Understanding of Scientism'

www.bethinking.org/science-christianity/intermediate/darwins-rottweiler-and-the-public-understanding.htm.
— 'The Faith-Based Dawkins'
www.bethinking.org/science-christianity/intermediate/the-faith-based-dawkins.htm.
—'Who's Afraid of the Big Bad Wolf?'
www.damaris.org/content/content.php?type=5&id=501.
— 'Who's Afraid of the Big Bad Wolf? Richard Dawkins' Failed Rebuttal of Natural Theology'
www.arn.org/docs/williams/pw_goddelusionreview2.htm.

Books

Baggett, David, Gary R. Habermas and Jerry L. Walls, eds. C.S. *Lewis as Philosopher: Truth, Goodness and Beauty* (Downers Grove, IL: IVP Academic, 2008).

Berlinski, David. *The Devil's Delusion: Atheism and Its Scientific Pretensions* (New York: Crown Forum, 2008).

Collins, Francis S. *The Language of God: A Scientist Presents Evidence for Belief* (New York: Free Press, 2006).

Downing, David C. *The Most Reluctant Convert: C.S. Lewis's Journey to Faith* (Downers Grove, IL: IVP, 2002).

Flew, Antony and Roy Abraham Varghese. *There Is a God* (London: HarperOne, 2009).

Lennox, John C. *God and Stephen Hawking: Whose Design Is It Anyway?* (Oxford: Lion, 2011).

— *God's Undertaker: Has Science Buried God?* (Oxford: Lion, 2007).

— *Gunning for God: A Critique of the New Atheism* (Oxford: Lion, 2011).

MacSwain, Robert, ed. *The Cambridge Companion to C.S. Lewis* (Cambridge University Press, 2010).

McGrath, Alister. *The Dawkins Delusion: Atheist Fundamentalism and the Denial of the Divine* (London: SPCK, 2007).

— *Dawkins' God: Genes, Memes, and the Meaning of Life* (Oxford: Blackwell, 2005).

— *The Twilight of Atheism: The Rise and Fall of Disbelief in the Modern World* (London: Rider, 2004).

— *Why God Won't Go Away: Engaging with the New Atheism* (London: SPCK, 2011).

Micklethwait, John and Adrian Wooldridge. *God Is Back: How the Global Rise of Faith Is Changing the World* (London: Allen Lane, 2009).

Stewart, Robert B., ed. *The Future of Atheism: Alister McGrath and Daniel Dennett in Dialogue* (London: SPCK, 2008).

Ward, Keith. *God, Chance and Necessity* (Oxford: OneWorld, 1996).

— *The God Conclusion: God and the Western Philosophical Tradition* (London: Darton Longman and Todd, 2009).

— *Is Religion Dangerous?* (Oxford: Lion, 2006).

— *Why There Almost Certainly Is a God: Doubting Dawkins* (Oxford: Lion, 2008).

Ward, Michael. *The Narnia Code: C.S. Lewis and the Secret of the Seven Heavens* (Milton Keynes: Paternoster, 2010).

Williams, Peter S. *A Sceptic's Guide to Atheism: God Is Not Dead* (Milton Keynes: Paternoster, 2009).

Journal article

Williams, Peter S. 'The Emperor's New Clothes: Pointing the Finger at Dawkins' Atheism.' Pages 29–33 in *Think* 9:24 (Spring 2010) http://journals.cambridge.org/action/displayAbstract?fromPage=online&aid=7191804.

2.

The Positively Blunt Sword of Scientism

> More of the substance and spirit of logical positivism
> persists than many would care to admit.
>
> *H.D. Lewis*[1]

Perhaps it's not so very strange to find parallels between C.S. Lewis the atheist and today's 'new atheists'. Lewis's career overlapped with that of highly influential Oxford atheists such as A.J. Ayer, Antony Flew, Gilbert Ryle and P.F. Strawson, as well as that of the Cambridge-educated philosopher Bertrand Russell; figures who taught, supervised or otherwise influenced the likes of Daniel Dennett and A.C. Grayling. Today's neo-atheists continue to be enamoured of 'what we might loosely call the Scientific Outlook, the picture of Mr [H.G.] Wells and the rest',[2] as Lewis once put it. Indeed, in 1924 Lewis noted that 'in [Bertrand Russell's essay] "Worship of a Free Man" I found a very clear and noble statement of what I myself believed a few years ago.'[3] According to Russell:

> That man is the product of causes which had no prevision of the end they were achieving; that his origin, his growth, his hopes and fears, his loves and his beliefs, are but the outcome of accidental collocations of atoms; that no fire, no heroism, no intensity of thought and feeling, can preserve an individual life beyond the grave; that all the labours of the ages, all the devotion, all the inspiration, all the noonday brightness of human genius, are destined to extinction in the vast death of the solar system, and that the

whole temple of Man's achievement must inevitably be buried beneath the debris of a universe in ruins – all these things, if not quite beyond dispute, are yet so nearly certain, that no philosophy which rejects them can hope to stand. Only within the scaffolding of these truths, only on the firm foundation of unyielding despair, can the soul's habitation henceforth be safely built.[4]

Today's neo-atheists are of course building their lives upon the same scaffolding (much of which can be traced back to Scottish sceptic David Hume, whose writing Lewis much admired). Some build with the same attitude of nihilistic 'true grit' that once attracted Lewis. Thus William B. Provine writes as what Lewis called 'a consistent pessimist',[5] stating: 'There are no gods, no purposes, and no goal-directed forces of any kind. There is no life after death. When I die . . . That's the end of me. There is no ultimate foundation for ethics, no ultimate meaning in life, and no free will for humans, either.'[6] Peter Atkins likewise affirms that (from his naturalistic perspective) when the sun dies: 'We shall have gone the journey of all purposeless stardust, driven unwittingly by chaos, gloriously but aimlessly evolved into sentience, born unchoosingly into the world, unwillingly taken from it, and inescapably returned to nothing.'[7]

Others build upon Russell's scaffolding with what Richard John Neuhaus calls a 'debonair nihilism',[8] an existential determination to ignore the meaninglessness of it all by enjoying the subjective bloom of the metaphorical roses along life's way. Hence, although Richard Dawkins agrees with Steven Weinberg's comment that 'the more the universe seems comprehensible, the more it seems pointless',[9] he nevertheless wants 'to guard against . . . people therefore getting nihilistic in their personal lives.'[10] Dawkins argues (correctly) that subjective human purposes lacking objective value are *compatible* with an objectively meaningless cosmos: 'You can have a very happy and fulfilled personal life even if you think the universe at large is a tale told by an idiot. You can still set up goals and have a very worthwhile life and not be nihilistic about it at a personal level.'[11] Likewise, A.C. Grayling affirms that 'the meaning of your life is the meaning you give it.'[12] But this is at best a pyrrhic victory over meaninglessness (and one only available to those capable of exercising such existential intentionality). As Terry

Eagleton observes, humans are contingent beings who depend both upon nature and each other:

> whatever [subjective] meaning I may forge for my own life is constrained from the inside by this dependency. We cannot start from scratch. It is not a matter of clearing away God-given meanings in order to hammer out our own, as Nietzsche seemed to imagine. For . . . we are woven through by the [subjective] meanings of others – [subjective] meanings we never got to choose, yet which provide the matrix within which we come to make sense of ourselves and the world. In this sense . . . the idea that I can determine the [subjective] meaning of my own life is an illusion.[13]

Even if the idea that I can determine the subjective meaning of my life weren't an illusion, the determination of subjective meaning can never deliver more than the self-deluded illusion of objective meaning. As French atheist André Comte-Sponville concludes: 'there is no way for a lucid atheist to avoid despair.'[14]

Dawkins likes to talk up the emotional rewards of science: 'All the great religions have a place for awe, for ecstatic transport at the wonder and beauty of creation. And it's exactly this feeling of spine-shivering, breath-catching awe – almost worship – this flooding of the chest with ecstatic wonder, that modern science can provide.'[15] However, given Russell's scaffolding, such value-laden terms as 'awe' and 'beauty' refer to *nothing but subjective personal reactions taking place within, and relative to, by-products of an evolutionary process lacking any intrinsic meaning or given purpose.* In the final analysis, Dawkins affirms that 'the universe we observe has precisely the properties we should expect if there is at bottom no design, no purpose, no evil and no good, nothing but pitiless indifference.'[16] As Lewis held (both as an atheist and a Christian): 'Either there is significance in the whole process of things as well as in human activity, or there is no significance in human activity itself . . . You cannot have it both ways. If the world is meaningless, then so are we . . .'[17] Thus Lewis explained that when he accepted Russell's naturalistic worldview: 'The two hemispheres of my mind were in the sharpest contrast. On the one side a many-islanded sea of poetry and myth; on the other a glib and shallow "rationalism". Nearly all that I loved I believed to be imaginary; nearly all that I believed to be real I thought grim and meaningless.'[18]

Ayer's Heirs

> The ideas of the school of Vienna . . . characterize rather well
> the average state of mind which . . . will no doubt prevail
> among scientists and, especially, among popularizers of sci-
> ence, with which we will have to deal for some time to come.
>
> *Jacques Maritain*[19]

Dr Edgar H. Andrews hits the nail on the head when he describes the new atheism as 'a cabal of academic atheists diligently reinventing the Vienna Circle . . . the 1920's philosophical school that invented logical positivism, a failed philosophy if ever there was one.'[20] A.C. Grayling's doctoral supervisor, A.J. Ayer, was at the heart of the 'positivist' movement. The positivists declared that talk about 'God' was *literally meaningless*, a view popularized by Ayer's 1936 book *Language, Truth and Logic*, which 'served as a sort of manifesto for this movement . . . The principle weapon employed by Ayer in his campaign against metaphysics was the vaunted Verification Principle of meaning.'[21] According to the verification principle, the meaning of any statement that wasn't true by definition (e.g. 2 + 2 = 4) lay in its ability to be empirically verified (at least in principle). To empirically verify something means to check it out with the physical senses (sight, hearing, touch, etc.). In other words, 'Socks exist' is a meaningful statement *because you can verify it* by seeing, hearing, touching, smelling or even tasting socks. But 'God exists' is a meaningless statement *because you can't verify it* by seeing, hearing, touching, smelling or tasting God. Thus, according to positivism, 'God exists' isn't a meaningful statement that's either true or false, but a use of language on a par with nonsense poetry (like the parts of 'Jabberwocky' Lewis Carroll didn't define). Ayer proclaimed:

> 'God' is a metaphysical term. And if 'God' is a metaphysical term,
> then it cannot even be probable that a god exists. For to say that
> 'God exists' is to make a metaphysical utterance which cannot be

either true or false . . . If a putative proposition fails to satisfy [the verification] principle, and is not a tautology, then . . . it is meta-physical, and . . . being metaphysical, it is neither true nor false but literally senseless.[22]

As Catholic philosopher F.C. Copleston observed in the 1950s: 'Ayer's writings [have] exercised a widespread influence, particularly perhaps on university students, for whom it possessed the charm of novelty and an atmosphere of daring.'[23] Atheist-turned-Christian Peter Hitchens, brother of the late Christopher Hitchens, gives a fascinating insight into the resulting 'scientistic' prejudices of his generation:

I have passed through the same atheist revelation that most self-confident members of my British generation – I was born in 1951 – have experienced. We were sure that we, and our civilization, had grown out of the nursery myths of God, angels and Heaven. We had . . . 'science', which explained everything that needed to be explained . . . This widely accepted dismissal of faith by the intelligent and educated seemed then to be definitive proof that the thing was a fake, mainly because I wanted such proof . . . There were, after all, plenty of Christian intellects available if I had desired reassurance that faith and intelligence were compatible. But I dismissed them as obvious dupes, who spoke as they did because it was their professional paid duty to do so. I had spotted the dry, disillusioned and apparently disinterested atheism of so many intellectuals, artists and leaders of our age . . . It did not cross my mind that they, like religious apologists, might have any personal reasons for holding to this disbelief. It certainly did not cross my mind that I had any low motives for it . . . Anything that had not yet been explained would no doubt soon be discovered. There were no mysteries . . . Science, summed up as the belief that what could not be naturalistically or materialistically explained was not worth taking seriously, simply appropriated them . . . I should stress that I was not actually taught these articles of the materialist faith, let alone the arguments which continue to rage around them. I was simply given the impression by adults that these things were the case, and that this was all settled forever. It was the faith of a faithless age. I had no idea, then, quite why so many of the older generation had set their faces so hard against religious belief. I was quite shocked when I later discovered the true state of affairs. They did not know half the things they claimed to know.[24]

No Longer Fashionable

Can the 'principle of verification' be verified?

H.D. Lewis[25]

Richard Dawkins implicitly rejects logical positivism when he objects to 'the erroneous notion that the existence or non-existence of God is an untouchable question, forever beyond the reach of science . . . Either he exists or he doesn't. It is a scientific question; one day we may know the answer, and meanwhile we can say something pretty strong about the probability.'[26] Dawkins says that science is 'the honest and systematic endeavour to find out the truth about the real world',[27] and this definition provides no grounds for the sort of airtight distinction between metaphysical philosophy and natural philosophy (as science used to be called) sought by positivism.

Dawkins clearly uses 'science' as a term of endearment restricted to any critical investigation of the 'real world' *grounded in empirical evidence*. Moreover, Dawkins *assumes* that the 'real world' can be described in exclusively naturalistic terms. By way of contrast, Intelligent Design theorists follow David Hume in distinguishing between conclusions science can and can't support without purely metaphysical extension.[28] Although Dawkins is sometimes less nuanced than Hume, Design theorists can give an unqualified welcome to Dawkins' statement that 'the presence or absence of a creative super-intelligence is unequivocally a scientific question . . . The methods we should use to settle the matter . . . would be purely and entirely scientific methods.'[29] As William Lane Craig explains:

Dawkins . . . implicitly rejects methodological naturalism and treats intelligent design as a scientific hypothesis which should be assessed like any other scientific hypothesis . . . Dawkins, then, finds himself in agreement with the most fundamental tenets of intelligent design theory: (i) that intelligent design is a scientific hypothesis which should be assessed as such, (ii) that it is illegitimate to exclude *a priori* from the pool of explanatory options hypotheses which appeal to final causes or even super-natural beings, and (iii) that the design inference is not to be equated with an inference to theism . . .[30]

However, a positive answer in respect of the existence of 'a creative super-intelligence' (a scientific conclusion, as Dawkins confirms) would provide obvious grist for the metaphysical mill of arguments for God. Still, the point of immediate relevance here is that the new atheism, no less than the theism it opposes, *is built upon verificationism's grave*, even as it continues to be haunted by its ghost.

Several factors conspired to render positivism 'no longer fashionable',[31] as Copleston declared just two decades after *Language, Truth and Logic* was published. For one thing, as Ayer himself admitted: 'If the assertion that there is a god is nonsensical, then the . . . assertion that there is no god is equally nonsensical.'[32] Ditto agnosticism. Indeed, although many who embraced positivism were materialists, 'materialism would have to be rejected as nonsense by a strict interpretation of logical positivism.'[33] After all, the mind-independent reality of matter is neither true by definition, nor something that can be empirically verified! Hence, although it was designed to define and promote scientific (empirical) knowledge claims over other (e.g. metaphysical) knowledge claims, the verification principle acted as a 'universal acid' that ate away the unavoidably philosophical foundations of science itself:

> Philosophers soon began to realize . . . that the Verification Principle was a double-edged sword. For it would force us to dismiss as meaningful not only theological statements but also a great many scientific statements as well, so that the principle cuts off at the knees science itself, in whose service this weapon had been wielded. As it turns out, physics is filled with metaphysical statements that cannot be empirically verified . . . If the ship of scientific naturalism was not to be scuttled, verificationism had to be cut loose.[34]

Given the anti-materialistic and anti-scientific implications of the verification principle, even the irreligious might be tempted to endorse atheist Kai Nielson's common-sense observation: 'Most claims that people make are not scientific; yet they can, for all that, be true or false.'[35] Indeed, atheist Luke Muehlhauser comments that 'in the 1950s and 60s, certain (atheistic) philosophers provided powerful criticisms of logical positivism, which led to its demise.'[36] For example, in a paper originally delivered at a meeting of the Oxford Socratic Club in the summer of 1950, Antony Flew cannily pointed out that:

> To assert that such and such is the case is necessarily equivalent to denying that such and such is not the case. Suppose then that we are in doubt as to what someone who gives vent to an utterance is asserting, or suppose that, more radically, we are sceptical as to whether he is really asserting anything at all, one way of trying to understand (or perhaps it will be to expose) his utterance is to attempt to find what he would regard as counting against, or as being incompatible with, its truth. For if the utterance is indeed an assertion, it will necessarily be equivalent to a denial of the negation of the assertion. And anything which would count against the assertion . . . must be part of (or the whole of) the meaning of the negation of that assertion. And to know the meaning of the negation of an assertion is, as near as makes no matter, to know the meaning of that assertion.[37]

In other words, one can show that a theological utterance has meaning without showing that it is verifiable, if one can show that it is falsifiable. Flew later explained: 'My primary purpose in "Theology and Falsification" was to spice up the bland dialogue between logical positivism and the Christian religion and to set discussion between belief and unbelief upon different and more fruitful lines . . . I was not saying that statements of religious belief were meaningless.'[38] That is, Flew wasn't setting up falsifiability as an alternative to the failing verification principle: 'I simply challenged religious believers to explain how their statements are to be understood, especially in the light of conflicting data. The paper elicited numerous responses . . . many of which helped me to sharpen – and at times, correct – my views.'[39] For example: 'Basil Mitchell, who succeeded C.S. Lewis as President of the Socratic Club, said that . . . the theological problem of evil arose precisely because the existence of pain seems to count against the truth that God loves humankind.'[40] By analogy, the claim that the earth is a globe 'excludes the possibility that it is flat'[41] and 'although it may appear flat, this apparent contradiction can be explained by the earth's great size, the perspective from which we are viewing it, and so on. So, once you add appropriate qualifications, the claim can be satisfactorily reconciled with phenomena that appear to contradict it. But if contradictory phenomena and associated qualifications keep multiplying, then the claim itself becomes suspect.'[42]

Flew eventually concluded that, like the statement 'The earth is a globe', the statement 'There is a God' is not only meaningful (since it can be 'satisfactorily reconciled with phenomena that appear to contradict it' without dying 'the death by a thousand qualifications'[43]), but also true.

Philosopher John Hick (who obtained his DPhil from Oxford in 1950) pointed out that, when made sufficiently precise, the statement 'God exists' *is* empirically verifiable (at least *in principle* and/or *indirectly*, which is all the verification criterion required). For example, he pointed out that 'the existence or non-existence of the God of the New Testament is a matter of fact, and claims as such eventual experiential verification.'[44] Hick observed that 'a set of expectations based upon faith in the historic Jesus as the incarnation of God, and in his teaching as being divinely authoritative, could be so fully confirmed in *post-mortem* experience as to leave no grounds for rational doubt as to the validity of that faith.'[45]

Hick's argument challenged the ability of the verification principle to draw a line of demarcation between 'scientific' knowledge-claims on the one hand and 'metaphysical' knowledge-claims on the other. Unless positivism is framed broadly enough to allow the sort of *indirect* verification utilized by Hick, many explanatory claims within science would lack meaning (because they concern entities that are verified indirectly). This being so, it may be argued that the God hypothesis is not only verifiable *in principle*, but also *in practice*, since although one cannot *directly* verify God's existence, several arguments for theism can be framed using the same scientific form of *indirect* verification. As Basil Mitchell comments:

> the Logical Positivist movement started as an attempt to make a clear demarcation between science and common sense on the one hand, and metaphysics and theology on the other. But work in the philosophy of science convinced people that what the Logical Positivists had said about science was not true, and, by the time the philosophers of science had developed and amplified their accounts of how rationality works in science, people discovered that similar accounts applied equally well to the areas which they had previously sought to exclude, namely theology and metaphysics.[46]

In 1967 American philosopher Alvin Plantinga (b. 1932) published *God and Other Minds*, which 'applied the tools of analytic philosophy to questions in the Philosophy of Religion with an unprecedented rigour and creativity.'[47] He argued by analogy with the rationality of belief in other minds (whose non-tautological existence can't be directly verified by empirical methods) that 'if my belief in other minds is rational, so is my belief in God.'[48] If belief in God is meaningless because it can't be directly verified, then so is belief in other minds. But, of course, positivists believe in other minds!

With the 1974 publication of *The Nature of Necessity*, Plantinga kick-started a philosophical re-evaluation of the traditional arguments for God by using modal logic to lay out a valid version of the 'ontological' argument (originally formulated in AD 1078 by Anselm).[49] Plantinga's work on the ontological argument got a theistic foot in the newly reopened door of metaphysics and served, as Roger Scruton acknowledges, 'the useful purpose of showing the rumours of God's death to be greatly exaggerated.'[50]

God and Other Minds and *The Nature of Necessity* tackled both prongs of the positivist's proposed dilemma: show that theism is either verifiable or tautologically true, or else accept banishment to the outer darkness of meaninglessness. In effect, Plantinga responded to the first prong that the demand for direct verification renders positivism self-contradictory (thereby opening up the possibility of indirect verification), and to the second prong that even if he can't prove that God's existence is tautologically true, he can prove that it is *rational to think that God's existence is tautologically true*, and that this is sufficient to demonstrate that God-talk is meaningful. For how can a truth-claim be rational without being meaningful?

The chief woe of positivism, explains R. Douglas Geivett, was self-contradiction; for the verification principle 'was neither empirically verifiable nor tautological.'[51] Craig comments:

> One need only ask oneself whether the sentence 'A meaningful sentence must be capable in principle of being empirically verified' is *itself* capable of being empirically verified. Obviously not; no amount of empirical evidence would serve to verify its truth. The Verification Principle is therefore by its own lights a meaningless combination of words, which need hardly detain us, or at best an arbitrary definition, which we are at liberty to reject. Therefore, the Verification Principle and the theory of meaning that it supported have been almost universally abandoned by philosophers of all stripes.[52]

The verification principle '*failed its own requirement* for factual meaningfulness,' notes William P. Alston, 'and thus was self-refuting.'[53]

Ayer himself mused: 'I just stated [the verification rule] dogmatically and an extraordinary number of people seemed to be convinced by my assertion.'[54] In 1973 he admitted:

> The very fact that [the verification principle] denied meaning to statements which many people regarded as meaningful could be taken as evidence that it was false. The only answer that could be made to this objection was that the principle was advanced as a stipulative definition. It did not describe how the word 'meaning' was commonly used, but prescribed how it should be. But then why should anyone follow the prescription if its implications were not to his taste? We have, in fact, seen that the verification principle is defective . . .[55]

Ayer recently wrote the obituary for the movement he'd led: 'Logical Positivism died a long time ago. I don't think much of *Language, Truth and Logic* is true. I think it is full of mistakes.'[56]

As Hugh J. McCann observes: 'The radical claims of logical positivism and the ordinary language movement have today very few defenders, and the movement that began with figures like Frege, Russell and Wittgenstein has long since broadened its scope to recover much of the historical heritage it once pretended to leave behind.'[57] Craig explains: 'The collapse of verificationism during the second half of the twentieth century was undoubtedly the most important philosophical event of the century. Its demise brought about a resurgence of metaphysics, along with other traditional problems of philosophy that had been hitherto suppressed. Accompanying this resurgence has come something new and altogether unanticipated: a renaissance in Christian philosophy.'[58]

Despite its ignominious destiny, *Language, Truth and Logic* 'was one of those books that galvanize a whole generation. Ambitious undergraduates commonly read it at a sitting. Their elders were appalled. When students tried to discuss the book at an Oxford seminar, the Master of Balliol flung it through the window . . .'[59] C.S. Lewis, who exhorts us to 'take a low view of "climates of opinion"'[60] and who became a Christian five years before Ayer's book came out, was fortunately with the elders on this one, spurning 'those plaguey philosophers whom we call Logical Positivists.'[61]

The Language of Religion

> All speech about supersensibles is, and must be,
> metaphorical in the highest degree.
>
> *C.S. Lewis*[62]

In a paper on 'The Language of Religion' Lewis argued that 'religious sayings . . . are significant: if you meet them with a certain good will, a certain readiness to find meaning.'[63] Lewis suggested that while 'some things said by religious people can't be treated exactly as we treat scientific statements' this isn't 'because they are statements of some special language. It would be truer to say that the scientific statements are in a special language.'[64] Indeed, Lewis avers that 'Scientific and Poetic language are two different artificial perfections of Ordinary [language].'[65] Lewis argues:

it seems to me to be a mistake to think that our experience in general can be communicated by precise and literal language [i.e. the language of empirical science] and that there is a special class of experience (say, emotions [or religious experience]) which cannot. The truth seems to me to be the opposite: there is a special region of experiences which can be communicated *without* Poetic language, namely, its 'common measurable features', but most experience cannot. To be incommunicable by Scientific language is, so far as I can judge, the normal state of experience . . . The very essence of our life as conscious beings, all day and every day, consists of something which cannot be communicated except by hints, similes, metaphors, and the use of those emotions . . . which are pointers to it.[66]

In other words, since the 'Scientific language' that describes our measurable, empirical experiences in 'precise quantitative [terms] which can be tested by an instrument'[67] is actually the *exception* to the general rule of 'Ordinary language' – i.e. the artificial perfection of 'Ordinary language' *on which it depends* – it follows that 'Scientific language' cannot, *on pain of self-contradiction*, be used to undermine the *meaning* of any propositions, *including religious propositions*, expressed in 'Ordinary language'.

If we can't communicate 'the very essence of our life as conscious beings . . . except by hints, similes, metaphors' etc., then we can't erect 'Scientific language' as the arbiter of linguistic meaning *without thereby rendering ourselves linguistically meaningless to ourselves*. But as Lewis argues in *Miracles*:

Very often when we are talking about something which is not perceptible by the five senses we use words which, in one of their meanings, refer to things or actions that are. When a man says that he grasps an argument he is using a verb (grasp) which literally means to take something in the hands, but he is certainly not thinking that his mind has hands or that an argument can be seized like a gun. To avoid the word *grasp* he may change the form of expression and say, 'I see your point,' but he does not mean that a pointed object has appeared in his visual field. He may have a third shot and say, 'I follow you,' but he does not mean that he is walking behind you along a road. Everyone is familiar with this linguistic phenomenon and the grammarians call it metaphor. But it is a serious mistake to think that metaphor is an optional thing which poets and orators may put into their work as a decoration and plain speakers can do without. The truth is that if we are going to talk at all about things which are not perceived by the senses, we are forced to use language metaphorically. Books on psychology or economics or politics are as continuously metaphorical as books of poetry or devotion. There is no other way of talking, as every philologist is aware.[68]

To back up this point, Lewis references the academic work of his friend Owen Barfield: 'Mr Barfield has shown, as regards the history of language, that words did not start by referring merely to physical objects and then get extended by metaphor to refer to emotions, mental states and the like. On the contrary, what we now call the "literal and metaphorical" meanings have both been disengaged by analysis from an ancient unity of meaning which was neither or both.'[69]

As Humphrey Carpenter explains:

> Barfield's arguments were printed in *Poetic Diction*, a short book by him that appeared in 1928 – though by that time Lewis knew its ideas well. Barfield examined the history of words, and came to the conclusion that mythology, far from being (as the philologist Max Muller called it) 'a disease of language', is closely associated with the very origin of all speech and literature. In the dawn of language, said Barfield, speakers did not make a distinction between the 'literal' and the 'metaphorical', but used words in what might be called a 'mythological' manner. For example, nowadays when we translate the Latin *spiritus* we have to render it either as 'spirit' or as 'breath' or as 'wind' depending on the context. But early users of language would not have made any such distinction between these meanings . . . This, in greatly simplified form, is what Barfield argued in *Poetic Diction*. He was not the only person to come to this conclusion: for example in Germany, Ernst Cassirer had said much the same thing independently. But it was said with particular force by Barfield, and his book impressed not just Lewis but also Tolkien . . . Perhaps it was as a result of reading Barfield's book that Tolkien made an

inversion of Muller's remark: 'Languages', he declared, 'are a disease of mythology.'[70]

On the one hand, then, if 'verification' requires 'Scientific language' that describes measurable, empirical experiences in 'precise quantitative [terms] which can be tested by an instrument', positivism makes a linguistic nonsense, not only of social sciences such as 'psychology or economics or politics' (which would be bad enough), but also of 'the very essence of our life as conscious beings, all day and every day'; and it's hard to imagine a worse recommendation for a philosophical school than that. On the other hand, if 'verification' *isn't* restricted to 'Scientific language' (but extends to 'Ordinary' and even 'Poetic language') then religious language is of the same type as, *and is thus no less meaningful than*, the language we must use in describing 'the very essence of our life as conscious beings': 'The language of religion,' Lewis affirms, 'seems to be, on the whole, either the same sort we use in ordinary conversation or the same sort we use in poetry, or somewhere between the two.'[71]

Moreover, Lewis observes that, at least when phrased in terms of 'Ordinary' and/or 'Poetic' language, expressions of Christian faith are 'closely connected with the grounds on which they are believed. There are usually two: authority and religious experience. Christians believe that Jesus Christ is the Son of God because He said so. The other evidence about Him has convinced them that He was neither a lunatic nor a quack.'[72] Furthermore: 'There is religious experience, ranging from the most ordinary experiences of the believer in worship, forgiveness, dereliction, and divine help, up to the high special experiences of the mystics. Through such experiences Christians believe that they get a sort of verification (or perhaps sometimes falsification) of their tenets.'[73] However, Lewis is keen to point out that 'such experience cannot be conveyed to [other believers], much less to unbelievers [who do not share the experience], except by language which shares to some extent the nature of Poetic language.'[74] It is this fact, thinks Lewis, that 'leads some people to suppose that it can be nothing but emotion. For of course, if you accept the view that Poetic language is purely emotional [or even purely "emotive", as Ayer might have said], then things which can be expressed only in Poetic language will presumably be emotions. But if we don't equate Poetic language with emotional language, the question is still open.'[75]

According to Lewis's philosophy of language:

> Poetic language does convey information, but it suffers from two disabilities in comparison with Scientific [language]. (1) It is verifiable or falsifiable only to a limited degree and with a certain fringe of vagueness . . . In that sense, Scientific statements are, as people say now, far more easily 'cashed'. But the poet might of course reply that . . . Scientific statements are cheques, in one sense, for very small amounts, giving us, out of the teeming complexity of every concrete reality only 'the common measurable features'. (2) Such information as Poetic language has to give can be received only if you are ready to meet it half way. It is no good holding a dialectical pistol to the poet's head and demanding how the deuce a river could have hair, or thought be green, or a woman a red rose. You may win, in the sense of putting him to a *non-plus*. But if he had anything to tell you, you will never get it by behaving that way. You must begin by trusting him. Only by doing so will you find out whether he is trustworthy or not.[76]

In other words, while Lewis recognizes that there's a sense in which at least some religious language isn't as easy to understand as 'Scientific language', he diagnoses those who would on that account dismiss the meaningfulness of religious claims as suffering from a pedantic lack of poetic sympathy and trust, an unjustifiably narrow understanding of language:

> We are invited to restate our belief in a form free from metaphor and symbol. The reason why we don't is that we can't. We can, if you like, say 'God entered history' instead of saying 'God came down to earth'. But, of course, 'entered' is just as metaphorical as 'came down'. You have only substituted horizontal or undefined movement for vertical movement. We can make our language duller; we cannot make it less metaphorical.[77]

Lewis's intransigence on the meaningfulness of God-talk means that his writings on religion retain a contemporary relevance that the work of contemporaries such as Ayer conspicuously lack; a fact that explains why Lewis was able to serve generations of scholars as a model of philosophical reflection upon God. Deeply rooted as he was in classical philosophy and ancient literature, Lewis wasn't swept off his feet by the rising, but soon retreating, tide of logical positivism. Nor, despite his respect for the natural and social sciences, was he tempted by the accompanying, corrosive spray of scientism.

Scientism: All Haft and No Blade

> Philosophy is dead. Philosophy has not kept up with
> modern developments in science . . . scientists have become
> the bearers of the torch of discovery in our
> quest for knowledge.
> *Stephen Hawking and Leonard Mlodinow*[78]

C.S. Lewis observed: 'it is widely believed that scientific thought does put us in touch with reality, whereas moral or metaphysical thought does not . . . But the distinction thus made between scientific and non-scientific thoughts will not easily bear the weight we are attempting to put on it.'[79] As Craig explains:

> during the 1950s and 60s . . . The overwhelmingly dominant mode of thinking was scientific naturalism. Physical science was taken as the final, and really only, arbiter of truth. Metaphysics had been vanquished, expelled from philosophy . . . Any problem that could not be addressed by science was simply dismissed as a pseudo-problem. If a question did not have a scientific answer, then it was not a real question – just a pseudo-question masquerading as a real question.[80]

There's an obvious similarity between this kind of positivistic scientism and the verificationism of so-called 'logical positivism'. Scientism simply attributes exclusive (or near-exclusive) rights over *knowledge*, rather than over *meaningfulness*, to empirical (scientific) verification. As atheist Bruce Sheiman notes: 'it is scientism, and not science that is opposed to theism . . . scientism is little more than atheism masquerading as science.'[81] Perhaps the conflation of science and scientism explains why so many neo-atheists are scientists who nevertheless feel qualified to pontificate upon metaphysical issues? This is what I mean by saying that neo-atheism is haunted by the ghost of positivism despite being built upon its grave.

The new atheism is resolutely positivistic in outlook. Michael Novak's comment that Daniel Dennett's 'concept of reason and science is so narrow that he seems trapped in something like early-period A.J. Ayer'[82] goes for the new atheist movement as a whole. Neo-atheism steers as close to the shores of logical positivism as it can get without actually landing. Indeed, from time to time, the occasional member of the flotilla finds himself running aground on the submerged reefs of verificationism. For example, Randy Everist observes that 'the [March 2011] debate between Lawrence Krauss and William Lane Craig brought out some of the claims of scientism in the New Atheist community. In a way, it is highly reminiscent of Logical Positivism with A.J. Ayer and the old-line atheists of the early-to-mid 20th century.'[83] During the 'Question and Answer' time physicist Lawrence Krauss stated: 'There are many things that I can't falsify . . . I'm willing to believe that there's much more to the universe than science is appropriate to describe, that's perfectly possible, but *science does what it does, and it determines nonsense from sense by testing.*'[84] An astonished Craig responded that Krauss:

> seems to hold to an epistemology which says that we should only believe that which can be scientifically proven, and . . . that itself is a self-contradictory position, because you can't scientifically prove that you should only believe that which can be scientifically proven. So when he says it 'distinguishes sense from nonsense', that's old-line verificationism, isn't it, and positivism, which went out with the 30's and 40's. It's a self-defeating position.[85]

As Craig commented afterwards: 'I am still amazed . . . when I enter into a debate with someone like a Lawrence Krauss, at how the epistemology of old-time verificationism and logical positivism *still* casts its long shadow over Western culture.'[86]

The Woes of Scientism

> Science is not the only way of knowing.
>
> *Francis Collins*[87]

The new atheists portray themselves as champions of reason in a struggle against the dogmas of blind religious faith; but they pay scant attention to the philosophy of science and consequently advance into battle with the false confidence of knights after the advent of gunpowder, trusting to the defensive and offensive power of equipment everyone else knows simply won't 'cut the mustard'. Their general attitude appears to be that, although empirical evidence can't sort the meaningful from the meaningless, it is nevertheless the only way to sort the true from the false and the worthy of consideration from those who needn't be taken seriously. In this they follow in the footsteps of Bertrand Russell, who once affirmed the self-contradictory statement that 'what science cannot tell us, mankind cannot know.'[88]

J.P. Moreland explains that there's a distinction to be drawn between 'strong' and 'weak' scientism:

> Strong scientism is the view that some proposition or theory is true or rational if and only if it is a well-established scientific proposition or theory that, in turn, depends upon its having been successfully formed, tested, and used according to appropriate scientific methodology. There are no truths apart from scientific truths, and even if there were, there would be no reason whatever to believe them. Advocates of weak scientism allow for the existence of truths apart from science and are even willing to grant that they can have some minimal, positive rationality status without the support of science. But advocates of weak scientism still hold that science is the most valuable, most serious, and most authoritative sector of human learning. Every other intellectual activity is inferior to science.[89]

Victor J. Stenger complains that 'critics accuse New Atheism of "scientism," which is the principle that science is the only means that can be used to learn about the world and humanity. They cannot quote a single new atheist who has said that.'[90] On the one hand, Stenger is conveniently ignoring 'weak scientism' here. Professor Sir Harry Kroto (a Fellow of the Royal Society who won the Nobel Prize for Chemistry in 1996) expressed both his anti-religious views and his faith in at least weak scientism while complaining about Lord Martin Rees (atheist, Astronomer Royal and recently retired President of the Royal Society) accepting the 2011 Templeton Prize:

> This news is really quite shocking . . . bad for science in general, bad for the Royal Society, bad for the UK – a basically secular country . . . Martin Rees is a brilliant astrophysicist and a personal friend, but I believe he has made a mistake in accepting £1 million from the Templeton Foundation. In doing so, he supports its primary aim, which is to undermine the most precious tenet of science: that it is *the only philosophical construct we have to determine truth with any reliability.*[91]

On the other hand, Oxford chemist Peter Atkins surely qualifies both as a neo-atheist (he says religion is 'just fantasy, basically. It's particularly empty of any explanatory content and is evil as well'[92]) and as a staunch advocate of 'strong scientism'. He states that *'the scientific method is the only means of discovering the nature of reality* . . . the only way of acquiring reliable knowledge.'[93] Stephen Hawking and Leonard Mlodinow likewise affirm strong scientism: 'philosophy is dead . . . Scientists have become the bearers of the torch of discovery in our quest for knowledge.'[94]

Richard Dawkins is adamant that 'scientists [are] the specialists in discovering what is true about the world and the universe . . .'[95] Dawkins poses the rhetorical question: 'Have you ever wondered how we know the things that we know?'[96] His answer (and he does seem to mean that it is *the* answer) is 'evidence.'[97] For Dawkins, all beliefs fall into one of two categories. On the one hand there is 'proper evidence-based belief.'[98] As he naïvely asserts in *The Magic of Reality: How We Know What's Really True* (Bantam, 2011):

> the only good reason to believe that something exists is if there is real evidence that it does . . . We come to know what is real, then, in one of three ways. We can detect it directly, using our five senses; or

indirectly, using our senses aided by special instruments such as telescopes and microscopes; or even more indirectly, by creating models of what *might* be real and then testing those models to see whether they successfully predict things that we can see (or hear, etc.), with or without the aid of instruments. Ultimately, it always comes back to our senses, one way or another.[99]

On the other hand, according to Dawkins, there is the improper methodology of blind faith: 'Faith is believing in something when there literally isn't a scrap of evidence. If there were a scrap of evidence, then it wouldn't be faith.'[100] On the basis of this flawed analysis, Dawkins issues self-defeating epistemological advice:

> Next time somebody tells you something that sounds important, think to yourself: 'Is this the kind of thing that people probably know because of evidence? Or is it the kind of thing that people only believe because of tradition, authority or revelation?' And next time somebody tells you that something is true, why not say to them: 'What kind of evidence is there for that?' And if they can't give you a good answer, I hope you'll think very carefully before you believe a word they say.[101]

Dawkins' philosophical claim that rational belief requires direct or indirect empirical evidence 'sounds important', but *it cannot be justified by direct or indirect empirical evidence*. Dawkins fails to grasp the self-contradictory consequences of taking his own advice, and consequently attempts to decapitate religion with one swipe of his scientistic sword: 'God cannot be proved by any scientific hypothesis. Therefore he does not exist.'[102] Of course, neither can the proposition that 'unless something can be proved by a scientific hypothesis it does not exist' be proved by any scientific hypothesis. By Dawkins' own standard, his objection to theism doesn't even exist! Dawkins' scientistic attack-plan begins with lopping off his own sword arm.

Indeed, despite protestations to the contrary, when Victor J. Stenger asserts both that 'science . . . does not require nor does it use any metaphysics',[103] and that 'science is belief in the presence of supportive evidence . . . faith is belief in the absence of supportive evidence',[104] he contrives to sound just like someone advocating strong scientism! In fairness to Stenger, perhaps he is really only a proponent of weak scientism who contradicts himself.

Unfortunately for neo-atheism, scientism is a deeply flawed philosophical position:

> Note first that strong scientism is self-refuting . . . scientism is a philosophical claim, *not* a scientific one . . . There are two more problems that count equally against strong and weak scientism. First, scientism (in both forms) does not adequately allow for the task of stating and defending the necessary [metaphysical] presuppositions for science itself to be practiced (assuming scientific realism). Thus, scientism shows itself to be a foe and not a friend of science . . . There is a second problem that counts equally against strong and weak scientism: *the existence of true and rationally justified beliefs outside of science*. The simple fact is that true, rationally justified beliefs exist in a host of fields outside science . . . Moreover, some propositions believed outside science ('red is a color', 'torturing babies is wrong', 'I am now thinking about science') are better justified than some believed within science . . .[105]

In point of fact, 'weak scientism' fails to avoid the self-contradiction of 'strong scientism' because it proposes a theory of knowledge wherein the supposedly *more reliable* form of knowledge (science) depends upon the supposedly *less reliable* form of knowledge (philosophy)! Weak scientism is analogous to the foolish man who built his house upon the sand rather than upon the rock (Matthew 7:24–27). As philosopher of science Del Ratzsch argues:

> if we are rationally justified in accepting science then we must be rationally justified in accepting those foundational presuppositions [that science depends upon]. But not being *results* of science, their rational justification cannot rest upon science, but must lie *beyond* science. Thus, if we take science and its results to be rationally justified, science is not the only source of rational justification. There must then evidently be some *deeper* source of rational justification.[105]

Robert C. Koons explains that:

> Much of the philosophy of science in the mid-twentieth century was taken up in a quixotic attempt to find a line of demarcation between science, on the one hand, and metaphysics and commonsense knowledge, on the other. Every such attempt to find necessary and sufficient conditions for counting something as 'scientific enquiry' or as a 'scientific theory' ended in utter failure . . . If science really were a distinctive mode of knowing, demonstrably superior to commonsense and all other methods, we might be under a kind of intellectual duty to base all of our beliefs on science alone. However, since science cannot be demarcated from the rest of knowledge, our ordinary ways of warranting beliefs are under no such cloud of suspicion and remain innocent until proven guilty.[107]

Sam Harris acknowledges that 'many people of faith make heroic sacrifices to relieve the suffering of other human beings',[108] but asks: 'is it necessary to believe anything on insufficient evidence in order to behave this way?'[109] Harris complains: 'While believing strongly, without evidence, is considered a mark of madness or stupidity in any other area of our lives, faith in God still holds immense prestige in our society.'[110] The odd thing about this complaint is that Harris inevitably believes many things 'strongly, without evidence' that it would nonetheless be rightly considered a mark of madness or stupidity if he *didn't* believe! As G.K. Chesterton remarked:

> let us clearly realize this fact, that we do believe in a number of things which are part of our existence, but which cannot be demonstrated . . . All sane men, I say, believe firmly and unalterably in a certain number of things which are unproved and unprovable . . . every sane man believes that the world around him and the people in it are real, and not his own delusion or dream . . .[111]

Harris presumably believes that the physical world is an objective, mind-independent reality that did *not* spring into existence five minutes ago (complete with false memories, tree rings that never grew, etc.). However, belief in a young but apparently old cosmos is, by hypothesis, compatible with all the available empirical evidence. So too is belief in a purely subjective cosmos (i.e. philosophical idealism). In both cases, our (surely 'strong') and obviously rational belief to the contrary is necessarily something we believe 'without evidence'!

The assumption that *all* beliefs must be evidenced by or justified on the basis of other beliefs before they count as rational entails an infinite regress that can never be accumulated. Hence it's clearly *not* the case that *all* beliefs have to be justified (let alone with empirical evidence) before they count as rational. As Lewis argued: 'You cannot produce rational intuition by argument, because argument depends upon rational intuition. Proof rests upon the unprovable which has to be just "seen".'[112] In *The Moral Landscape* (Bantam, 2011) Sam Harris acknowledges that there are many things in which he believes strongly and rationally but without scientific evidence:

> Science cannot tell us why, *scientifically*, we should value . . . well-being . . . it is essential to see that the demand for *radical* justification leveled by the moral skeptic could not be met by science. Science is defined with reference to the goal of understanding the processes at work in the universe. Can we justify this goal scientifically? Of course not . . . What evidence could prove that we should value evidence?[113]

In other words, science depends upon the rationality of our trust in a host of assumptions about the nature of reality and our cognitive access to reality *that science itself is necessarily incapable of warranting*. As Moreland explains:

> A dogmatic claim of scientism (e.g. 'only what can be known by science or quantified and tested empirically is true and rational') is self-refuting. The statement itself is not a statement of science, but a second-order philosophical statement about science. The statement cannot be tested empirically, quantified, and so on . . . Justifying science by science is question begging. The validation of science is a philosophical issue . . . and any claim to the contrary will itself be philosophical.[114]

It is thus a demonstrable fact that the new-atheists' weapon of choice, the sword of scientism, 'is all haft and no blade.'[115]

Whose Faith Is Blind?

> But they are much deceived, who think that we believe in
> Christ without any proofs.
>
> *Augustine*[116]

The flip side of the neo-atheists' commitment to a scientistic vision of rationality is their blanket portrait of religious belief as being, by definition, a matter of irrational, 'blind faith'. As John Lennox rightly complains:

> the New Atheists are classic examples of the very thing that they despise: they are characterized by the blind faith that all faith is blind faith . . . It is the New Atheist concept of faith that is a del-usion in the precise sense they assign to that term: a persistent false belief held in the face of strong contradictory evidence. Against all the evidence (do they not even bother to consult dictionaries?) they irrationally reduce all faith to blind faith, and then subject it to ridicule.[117]

Victor J. Stenger asserts: 'Faith is always foolish . . . Science is belief in the presence of supportive evidence . . . faith is belief in the absence of supportive evidence and even in the light of contrary evidence.'[118] Christopher Hitchens portrays all religion as 'a surrender of reason in favour of faith.'[119] A.C. Grayling states: 'Faith is a stance or an attitude of belief independent of, and characteristically in the countervailing face of, evidence. It is non-rational at best, and is probably irrational given that it involves deliberate ignoring of evidence, or commitment despite lack of evidence.'[120] Daniel Dennett opines:

> religion [is] the greatest threat to rationality and scientific progress . . . religion . . . doesn't just disable, it honours the disability. People are revered for their capacity to live in a dream world, to shield their minds from factual knowledge and make the major decisions in their lives by consulting voices in their heads that they call forth by rituals designed to intoxicate them . . . This imperviousness to reason is, I think, the property that we should most fear in religion. Other institutions or traditions may encourage a certain amount of irrationality . . . but only religion demands it as a sacred duty.[121]

Richard Dawkins criticizes faith for requiring 'blind trust, in the absence of evidence, even in the teeth of evidence.'[122] He proclaims:

> Fundamentalist religion is hell-bent on ruining the scientific education of countless thousands . . . Non-fundamentalist, 'sensible' religion may not be doing that. *But it is making the world safe for fundamentalism by teaching* . . . *that unquestioned faith is a virtue* . . . if children were taught to question and think through their beliefs, instead of being taught the superior virtue of faith without question, it is a good bet that there would be no suicide bombers.[123]

As Richard Norman observes: 'For Dawkins the problem is that all religious believers are committed to faith rather than reason . . . So for him the difference between the so-called moderate, sensible religious believers and the fundamentalists is a minor one . . . it's religion as such that is the problem.'[124] Hence Dawkins explains: 'I do everything in my power to warn people against faith itself, not just against so-called "extremist" faith. The teachings of "moderate" religion, though not extremist in themselves, are an open invitation to extremism.'[125]

Exegesis over Eisegesis

> The first demand any work of art makes upon us is surrender. Look. Listen. Receive. Get yourself out of the way.
>
> *C.S. Lewis*[126]

Ironically, it's the neo-atheist portrait of all religious faith as a matter of blind faith (as if 'blind' were a redundant term) that is itself a conspicuous example of blind faith. As A.C. Grayling rightly warns:

> It is quite hard sometimes to hear things. We make ourselves deaf and blind by means of our unrecognised prejudices and assumptions. We acquire such rooted ways of thinking about the world, such natural prejudices, natural blindfolds and ear-plugs, bad

mental habits . . . that we too often do not see and hear things we ought to if we are to get the rounded picture.[127]

The blinding power of unrecognized prejudice is nicely illustrated by Sam Harris's investigation into the biblical concept of faith in *The End of Faith*: 'What is faith, then? Is it something other than belief? The Hebrew term *'emuna* (verb *'mn*) is alternatively translated as "to have faith," "to believe," or "to trust." The Septuagint, the Greek translation of the Hebrew Bible, retains the same meaning in the term *pisteuein*, and this Greek equivalent is adopted in the New Testament.'[128]

In Greek mythology *Pistis* was the spirit (*daimona*) of trust, honesty and good faith. Her Roman name was *Fides*, from which the English word 'faith' derives. There's nothing about these terms that requires faith (belief/trust) to be 'blind' or incompatible with reason or evidence! Unfortunately, despite his linguistic background check, Harris immediately misinterprets a well-known verse from the New Testament: 'Hebrews 11:1 defines faith as "the assurance of things hoped for, the conviction of things not seen." Read in the right way, this passage seems to render faith entirely self-justifying . . .'[129]

Now, as C.S. Lewis advised: 'We want to find the sense the author intended . . . in ordinary language the sense of a word is governed by the context and this sense normally excludes all others from the mind.'[130] In Hebrews 10 the (unknown) writer encourages Christians to *persevere in their faith despite worldly persecutions* (not despite evidence to the contrary) in light of the promise of heaven:

> Remember those earlier days after you had received the light, when you endured in a great conflict full of suffering. Sometimes you were publicly exposed to insult and persecution; at other times you stood side by side with those who were so treated. You suffered along with those in prison and joyfully accepted the confiscation of your property, because you knew that you yourselves had *better and lasting possessions* [i.e. their relationship with God through Jesus in the Holy Spirit and the promise of heaven]. So do not throw away your confidence; it will be richly rewarded. You need to persevere so that when you have done the will of God, *you*

will receive what he has promised (Hebrews 10:32–36 [NIV 2011], my italics).

It's the fulfilment of the promise mentioned in Hebrews 10:36 that Hebrews 11:1 has in mind. Read in context, then, Hebrews 11:1 says that having faith (i.e. belief) in God means trusting him to deliver on his promise of heaven ('faith is being sure of what we hope for') without needing to personally see the fulfilment of that promise in the present time of persecution ('and certain of what we do not see').

The Greek word translated as 'assurance' (or 'being sure') in Hebrews 11:1 is *hypo'stasis*, a term that commonly appears in ancient business documents, where it describes a covenant as an exchange of guarantees concerning the future transfer of goods described in a contract. The Greek word *e'legkhos*, translated as 'conviction' or 'certainty' in Hebrews 11:1, conveys the idea of *bringing forth evidence to demonstrate something* (particularly something contrary to what superficially appears to be the case). Hence Hebrews 11:1 does *not* say or imply that faith means trusting God *in the absence of any supposed reason to trust him!* Rather, Hebrews 11:1 says that having faith means adhering to the covenant relationship that exists between God and the believer in the *rationally warranted* expectation that God will bring his promises to completion. In times of persecution such faith bears witness to 'the reason for the hope' the Christian has in Jesus (cf. 1 Peter 3:15). Sam Harris clearly reads his own assumptions *into* Hebrews 11:1, riding roughshod over its natural meaning in context.

Harris goes on to misinterpret the story of doubting Thomas (John 20:24-31) as demonstrating that 'ignorance is the true coinage of this realm – "Blessed are those who have not seen and have believed" (John 20:29) . . .'[131] In point of fact, Jesus commends people who believe *without demanding to see for themselves*, not those who 'believe without evidence',[132] as A.C. Grayling erroneously concludes: 'Faith is commitment to belief in something either in the absence of evidence or in the face of countervailing evidence. It is accounted a "theological virtue" precisely for this reason, as the New Testament story of Doubting Thomas is designed to illustrate.'[133]

Note that earlier in John's gospel Jesus himself affirms evidence-based faith: 'believe on the evidence of the miracles' (John 14:11). Indeed, before the resurrected Jesus offered himself for empirical examination, Thomas wasn't asked to believe *without evidence*; for although 'Thomas (also known as Didymus), one of the Twelve, was not with the disciples when Jesus came', nevertheless 'the other disciples told him, "We have seen the Lord!"' (John 20:24—25.) So, all the other disciples are portrayed as believing in the resurrection of Jesus *on the basis of first-hand empirical experience*, while the *evidence of their eyewitness testimony* given to Thomas was certainly no worse than the evidence available to believers and non-believers alike today.[134] Moreover, the reason given for recounting the story of doubting Thomas by the Gospel of John itself is that this incident is among the *evidence* for the truth of the Christian understanding of Jesus: 'Jesus did many other miraculous signs in the presence of his disciples, which are not recorded in this book. But these are written that you may believe that Jesus is the Christ, the Son of God, and that by believing you may have life in his name' (John 20:30–31). As Roger Steer observes:

> There was no expectation that the sceptical disciple should exercise blind trust in the absence of evidence . . . of course, generations of people since then have been invited to exercise faith without the privilege of sight granted to Thomas, but the point is that through the centuries followers of Christ have never been required to take a step – or make a leap – which is blind or irrational.[135]

Putting the Record Straight

The new-atheist *eisegesis* of the biblical meaning of 'faith' is wholly at odds with Scripture's repeated insistence upon the importance of reason and evidence:

- The prophet Samuel stood before Israel and said: 'I am going to confront you with *evidence* before the LORD' (1 Samuel 12:7).
- God says to humans: 'let us *reason* together' (Isaiah 1:18).

- Jesus said the greatest commandment included the require-ment to 'love the Lord your God . . . *with all your mind'* (Matthew 22:37).
- Jesus said: *'believe on the evidence* of the miracles' (John 14:11).
- Paul *'reasoned . . . explaining* and *proving'* (Acts 17:2–3).
- Paul himself wrote of *'defending* and *confirming* the gospel' (Philippians 1:7).
- Paul urges Christians to *'stop thinking like children.* In regard to evil be infants, but *in your thinking be adults'* (1 Corinthians 14:20).
- Paul advises Christians to 'be ready to *give answers* to anyone who asks questions' (Colossians 4:6 [CEV]).
- Peter likewise commands Christians to 'always be prepared to *give an answer* to everyone who asks you to give the *reason* for the hope that you have . . .' (1 Peter 3:15).[136]

Hence Alister McGrath complains:

[Dawkins'] arbitrary and idiosyncratic definition [of 'faith'] sim-ply does not stand up to serious investigation. In fact, it is itself an excellent example of a belief tenaciously held and defended 'in the absence of evidence, even in the teeth of evidence' . . . the classic Christian tradition has always valued rationality, and does not hold that faith involves the complete abandonment of reason or believing in the teeth of evidence. Indeed, the Christian tradition is so consistent on this matter that it is difficult to understand where Dawkins has got the idea of faith as 'blind trust' from.[137]

McGrath has personally experienced the pernicious conse-quences of the new atheists' prejudicial mischaracterization of faith:

On several occasions I've been earnestly told by New Atheist foot soldiers that I have no business being a professor in a leading British university. After all, they inform me, I believe in God and am therefore stupid, evil and mentally unstable. I ought to be locked up for the public good. When I'm openly abused in this way, I find my most vociferous defenders are moderate atheists – often academics – who are sickened by such mindless hostility and alarmed at the damage it's inflicting on the public image of atheism.[138]

For example, atheist philosopher Keith M. Parsons comments that 'a dichotomy between faith and evidence is grossly simplistic. Faith need not be blind and science is not always quite as evidence-driven as simplistic stereotypes imply.'[139] Atheist Richard Norman cautions: 'faith means different things to different religious believers, and from the fact that they claim to have faith you can't infer that they are all irrationalists who believe things on "blind faith" without any evidence . . .'[140] As Moreland explains:

> The essence of faith – biblical or otherwise – is confidence or trust, and one can have faith in a thing (such as a chair) or a person (such as a parent, the president, or God), and one can have faith in the truth of a proposition . . . When trust is directed toward a person/thing, it is called 'faith in'; when it is directed toward the truth of a proposition, it is called 'faith that.' . . . It is a great misunderstanding of faith to oppose it to reason or knowledge. Nothing could be further from the truth. In actual fact, faith – confidence, trust – is rooted in knowledge.[141]

Hence Moreland defines faith as 'a trust in and commitment to what we have reason to believe is true.'[142] C.S. Lewis concurs:

> I think we must introduce into the discussion a distinction between two senses of the word *Faith*. This may mean (a) a settled intellectual assent. In that sense faith (or 'belief') in God hardly differs from faith in the uniformity of nature or in the consciousness of other people . . . It may also mean (b) a trust, or confidence, in the God whose existence is thus assented to. This involves an attitude of the will. It is more like our confidence in a friend.[143]

Lewis observes that 'Faith-A [belief] . . . is a necessary precondition of Faith-B [trust]'[144] and that 'philosophical arguments for the existence of God are presumably intended to produce Faith-A.'[145] Thus Lewis was no advocate of blind faith: 'I define Faith [i.e. Faith-B, trust] as the power of continuing to believe what we once honestly thought to be true [i.e. Faith-A, belief] until cogent reasons for honestly changing our minds are brought before us.'[146] Lewis thought of faith as 'the art of holding onto things your reason has once accepted, in spite of your changing moods.'[147] For moods change whatever view your reason takes:

> Now that I am a Christian I do have moods in which the whole thing looks very improbable: but when I was an atheist I had moods in which Christianity looked terribly probable . . . unless you teach your moods 'where to get off,' you can never be a sound Christian or even a sound atheist, but just a creature dithering to and fro, with its beliefs really dependent on the weather and the state of its digestion.[148]

Thus, in response to Grayling's misunderstanding of the 'theological virtue' of faith, Lewis would be keen to explain that:

> When we exhort people to Faith as a virtue, to the settled intention of continuing to believe certain things, we are not exhorting them to fight against reason . . . If we wish to be rational, not now and then, but constantly, we must pray for the gift of Faith, for the power to go on believing not in the teeth of reason but in the teeth of lust and terror and jealousy and boredom and indifference that which reason, authority, or experience, or all three, have once delivered to us for truth.[149]

Lewis didn't think his definition of faith was idiosyncratic:

> Nearly everyone I know who has embraced Christianity in adult life has been influenced by what seemed to him to be at least probable arguments for Theism . . . Even quite uneducated people who have been Christians all their lives not infrequently appeal to some simplified form of the Argument from Design. Even acceptance of tradition implies an argument which sometimes becomes explicit in the form 'I reckon all those wise men wouldn't have believed in it if it weren't true.'[150]

Moreover, as Sean McDowell and Jonathan Morrow explain: 'The fact that some Christians may have blind faith is not the same as

Christianity itself valuing blind faith and irrationality. Mainstream Christianity has always emphasized that faith and reason go together. Indeed, *biblical faith is trust in God because he has shown himself to be reliable and trustworthy*. Faith is not belief in spite of the evidence, but belief in light of the evidence.'[151]

Thus, although a person's faith *that* there is a God ('Faith-A') may have grounds that are more or less sophisticated and/or rationally compelling, *contra* the new atheists, there's nothing inherent within the definition of Christian faith that requires it to be sustained without rational warrant, let alone in the teeth of (overwhelming) evidence to the contrary. Indeed, for Lewis himself:

> Faith . . . does not flow from philosophical arguments alone; nor from experience of the Numinous alone; nor from moral experience alone; nor from history alone; but from historical events which at once fulfil and transcend the moral category, which link themselves with the most numinous elements in paganism, and which (as it seems to me) demand at their presupposition the existence of a Being who is more, but not less, than the God whom many reputable philosophers think they can establish.[152]

Conclusion

In the chapters to come we will retrace Lewis's exploration of the numinal, philosophical, moral and historical evidence that slowly convinced him to abandon his faith that atheism was true and to replace it with the faith that Christian theism is true. Along the way, we'll bring the arguments that shaped Lewis's spiritual journey into dialogue with today's new atheists.

* * *

Recommended Resources

By C.S. Lewis:
'De Futilitate', in *Christian Reflections* (ed. Walter Hooper; London: Fount, 1991)
'Is Theism Important?', in *C.S. Lewis Essay Collection: Faith, Christianity and the Church* (ed. Lesley Walmsley; London: HarperCollins, 2002)
'The Language of Religion', in *C.S. Lewis Essay Collection: Faith, Christianity and the Church* (ed. Lesley Walmsley; London: HarperCollins, 2002)

Video

Craig, William Lane. 'Origins of the Universe: Has Stephen Hawking Eliminated God?'
www.reasonablefaith.org/site/News2?page=NewsArticle&id=9227.

Audio

Williams, Peter S. 'Blind Faith in Blind Faith'
www.damaris.org/cm/podcasts/618.
— 'Hawking and the Grand Designer'
www.damaris.org/cm/podcasts/566.
— 'Is Science the Only Way to Know Anything?'
www.damaris.org/cm/podcasts/619.

Online papers

Invagen, Peter Van. 'Is It Wrong Everywhere, Always, and for Anyone to Believe Anything on Insufficient Evidence?'
http://comp.uark.edu/~senor/wrong.html.
Plantinga, Alvin. 'Reason and Belief'
http://philosophy.nd.edu/people/all/profiles/plantinga-alvin/documents/ReasonandBelief.pdf.
Russell, Bertrand. 'A Free Man's Worship'
www.philosophicalsociety.com/Archives/A%20Free%20Man's%20Worship.htm.

Books

Alston, William P. 'Religious Language and Verificationism.' Pages 17–32 in *The Rationality of Theism* (ed. Paul Copan and Paul K. Moser; London: Routledge, 2003).

Beckwith, Francis J., William Lane Craig and J.P. Moreland, eds. *To Everyone an Answer: A Case for the Christian Worldview* (Downers Grove, IL: IVP 2004).

Carter, Joe and John Coleman. *How to Argue Like Jesus: Learning Persuasion from History's Greatest Communicator* (Wheaton, IL: Crossway, 2009).

Craig, William Lane and J.P. Moreland, eds. *Naturalism: A Critical Analysis* (London: Routledge, 2000).

Flew, Antony. 'Theology and Falsification.' Pages 224–8 in *The Existence of God* (ed. John Hick; London: Collier, 1964).

Groothuis, Douglas. *On Jesus* (London: Thompson Wadsworth, 2003).

Horner, David A. *Mind Your Faith: A Student's Guide to Thinking and Living Well* (Downers Grove, IL: IVP Academic, 2011).

Koons, Robert C. 'Science and Theism: Concord, Not Conflict.' Pages 72–86 in *The Rationality of Theism* (ed. Paul Copan and Paul K. Moser; London: Routledge, 2003).

Kreeft, Peter. *Socrates Meets Hume: The Father of Philosophy Meets the Father of Modern Skepticism* (San Francisco: Ignatius, 2010).

Lennox, John. *Gunning for God: Why the New Atheists Are Missing the Target* (Oxford: Lion, 2011).

McDowell, Sean, ed. *Apologetics for a New Generation: A Biblically and Culturally Relevant Approach to Talking about God* (Eugene, OR: Harvest House, 2009).

McGrath, Alister. *The Passionate Intellect: Christian Faith and the Discipleship of the Mind* (Downers Grove, IL: IVP, 2010).

Monton, Bradley. *Seeking God in Science: An Atheist Defends Intelligent Design* (Toronto, Ontario: Broadview, 2009).][;][

Moreland, J.P. *Love God with All Your Mind: The Role of Reason in the Life of the Soul* (Colorado Springs: NavPress, 1997).

— and William Lane Craig. *Philosophical Foundations for a Christian Worldview* (Downers Grove, IL: IVP, 2003).

— and Mark Matlock. *Smart Faith: Loving Your God with All Your*

Mind (Colorado Springs: Think, 2005).

Plantinga, Alvin. *God and Other Minds: A Study of the Rational Justification of Belief in God* (Cornell University Press, new edn, 1990).

— *The Nature of Necessity* (Oxford: Clarendon Press, new edn, 1978).

3.

A Desire for Divinity?

Nature does nothing in vain.
A.C. Grayling, The Good Book[1]

Augustine lamented: 'I looked for pleasure, beauty, and truth not in [God] but in myself and his other creatures, and the search led me instead to pain, confusion, and error.'[2] Augustine's search eventually led him to believe that the true object of his desire was God, and to the exclamation: 'Late have I loved you, beauty so old and so new: late have I loved you!'[3] With the benefit of hindsight Augustine famously wrote: 'You made us for yourself, Lord; and our hearts are restless until they come to rest in you.'[4] Contemporary philosopher John Haldane comments:

> I have read this sentence many times: when things have been going well and when they have been going badly; when I have been confident in my beliefs and when I have doubted them; when feeling lifted by grace and when feeling burdened by sin. Augustine's words seem ever apt, and I ask myself why that should be. The answer is just a repetition of the words themselves: 'our hearts are restless until they come to rest in you.' Our striving and struggling, wishing and wanting, seek completion in something that is itself complete . . . something that made us for itself, not as an act of narcissism but as one of gratuitous generosity, and something that has the power to redeem innocent suffering. Should our yearnings be without the possibility of completion then we are indeed without point or purpose; but should these longings be purposeful in something close to the terms in which they represent themselves, then we can hope to enter into the eternal company of God. That is the

prospect offered by the theism I have been concerned to argue for, and it is, I believe, the best explanation of our heart's desire and of the possibility that evil is neither without point nor just response.[5]

A similar search for a transcendent something sensed within or through aesthetic experience was a golden thread running through the life of C.S. Lewis, who did much to develop what has since come to be known as the 'argument from desire' (AFD).

A Divine Romance

> As a deer longs for a stream of cool water,
> so I long for you, O God.
> Psalm 42:1 GNB

As Peter Kreeft explains, the AFD 'is more than an argument . . . it is also a meditation, an illumination, an experience, an invitation to an experiment with yourself, a pilgrimage.'[6] However, while it is more than an argument, it is not less. As an argument, this meditation can be summarized as follows:

Premise One: Every innate desire points to a corresponding object of satisfaction
Premise Two: We have innate desires that only God could satisfy
Conclusion: Therefore, God exists

This argument can easily be phrased inductively (by proposing that nature *probably* makes no innate human desire in vain, and so on). As Phil Fernandes writes: 'This argument is not meant to be an air-tight proof, but it does seem to have a high degree of probability since everything else man genuinely needs does in fact exist.'[7]

Sehnsucht

Let us deploy the German term *Sehnsucht* to describe that family of responses to the world linked by a combined sense of longing for, and displacement or alienation from, the object of desire. *Sehnsucht* is 'nostalgic longing', and it arises when experience of something within the world (particularly beauty) awakens in us a desire for something beyond what the natural world can offer as a corresponding object of desire: 'The thing I am speaking of is not an experience,' wrote Lewis. 'You have experienced only the want of it.'[8] *Sehnsucht* directs our attention towards the transcendent, that which 'goes beyond' our present experience.

The power of fairy tales lies in their ability to transport us into a world transparently imbued with *Sehnsucht*. Consider the experience of beauty that sustains Sam the Hobbit in the midst of Mordor's deathly landscape, from *The Return of the King*, by Lewis's friend J.R.R. Tolkien:

> There, peeping among the cloud-wrack above a dark tor high up in the mountains, Sam saw a white star twinkle for a while. The beauty of it smote his heart, as he looked up out of the forsaken land, and hope returned to him. For like a shaft, clear and cold, the thought pierced him that in the end the Shadow was only a small and passing thing: there was light and high beauty forever beyond its reach.[9]

Or take this passage from another book Lewis loved, *The Wind in the Willows*:

> A bird piped up suddenly, and was still; and a light breeze sprang up and set the reeds and bulrushes rustling. Rat, who was in the stern of the boat, while Mole sculled, sat up suddenly and listened with a passionate intentness. Mole, who with gentle strokes was just keeping the boat moving while he scanned the banks with care, looked at him with curiosity.
> 'It's gone!' sighed the Rat, sinking back in his seat again. 'So beautiful and strange and new! Since it was to end so soon, I almost wish I never had it. For it has roused a longing in me that is pain, and nothing seems worth while but just to hear that sound once more and go on listening to it forever.'[10]

Lewis warns: 'The books or the music in which we thought the beauty was located will betray us if we trust them; it was not in them, it only came *through* them, and what came through them was longing . . . Do what we will, then, we remain conscious of a desire which no natural happiness will satisfy.'[11] Of course, there is beauty in books and music, as there is in nature; but these things also stir within us a desire for a beauty greater than themselves that we seem to apprehend *through* the act of apprehending their beauty. As C.E.M. Joad mused: 'aesthetic emotion is at once the most satisfying and the most unsatisfying of all the emotions known to us; satisfying because of what it gives, unsatisfying because it gives so briefly, and, in the act of giving hints at greater gifts withheld'.[12] It is as if finite beauty is a derived quality that draws our aesthetic attention into the Platonic heaven of underived and absolute beauty:

> we want so much more – something the books on aesthetics take little notice of. But the poets and the mythologies know all about it. We do not want merely to see beauty, though, God knows, even that is bounty enough. We want something else which can hardly be put into words – to be united with the beauty we see . . . to receive it into ourselves . . . to become part of it . . . At present we are on the outside of the world, the wrong side of the door. We discern the freshness and purity of morning, but they do not make us feel fresh and pure. We cannot mingle with the splendors we see. But all the leaves of the New Testament are rustling with the rumor that it will not always be so. Some day, God willing, we shall get *in*. When human souls have become as perfect in voluntary obedience as the inanimate creation is in its lifeless obedience, then they will put on its glory, or rather that greater glory of which Nature is only the first sketch.[13]

The argument from desire claims that the most plausible interpretation of *Sehnsucht* is that it is a satisfiable desire for an eternal relationship with God. Lewis discussed the experience of *Sehnsucht* in three different contexts, which Peter Kreeft labels as 'autobiographical', 'practical-pastoral' and 'logical'.[14] These contexts are exemplified by Lewis's autobiography *Surprised by Joy*, the introduction to his semi-autobiographical allegorical novel *The Pilgrim's Regress*, and the theology-cum-apologetics of *Mere Christianity*.

Surprised by Joy

Lewis's autobiography *Surprised by Joy* (a title taken from a poem by Wordsworth) is concerned to describe his experience of 'an unsatisfied desire which is itself more desirable than any other satisfaction. I call it Joy . . .'[15] Lewis found that 'Joy' was occasioned by his appreciation of various aspects of reality, but pointed beyond such experiences and couldn't be contained within them: 'Only when your whole attention and desire are fixed on something else – whether a distant mountain, or the past, or the gods of Asgard – does the "thrill" arise. It is a by-product. Its very existence presupposes that you desire not it but something other and outer.'[16] 'Joy' is thus a state of consciousness that is occasioned by various objects of experience, but which is not a desire for any of the objects of experience that occasion it. Nor is it merely a mediated experience of a transcendent reality, nor even a desire to experience the 'thrill' of being in this particular state of mind, but rather it is *a desire for some transcendent object of satisfaction*. As Simone Weil notes: 'When we possess a beautiful thing, we still desire something . . . We want to get behind the beauty, but it . . . like a mirror sends back our own desire for goodness. It is a . . . mystery that is painfully tantalizing.'[17]

Lewis traces his life via a series of lived experiments wherein he pursues 'Joy' and discovers that one object of attention after another occasions this desire but fails to fulfil it: 'What I like about experience is that it is such an honest thing. You may take any number of wrong turnings; but keep your eyes open and you will not be allowed to go very far before the warning signs appear. You may have deceived yourself, but experience is not trying to deceive you. The universe rings true wherever you fairly test it.'[18]

Lewis describes his spiritual life as a series of 'wrong turnings' in pursuit of the reality that would satisfy the desire he calls 'Joy', and how his eventual admission of God's existence, and subsequent conversion to Christianity, brought him to the conclusion that 'Joy' was the desire for a proper relationship with God – a destination that cannot be fully attained until heaven, but which (partly by a process of experiential elimination) can be located and glimpsed from within the present world:

But what, in conclusion, about Joy? for that, after all, is what the story has mainly been about. To tell you the truth, the subject has lost nearly all interest for me since I became a Christian. I cannot, indeed, complain, like Wordsworth, that the visionary gleam has passed away. I believe (if the thing were at all worth recording) that the old stab, the old bitter-sweet, has come to me as often and as sharply since my conversion as at any time of my life whatever. But I now know that the experience, considered as a state of my own mind, had never had the kind of importance I once gave it. It was valuable only as a pointer to something other and outer. While that was in doubt, the pointer naturally loomed large in my thoughts. When we are lost in the woods the sight of a signpost is a great matter. He who first sees it cries 'Look!' The whole party gathers round and stares. But when we have found the road and are passing signposts every few miles, we shall not stop and stare. They will encourage us and we shall be grateful to the authority that set them up. But we shall not stop and stare, or not much; not on this road, though their pillars are of silver and their lettering of gold. 'We would be at Jerusalem.'[19]

If we experience a desire that remains unsatisfied by worldly objects of desire, but the desire is partially satisfied by an apparently transcendent object of desire (just as a large thirst is partially satisfied by a small drink) – an object which not only provides a coherent explanation of our desire, but of the failure of worldly goods to satisfy it, and of the partial nature of the satisfaction offered here and now, and which offers the possibility of future total satisfaction – then we are *prima facie* justified in concluding that this apparent object is indeed the real object of our desire.

The Pilgrim's Regress

Absence does not mean non-existence; and a man drinking
a toast of absent friends does not mean that from his life all
friendship is absent. It is a void but it is not a negation; it is
something as positive as an empty chair.
G.K. Chesterton[20]

In this allegorical novel Lewis traces his spiritual journey 'from "popular realism" to "Philosophical Idealism"; from Idealism to

Pantheism; from Pantheism to Theism; and from Theism to Christianity.'[21] Central to Lewis's story is 'a particular recurrent experience which dominated my childhood and adolescence and which I hastily called "Romantic" because inanimate nature and marvellous literature were among the things that evoked it. I still believe that the experience is common, commonly misunderstood, and of immense importance . . .'[22] Lewis describes the experience he called 'Romantic' (which is one and the same as the experience he later called 'Joy'):

> The experience is one of intense longing. It is distinguished from other longings by two things. In the first place, though the sense of want is acute and even painful, yet the mere wanting is felt to be somehow a delight. Other desires are felt as pleasures only if satisfaction is expected in the near future: hunger is pleasant only when we know (or believe) that we are soon going to eat. But this desire, even when there is no hope of possible satisfaction, continues to be prized, and even to be preferred to anything else in the world, by those who have once felt it. This hunger is better than any other fullness; this poverty better than all other wealth. And thus it comes about, that if the desire is long absent, it may itself be desired, and that new desiring becomes a new instance of the original desire . . . In the second place, there is a peculiar mystery about the *object* of this Desire. Inexperienced people (and inattention leaves some inexperienced all their lives) suppose, when they feel it, that they know what they are desiring. Thus if it comes to a child while he is looking at a far off hillside he at once thinks 'if only I were there'; if it comes when he is remembering some event in the past, he thinks 'if only I could go back to those days' . . . But every one of these impressions is wrong . . . I know them to be wrong not by intelligence but by experience . . . For I have myself been deluded by every one of these false answers in turn, and have contemplated each of them earnestly enough to discover the cheat . . .[23]

According to Lewis, the 'cheat' is that 'every one of these supposed *objects* of the Desire is inadequate to it. An easy experiment will show that by going to the far hillside you will get either nothing, or else a recurrence of the same desire which sent you thither.'[24]

Not only is each of the supposed earthly objects of the 'Romantic' desire inadequate to it, but it is a defining feature of the 'Romantic' desire that it is occasioned by all manner of earthly objects (occasions that may vary from person to person) which may be mistaken as the object of the desire but which are discovered by bitter experience not to be the object of the desire:

> Lust can be gratified. Another personality can become to us 'our America, our New-found-land'. A happy marriage can be achieved. But what has any of the three, or any mixture of the three, to do with that unnameable something, desire for which pierces us like a rapier at the smell of a bonfire, the sound of wild ducks flying overhead, the title of *The Well at the World's End*, the opening lines of *Kubla Khan*, the morning in late summer, or the noise of falling waves?[25]

Richard Dawkins notes: 'It is often said that there is a God-shaped gap in the brain [actually, following Pascal, it is the heart which is traditionally mentioned] which needs to be filled . . .'[26] and he poses the rhetorical question: 'could it be that God clutters up a gap that we'd be better off filling with something else? Science, perhaps? Art? Human friendship? Humanism? Love of this life in the real world, giving no credence to other lives beyond the grave?'[27] Dawkins' question is ill-formed precisely because it is *in the very appreciation of* science, art, human friendship and so on that we discover an unsatisfied desire for something 'more'.

The winding path of Lewis's own spiritual journey was determined by his pursuit of the proper object of this 'Romantic' longing:

> It appeared to me therefore that if a man diligently followed this desire, pursuing the false objects until their falsity appeared and then resolutely abandoning them, he must come at last to the clear knowledge that the human soul was made to enjoy some object that is never fully given – nay, cannot even be imagined as given – in our present mode of subjective and spatio-temporal experience. This Desire was, in the soul, as the Siege Perilous in Arthur's castle – the chair in which only one could sit. And if

nature makes nothing in vain, the One who can sit in this chair must exist.[28]

A.C. Grayling's 'secular Bible', *The Good Book*, affirms that 'nature does nothing in vain',[29] but as Peter Kreeft comments: '*If* nature makes nothing in vain, if you admit the premise, the conclusion necessarily follows. Of course, one who wants to refuse to admit the conclusion at all costs will deny the premise – but at the cost of a meaningful universe, a universe in which desires and satisfactions match.'[30] A universe in which innate desires and satisfactions do not match would be 'absurd' in the technical sense of the term explored in *The Myth of Sisyphus* by French existentialist Albert Camus: 'absurdity springs from a comparison . . . between a bare fact and a certain reality, between an action and the world that transcends it. The absurd is essentially a divorce. It lies in neither of the elements compared; it is born of their confrontation.'[31] That is, an absurd universe is one which fails to form a coherent whole because there is a divorce between the innate needs of human beings and what the universe has to offer by way of satisfaction for those needs. As Stephen T. Davies explains:

> Camus's basic assumption was that life is absurd . . . We long for some sort of Meaning in Life, but there is none . . . We want there to exist a kindly, loving God, but no such being exists . . . We hope for life after death, but death is the end of our existence. We long for some sort of grand, over-arching explanation of life and history and human existence, but no such over-arching explanation is available.[32]

The argument from desire can be phrased so as to bring out the underlying dilemma about the absurdity of a universe that contains a fundamental mismatch between innate desires and satisfactions:

1) Unless every innate desire has a corresponding object of satisfaction the universe is existentially absurd
2) The universe is not existentially absurd
3) Therefore, every innate desire has a corresponding object of satisfaction

4) Humans have an innate desire for the divine (i.e. an innate desire most plausibly interpreted as a desire for God and/or for satisfactions only available if God exists)
5) Therefore, divinity exists

One can escape this argument by claiming that the universe is existentially absurd, but where's the sense in doing that?!

Mere Christianity
> There is in man a restlessness of ambition; an interminable longing after nobler and higher things . . . a dissatisfaction with the present, which never is appeased by all that the world has to offer.
> *Thomas Chalmers*[33]

In *Mere Christianity* Lewis makes the AFD the centrepiece of his chapter on the theological virtue of 'hope'. Asserting that 'looking forward to the eternal world is not (as some modern people think) a form of escapism or wishful thinking, but one of the things a Christian is meant to do',[34] Lewis affirms:

> Most people, if they had really learned to look into their own hearts, would know that they do want, and want acutely, something that cannot be had in this world. There are all sorts of things in this world that offer to give it to you, but they never quite keep their promise. The longings which arise in us when we first fall in love, or first think of some foreign country, or first take up some subject that excites us, are longings which no marriage, no travel, no learning, can really satisfy.[35]

Humans have a desire that, while it may be awoken by the things of this world, is, if we are honest with ourselves, left perpetually unsatiated by the things of this world: 'There was something we grasped at, in the first moments of longing, which just faded away in the reality . . . something has evaded us.' [36] Lewis observes that there are three ways of dealing with this unsatisfied sense of longing, two of which he argues are to be avoided, leaving us with one response which is to be embraced.

Lewis calls the first way:

The Fool's Way – He puts the blame on the things themselves. He goes on all his life thinking that if only he tried another woman, or went on a more expensive holiday, or whatever it is, then, this time, he really would catch the mysterious something we are all after. Most of the bored, discontented, rich people in the world are of this type. They spend their whole lives trotting from woman to woman . . . continent to continent, hobby to hobby, always thinking that the latest is 'the Real Thing' at last, and always disappointed.[37]

Those who blame the immanent objects of satisfaction provided by this world for their inability to answer the transcendent longing they occasion are 'fools' in that they ignore (perhaps because they are begging the question against the possibility of a transcendent object of satisfaction) an ever-mounting inference from experience against their assumption that this desire has an earthly satisfaction. This inductive argument means that one needn't *exhaustively* pursue the 'lived dialectic' of Lewis's argument from desire to reach the justifiable (if falsifiable) conclusion that the desire in question has no this-worldly object of satisfaction. Moreover, the hypothesis that relationship with God is the object of the 'Romantic' desire, a desire *occasioned* but not *answered* by our relationship with various aspects of the creation that reflect its Creator, explains why it is that those who continue to seek satisfaction for this desire in the created realm are repeatedly disappointed. As Pascal wrote:

Man tries unsuccessfully to fill this void with everything that surrounds him, seeking in absent things the help he cannot find in those that are present, but all are incapable of it. This infinite abyss can be filled only with an infinite, immutable object, that is to say, God himself. He alone is our true good. From the time we have forsaken him, it is a curious thing that nothing in nature has been capable of taking his place.[38]

Lewis calls the second way:

The Way of the Disillusioned 'Sensible Man' – He soon decides that the whole thing was moonshine. 'Of course,' he says, 'one feels like that when one is young. But by the time you get to my age you've given up on chasing the rainbow's end.' And so he settles down and learns not to expect too much and represses the part of himself which used, as he would say, 'to cry for the moon.'[39]

Richard Dawkins takes the way of the disillusioned 'sensible man' when he writes about filling the 'God-shaped gap' with 'life in the real world'.[40] Lewis regards this as an improvement upon the way of the fool, for it 'makes a man much happier and less of a nuisance to society. It tends to make him a prig (he is apt to be rather superior towards what he calls "adolescents"), but, on the whole, he rubs along fairly comfortably.'[41] Lewis's critique of the 'sensible man' is both ethical and pragmatic. He argues that the way of the sensible man 'would be the best line we could take if man did not live forever. But supposing infinite happiness really is there, waiting for us? Supposing one really can reach the rainbow's end? In that case, it would be a pity to find out too late (a moment after death) that by our supposed "common sense" we had stifled in ourselves the faculty of enjoying it.'[42]

If there's no possibility of infinite happiness beyond our earthly existence, then we won't be around to discover that the way of the 'sensible man' was right and that the way of the Christian (Lewis's third option) was wrong. On the other hand, if there is such a possibility, then we will be around to discover that the way of the 'sensible man' was wrong and the way of the Christian right. In practical terms, then, we have little if anything to lose, and much to gain, by at least exploring the Christian response to our unsatisfied desire in this life.

Of the third, 'Christian Way', Lewis additionally writes:

> The Christian says, 'Creatures are not born with desires unless satisfaction for those desires exists. A baby feels hunger: well, there is such a thing as food. A duckling wants to swim: well, there is such a thing as water. Men feel sexual desire: well, there is such a thing as sex. If I find in myself a desire which no experience in this world can satisfy, the most probable explanation is that I was made for another world. If none of my earthly pleasures satisfy it, that does not prove that the universe is a fraud. Probably earthly pleasures were never meant to satisfy it, but only to arouse it, to

suggest the real thing. If that is so, I must take care, on the one hand, never to despise, or be unthankful for, these earthly blessings, and on the other, never to mistake them for the something else of which they are only a kind of copy, or echo, or mirage. I must keep alive in myself the desire for my true country, which I shall not find till after death . . .'[43]

These comments constitute a further argument against the way of the 'sensible man'. Lewis begins with the premise that creatures don't have innate desires (desires they are 'born with') unless satisfaction for those desires exists. The examples he gives provide inferential support for this claim. As Thomas Chalmers observed:

> For every desire or every faculty, whether in man or in the inferior animals, there seems a counterpart object in external nature . . . there exists a something without that is altogether suited to it, and which seems to be expressly provided for its gratification. There is light for the eye; there is air for the lungs; there is food for the ever-recurring appetite of hunger; there is water for the appetite of thirst . . . in a word, there seems not one affection in the living creature, which is not met by a counterpart. . .[44]

Given this premise, Lewis argues that the existence of a desire that experience leads us to infer (*contra* the blind faith of the 'fool') cannot be satisfied by any object in the present world, supports the conclusion (*contra* the cynicism of the 'sensible man') that the desire in question has a satisfaction *obtainable in another world*. As C. Stephen Evans argues:

> The fact that people in general have a need for water is strong evidence that there is such a thing as water, though this does not imply that an individual person will get water on any specific occasion. In a similar manner, the fact that we have a deep need to believe in and find God strongly suggests that God is real, though of course this does not mean that any one of us will actually discover God and establish a relationship with him. It would be very odd indeed if we had a fundamental need for something that did not exist.[45]

The Blind Faith of Neo-Atheists

> Ignorance more frequently begets confidence
> than does knowledge.
> *Charles Darwin*[46]

While various objections that deserve a response have been raised against the argument from desire, very few of these objections are to be found in neo-atheist works. Richard Dawkins' brief and confused comments about filling the purported 'God-shaped gap' with 'life in the real world'[47] are about as close as any of the new atheists come to directly engaging with the argument from desire. This is surely rather strange given the prominence accorded to Lewis as a Christian apologist in new-atheist writings and the prominent role this argument plays in Lewis's thought.

Indeed, if their atheism is to escape characterization as a belief held in the teeth of contrary evidence, the new atheists really must put more effort into rebutting natural theology (that is, arguments for God). The shocking fact of the matter is that the new atheists mainly deal with arguments for God (such as the argument from desire) *by ignoring them.* As James E. Taylor comments in his article on 'The New Atheists' in the peer-reviewed *Internet Encyclopedia of Philosophy*:

> Since atheism continues to be a highly controversial philosophical position, one would expect that the New Atheists would devote a fair amount of space to a careful (and, of course, critical) consideration of arguments for God's existence and that they would also spend a corresponding amount of time formulating a case for the non-existence of God. However, none of them addresses either theistic or atheistic arguments to any great extent. Dawkins does devote a chapter apiece to each of these tasks, but he has been criticized for engaging in an overly cursory evaluation of theistic arguments and for ignoring the philosophical literature in natural theology.[48]

Similarly, Alvin Plantinga complains that '[Daniel] Dennett . . . doesn't know anything about contemporary analytic philosophy of religion, but that doesn't stop him from making public declarations on the subject.'[49] In his review of *The God Delusion* for *Free Inquiry*, Dennett nonchalantly admits to dropping the ball with respect to the arguments for theism in his book *Breaking the Spell* and declares himself content to simply pass the ball to Dawkins:

> I give short shrift to the task of rebutting the standard arguments for the existence of God [in *Breaking the Spell*] so I welcome the characteristically trenchant and imaginative demolitions that Dawkins has assembled. If you encounter people who think it might still be intellectually respectable to believe in God in any literal sense, direct them to *The God Delusion*, where they will get their heads dismantled – and reassembled with a different perspective.[50]

This is a truly astonishing statement, for as Jeremy Pierce comments: 'Dawkins is not a philosopher, never mind a well-trained one, and what he says demonstrates that he is hardly familiar with the literature in philosophy of religion. He regularly commits easy-to-spot fallacies . . .'[51] Likewise, Dr James Hannam complains that *The God Delusion* is:

> under-researched, under-argued and appears to have been dashed off the cuff. Few scholarly references are given . . . no effort is made to understand counterarguments . . . The treatment of the traditional proofs of God's existence is largely an attack on straw men. The cosmological argument is far stronger than Dawkins gives it credit for and he does not bother [to] interact with its modern proponents like William Lane Craig. On the ontological argument, Alvin Plantinga is the man to go to, but Dawkins goes nowhere near him . . . This refusal to engage with the serious literature is evident throughout *The God Delusion*, whether the subject is biblical studies, anthropology, ethics or philosophy.[52]

Nevertheless, according to Dennett: 'Dawkins set out to expose and discredit every source of the God delusion, and even when he is going over familiar ground . . . he almost invariably finds some novel twist that refreshes our imaginations.'[53] In point of fact, the most 'novel' aspect of Dawkins' treatment of the arguments for

God is the way in which he repeatedly misstates the arguments so as to give himself a fair fight against a random collection of straw men. It is truly shocking to see a professional philosopher like Dennett portraying Dawkins as 'flattening all the serious arguments for the existence of God . . .'[54] Sure, of the new-atheist books published thus far, *The God Delusion* makes the most fulsome attempt to grapple with natural theology; but that's not saying a lot! In chapter three ('Arguments for God's Existence') Dawkins devotes just thirty-seven pages to *ten* arguments for God (eleven if one counts the Baysean method of assessing arguments as a cumulative argument in its own right. He also discusses Pascal's 'wager', but that's an argument for belief in God rather than an argument for God's existence). By contrast, the Last Seminary website groups philosophy of religion papers in the field of natural theology into *fourteen general categories of theistic argument*, many of which contain significant subcategories.[55] Philosophers Peter Kreeft and Ronald K. Tacelli summarize 'Twenty Arguments for the Existence of God'[56] (including Pascal's wager) in their *Handbook of Christian Apologetics* (IVP, 1994). Alvin Plantinga once sketched out 'a couple of dozen or so'[57] arguments for God's existence that he thought deserved careful consideration. Hence, even if Dawkins' critique of the arguments he does consider were the decisive refutations portrayed by Dennett, *The God Delusion* still wouldn't merit P.Z. Myers' inflated appraisal as 'a thorough overview of the logic of belief and disbelief [that] reviews, dismantles, and dismisses the major arguments for the existence of the supernatural and deities.'[58]

In *The God Delusion* Dawkins recounts how 'Bertrand Russell was asked what he would say if he died and found himself confronted by God, demanding to know why Russell had not believed in him. "Not enough evidence, God, not enough evidence," was Russell's (I almost said immortal) reply.'[59] Dawkins clearly sees himself following in Russell's footsteps in the same hypothetical situation. Hypothetically, it seems to me that God would be perfectly within his rights to observe that it wasn't the evidence that was lacking so much as Dawkins' willingness to examine it.

Of course, Dawkins conspicuously fails to rebut even the theistic arguments he does consider. Plantinga's professional verdict on Dawkins-the-philosopher is to the point: 'You might say that some of his forays into philosophy are at best sophomoric, but that would be unfair to sophomores; the fact is . . . many of his arguments would receive a failing grade in a sophomore philosophy class.'[60] Philosopher Barney Zwartz agrees that Dawkins 'is not nearly as good a philosopher as he supposes . . . On nearly every page I found myself wanting to argue, not just with his arguments (or mere assertions), but with the often slipshod or superficial way he puts them . . . He is spectacularly inept when it comes to the traditional philosophical arguments for God . . .'[61] Michael Ruse acknowledges:

> It is not that the atheists are having a field day because of the brilliance and novelty of their thinking. Frankly – and I speak here as a non-believer myself, pretty atheistic about Christianity and skeptical about all theological claims – the material being churned out is second rate. And that is a euphemism for 'downright awful.' . . . Dawkins is brazen in his ignorance of philosophy and theology (not to mention the history of science) . . . Dawkins . . . is a man truly out of his depth.[62]

Atheist Thomas Nagel laments: 'Dawkins dismisses, with contemptuous flippancy, the traditional . . . arguments for the existence of God offered by Aquinas and Anselm. I found these attempts at philosophy, along with those in a later chapter on religion and ethics, particularly weak . . .'[63] As Jay Tolson comments: 'Philosophical arguments for or against God are more sophisticated than one might learn from Dawkins, who sometimes comes close to confirming Francis Bacon's adage that a little philosophy inclineth man's mind to atheism, but depth in philosophy bringeth men's minds about to religion.'[64]

Contrast the amateur philosophizing of *The God Delusion* with the professional papers collected in *The Blackwell Companion to Natural Theology* (Wiley-Blackwell, 2009), a book described by atheist Quentin Smith as 'required reading for philosophers of religion'.[65] Of the nine chapters that present theistic arguments in this significant volume, how many would be familiar on the basis of having read *The God Delusion*? Five. Actually, that's a rather generous count. Dawkins only takes on a straw-man version of the 'first cause' *Kalam* cosmological argument, defended in the Blackwell companion by William Lane Craig and James D. Sinclair.[66] Dawkins doesn't even bother laying out the sort of argument from religious experience defended by Kai-Man Kwan before dismissing religious experience with a logically fallacious flick of the wrist (Dawkins makes an invalid leap from the premise that some experiences are illusory to the conclusion that all religious experiences are illusory). In light of Mark D. Linville's discussion of the moral argument,[67] Dawkins' comments on the subject are obviously rather superficial red herrings. Dawkins ignores the sophisticated modern type of modal ontological argument defended by Robert E. Maydole, in favour of trashing the weaker of Anselm's eleventh-century original formulations thereof (which he dismisses by relying upon the long-rebutted criticisms of Hume and Kant). However, the main point here isn't Dawkins' penchant for attacking straw men with rubber daggers, but his failure to 'cover the waterfront'. Anyone who could mistake *The God Delusion* for the thorough overview lauded by Daniel Dennett or P.Z. Myer simply wouldn't know about the argument from desire, or 'the argument from consciousness' (defended in the Blackwell volume by J.P. Moreland), or 'the argument from reason' (defended therein by Victor Reppert), whereas these were precisely the considerations that weighed most heavily with C.S. Lewis. Finally, Dawkins completely ignores the 'minimal facts' argument for Jesus' resurrection marshalled in the Blackwell companion by Timothy and Lydia McGrew.[68] In reality, then, Dawkins' review of natural theology is anything but 'thorough' in either breadth or depth. And remember, Dawkins provides the most conscientious new-atheist engagement with natural theology! As Paul Copan complains: 'the new atheists are remarkably out of touch with [contemporary] sophisticated theistic arguments for God's existence.'[69]

Fortunately for our purposes, although the new atheists *generally* fail to engage directly with the arguments that changed Lewis's mind, they do at least comment upon related issues in a way that can be taken as an *indirect* engagement with the relevant arguments. While we'll have to do rather a lot of 'filling in' for the new atheists in posing objections to the AFD in this chapter, future chapters will deliver a greater degree of dialogue between Lewis and the neo-atheists.

Seven objections to the argument from desire

1. The 'wishful thinking' objection

As new atheist Peter Atkins rightly observes: 'longing is not itself an adequate proof of the existence of what is longed for.'[70] However, the argument from desire depends upon the distinction between innate and artificial desires:

> The major premise implicitly distinguishes desires into two kinds: innate and conditioned, natural and artificial. We naturally desire things like food, drink, sex, knowledge, friendship, and beauty, and we naturally turn away from things like starvation, ignorance, loneliness, and ugliness. We also desire things like Rolls Royces, political offices, flying through the air like Superman, a Red Sox world championship, and lands like Oz. But there are two differences between the two lists. First, we do not always recognize corresponding states of deprivation of the second, as we do the first. And, most important, the first list of desires all come from within, from our nature, while the second come from without, from society, or advertising, or fiction.[71]

Although artificial desires don't necessarily have a correlating object of desire (Rolls Royces exist but Narnia does not), it is possible to argue that *innate* desires necessarily (or at least probably) correlate with answering objects of desire. After all: 'the existence of desires in the first class, in every discoverable case, does mean that the objects desired exist.'[72] As Richard Purtill argues:

> Hunger is natural; food, which is its object, exists. Sexual desire is normal; sexual satisfaction is possible. And if there is in our nature a desire for something that no finite object will satisfy, then we can argue that something exists that will satisfy that longing. The inference is not certain, but it is overwhelmingly probable; longings do not exist unless they can be satisfied . . . The price one pays for [rejecting] this line [of argument] is that it makes the desires in question unsatisfiable in principle. If our 'infinite

longings' do not mean that an infinite object exists to satisfy them, then they mean that [uniquely in this case] we shall never be satisfied . . . it is possible to resist the pull towards God in our . . . experience . . . but if we do so we invalidate those experiences themselves.[73]

From the premise that all innate desires (probably) have satisfactions, one may validly conclude, via the minor premise that humans have a desire for communion with God which is more plausibly to be considered innate than artificial, that God (probably) exists. As Steve Lovell writes: 'Once the meaning of these premises is made clear, it will be evident that the argument is a valid one, that if the premises are true then the conclusion must also be true.'[74]

2. The 'begging the question' objection

Atheist John Beversluis thinks that far from being logically valid, Lewis's argument from desire is guilty of begging the question:

[Lewis's] reasons for thinking that [Joy has a real object] were, first, that Joy is a natural desire, and second, that every natural desire has a real object. But this is puzzling. How could Lewis have known that every natural desire has a real object *before* knowing that Joy has one? I can legitimately claim that every student in the class has failed the test only if I first know that each of them has individually failed it. The same is true of natural desires.[75]

However, Beversluis's objection a) only applies to the deductive formulation of Lewis's argument (indeed, this objection applies to all deductive arguments, and does so by assuming the truth of empiricism[76]) and b) even then, ignores the fact that the premises of a deductive argument can themselves be justified inductively. As Edward M. Cook comments: 'If every known natural desire has an object, that is a good reason for thinking that Joy has one too, although it does not logically entail it. Beversluis is accusing the Argument from Desire of failing to provide the certainty of a deductive argument, all the while failing to notice that it provides all the certainty proper to an inductive one.'[77] Moreover, the 'absurdity' version of the argument from desire turns on the very issue of whether or not every natural desire has a real object. Hence Beversluis's objection amounts to his being prepared to pay the price of agreeing with Camus that the universe is absurd. This is a philosophical price that many thinkers are simply not prepared to pay.

Then again, if the universe were absurd, just how much confidence should Beversluis place in his ability to rationally assess philosophical arguments? Isn't there something fundamentally incoherent about wanting one's own thinking to be reliable on the one hand while believing that the universe as a whole is unreliable to the point of absurdity on the other hand? As Lewis argued:

> Surely the dilemma is plain. Either there is significance in the whole process of things as well as in human activity, or there is no significance in human activity itself. It is an idle dream, at once cowardly and arrogant, that we can withdraw the human soul, as a mere epiphenomenon, from a universe of idiotic force, and yet hope, after that, to find for her some *faubourg* where she can keep a mock court in exile. You cannot have it both ways. If the world is meaningless, then so are we; if we mean something, we do not mean alone.[78]

We are touching here upon what has come to be known as 'the argument from rationality', an argument that will occupy our attention in chapter four.

3. The 'We don't necessarily get what we want' objection

According to Beversluis: 'the phenomenon of hunger simply does not prove that man inhabits a world in which food exists. . . What proves that we inhabit a world in which food exists is the discovery that certain things are in fact eatable. . . The Desire in and of itself proves nothing.'[79] However, we would surely be very surprised to discover a species with a desire for sex but which lacked reproductive organs! But why would we be surprised, unless desire does in fact prove something?

Jacques Maritain's formulation of the argument from desire specifically circumvents this objection:

Because this desire which asks for what is impossible to nature is a desire of nature in its profoundest depths, it cannot issue in an absolute impossibility. It is in no wise necessary that it *be* satisfied, since it asks for what is impossible for nature. But it is necessary that by some means (which is not nature) it be *able* to be satisfied, since it necessarily emanates from nature. In other words it is necessary that an order superior to nature be possible in which man is capable of that of which nature is incapable but which it necessarily desires.[80]

As Lewis argued:

A man's physical hunger does not prove that man will get any bread; he may die of starvation . . . But surely a man's hunger does prove that he comes of a race which repairs its body by eating and inhabits a world where eatable substances exist. In the same way, though I do not believe (I wish I did) that my desire for Paradise proves that I shall enjoy it, I think it a pretty good indication that such a thing exists and that some men will.[81]

4. The 'contrary desire' objection

As an unbeliever, Lewis saw God as a 'transcendental Interferer'; hence he recalls: 'That which I greatly feared had at last come upon me. In the Trinity Term of 1929 I gave in, and admitted that God was God, and knelt and prayed: perhaps, that night, the most dejected and reluctant convert in all England.'[82] He also saw himself as 'the Prodigal Son . . . brought in kicking, struggling, resentful, and darting his eyes in every direction for a chance of escape . . .'[83] Beversluis asks: 'If Joy's object really is God, and if all desire is really desire for him, why when he was brought face to face with him did Lewis *cease* to desire him and search for a way of escape?'[84] According to Beversluis: 'Either God is the ultimate object of desire or he is not. If he is, then it makes no sense to talk about shrinking from him the moment he is found.'[85] Beversluis assumes that the AFD does not apply to any desire that can be brought into conflict with a contrary desire. However, this assumption doesn't seem to be true. As Adam Barkman observes: 'people can at once desire something for one reason and in one way, and yet also feel frightened of it for another reason and in another way.'[86] For example, the desire for social interaction is surely an innate human desire; but people can certainly exhibit the contrary desire of the agoraphobic. Hence Peter Kreeft calls this 'just about the silliest and shallowest objection I have ever read.'[87] He asks: 'How did a virgin feel about her wedding night in the days before the sexual revolution? Was there not often a fear of the great, the mysterious, the unknown, the "bigger than both of us", as well as a deep desire for it?'[88] However much a wild animal may desire to be freed from a trap, it will nevertheless initially fear the approach of the only being capable of bringing that desire to fruition.

5. The 'continuing desire' objection

Another objection might be that religious belief doesn't reliably or fully satisfy our supposed need for God. When you are hungry, eating (enough) food stops you being hungry (for a while). Although people feel a desire for God, purported religious experience doesn't seem to satiate that desire. This, it might be held, counts against taking the desire for God as based upon a real need for God. However, this objection is like arguing that since a little food does not satiate people's hunger for ever, hunger is not the result of a need for food!

The analogy with hunger, like all analogies, is misleading if pushed too far, because while food is a limited good, a relationship with God crucially includes unlimited goods (e.g. knowledge and appreciative love of the divine beauty). While we can have enough or even too much of a limited good, we can never have enough or too much of an unlimited good like God; so pointing out that believers can't get enough of God to sate their desire for God doesn't count against the AFD. The theistic hypothesis is that eternal life (which requires the existence of God) is the human *telos*, without which we would be ultimately unfulfilled. Eternal life is something that can begin here and now, but Christians have never claimed that eternal life can truly flourish until the advent of the 'new heavens and the new earth'. In heaven then, it is claimed, the eternal life that begins here and now can progress to a higher or deeper level because the limiting factor of sin will be stripped away. In the meantime, the fact that purported experiences of God at least *partially meet certain needs within people better than the alternatives* is evidence that heaven is the human *telos*, just as the fact that a little food takes the edge off hunger proves that enough food will satiate it.

6. The 'I'm happy as I am' objection

There's all the difference in the world between a profession of genuine earthly satisfaction (the denial of any innate desire that could be interpreted as a desire for God) and what Lewis called:

> The Way of the Disillusioned 'Sensible Man' [who] decides that the whole thing was moonshine. 'Of course,' he says, 'one feels like that when one is young. But by the time you get to my age you've given up on chasing the rainbow's end.' And so he settles down and learns not to expect too much and represses the part of himself which used, as he would say, 'to cry for the moon.'[89]

Those who know they are settling for second best know that they once hoped for more; hence Peter Kreeft suggests that the 'I'm happy as I am' objection 'verges on culpable dishonesty . . . and requires something more like exorcism than refutation.'[90]

Many atheists openly admit the existence of a yearning for a transcendent reality that they deny:

- According to Albert Camus: 'For anyone who is alone, without God and without a master, the weight of days is dreadful.'[91]
- Friedrich Nietzsche wrote of Dante and Spinoza that 'their way of thinking, compared to mine, was one which made solitude bearable; and in the end, for all those who somehow still had a "God" for company . . . My life now consists in the wish that it might be otherwise with all the things that I comprehend, and that somebody might make *my* "truths" appear incredible to me.'[92]
- Jean-Paul Sartre wrote: 'I needed God . . . I reached out for religion, I longed for it, it was the remedy.'[93] But as Arthur F. Holmes recounts: 'The novels and plays of Jean-Paul Sartre portray man's futile attempt to create meaning . . . underlying his pessimism is an outright denial of the existence of God . . .

Either God exists and thereby guarantees life's meaning and wholeness, or else God does not exist, religion is irrelevant, and life falls apart.'[94] For Sartre, atheism was consequently 'a cruel and long-range affair'.[95]

- Bruce Sheiman admits: 'I want to believe that the reason we finite beings reach out to an ineffable and unfathomable Absolute is because we are *Imago Dei*. I want to believe that our timeless quest for goodness and transcendence has its Omega Point in God . . . even though I cannot believe in God, I still feel the need for God.'[96]
- H.G. Wells admitted: 'Unless there is a more abundant life before mankind, this scheme of space and time is a bad joke beyond our understanding, a flare of vulgarity, an empty laugh braying across the mysteries.'[97]

Bertrand Russell professed to believe that:

> man is the product of causes that had no prevision of the end they were achieving . . . his origin, his growth, his hopes and fears, his loves, his beliefs, are but the outcome of accidental collocations of atoms . . . [while] the whole temple of man's achievement must inevitably be buried beneath the debris of a universe in ruins . . . Only within the scaffolding of these truths, only on the firm foundation of unyielding despair, can the soul's habitation, henceforth, be safely built.[98]

But how can Russell's 'scaffolding of . . . unyielding despair' be a 'firm foundation' upon which to build a life? Surely, 'this is psychologically impossible and logically contradictory; despair is not a "firm foundation" but precisely the lack of one.'[99] As Russell admitted:

> Even when one feels nearest to other people, something in one seems obstinately to belong to God, and to refuse to enter into any earthly communion – at least that is how I should express it if I thought there was a God. It is odd, isn't it? I care passionately for this world and many things and people in it, and yet . . . what is it all for? There must be something more important, one feels, though I don't believe there is.[100]

Russell said of his life that 'the centre of me is always and eternally a terrible pain – a curious wild pain – a searching for something beyond what the world contains.'[101]

7. The 'I'd be happy if only . . .' objection

To those who maintain that while they aren't happy now (in the sense of being wholly fulfilled) they would be happy if only they could obtain some worldly object of satisfaction (money, sex, power, fame, etc.), the reply is of course: '"Try it. You won't like it." Billions of people have performed trillions of "if only" experiments with life, and they all had the same result: failure.'[102]

Conclusion

> Now a man must be lacking something if he
> misses it, mustn't he?
> *Boethius*

None of the above attempts at rebutting the argument from desire is cogent, and so the argument is left standing. Clark H. Pinnock frames the AFD in terms of our implicit ultimate commitments:

> We might say that when the word *God* is used, one thing it has reference to is what Schubert M. Ogden calls 'the objective ground in reality itself of our ineradicable confidence in the final worth of our existence' . . . I would suggest that we reflect on our attitudes and actions. Do they not imply this very confidence, even if we have not actually taken the step of explicit faith in God? There is a sense in which the decision to believe renders explicit the seeds of faith already present, implicit in the confidence [secular] humanists and Christians both manifest towards the goodness and worthwhileness of life. By virtue of continuing to live and act, even the atheist shows he must in *some* sense believe in God and cannot in *every* sense deny him . . . Confessing the atheist's creed is certainly possible; but living consistently on the basis of it is practically impossible. What I am asking you as a reader to do, then, is to clear up this inconsistency by the decision to trust in God and to bring about harmony between your explicit beliefs and the underlying confidence in life's meaning that you sense.

Should you decide in the other direction, to bring about consistency by working your unbelief in God more deeply into the fabric of your everyday life, I predict great sadness and self-destruction . . .[103]

Pinnock's appeal here is made to 'the whole person', and to what might be termed the 'wisdom' of belief:

Proverbs . . . constantly asks us to consider wisdom which promises to make life good and valuable in the context of the fear [i.e. awed respect] of the Lord. Referring to wisdom, Proverbs says, 'The man who finds me finds life, and the Lord will be pleased with him. The man who does not find me hurts himself; anyone who hates me loves death' (Proverbs 8:35–36).[104]

Philosopher Stephen D. Schwarz lays out our ultimate existential options:

All these questions point to God. Or rather they point to the great alternative: God is, and there is ultimate meaning – or God is not, and existence is ultimately absurd . . . We can make a commitment to 'existence is ultimately meaningful' and risk that perhaps it is ultimately absurd. Or we can make a commitment to 'existence is ultimately absurd,' and it may turn out that it is ultimately meaningful. Which 'way of going wrong' is worse? In the first (existence is ultimately absurd), our error is just one more absurdity; does that really matter? Can anything *ultimately* matter in a reality that is ultimately absurd? But in the second (existence is ultimately meaningful), our error stands in drastic contrast to the meaningfulness of existence. Our commitment puts us outside the mainstream of existence. God is, but we are not part of his plan; that cannot be other than a terrible consequence for us. Is it not better to believe in, or seek, or hope for ultimate meaningfulness, with the risk that we may lose; than to despair of ultimate meaningfulness . . . with the terrible risk that existence is, after all, ultimately good? That, I think, is the ultimate decision each person has to make: *Either*, a commitment to ultimate absurdity, that all will be lost in the end, that the powers of Darkness and the Impersonal will triumph over us and everything that we cherish:

love, beauty, truth, meaning, goodness, being, hope. *Or*, a commitment to ultimate meaning, the triumph of Love, Beauty, Truth, meaning, Goodness, Being, Hope.[105]

Schwarz may at first glance seem to be advancing a version of Pascal's 'wager', encouraging us to 'bet' upon life being meaningful because we have everything to gain and nothing to lose thereby. However, the argument cuts deeper than that. It shows that we face a forced, either-or decision: On the one hand, we can embrace the absurd, incoherent and ultimately meaningless-if-true claim that 'reality is absurd and inconsistent, but we should be consistent by denying the meaningfulness of existence'. On the other hand, we can embrace the reasonable, coherent and meaningful-if-true claim that 'reality is rational and consistent, and we should be consistent by affirming the ultimate meaningfulness of existence'. Nihilism is the truth claim that 'everything, *including every truth claim*, and therefore *including this truth claim*, is absurd and without objective meaning'! In other words, in light of our self-knowledge about human nature, our choice is between a theism that can be coherently affirmed and a nihilism that cannot be coherently affirmed.

For Lewis, the argument from desire is a philosophical expression of a lived experience, a winding pilgrimage that he himself took as a young man, and one that converged upon a conclusion supported by independent philosophical arguments that together formed a cumulative case for God:

> I knew only too well how easily the longing accepts false objects and through what dark ways the pursuit of them leads us: but I also saw that the Desire itself contains the corrective of all these errors. The only fatal error was to pretend that you had passed from desire to fruition, when, in reality, you had found either nothing, or desire itself, or the satisfaction of some different desire. The dialectic of desire, faithfully followed, would retrieve all mistakes, head you off from all false paths, and force you not to propound, but to live through, a sort of ontological proof. This lived dialectic, and the merely argued dialectic of my philosophical progress, seemed to have converged on one goal . . .[106]

Recommended Resources

By C.S. Lewis:
Mere Christianity (London: Fount, 1997)
The Pilgrim's Regress (London: Fount, 1977)
Surprised by Joy (London: Fount, 1998)
'The Weight of Glory', in *C.S. Lewis Essay Collection: Faith, Christianity and the Church* (ed. Lesley Walmsley; London: HarperCollins, 2002)

Video

Fraser, Brooke. 'C.S. Lewis Song'
    www.youtube.com/watch?v=qT-sso5AhmA&feature=related.
Kreeft, Peter. 'Desire'
    www.youtube.com/watch?v=_Z9q8zazy68.
Lindsey, Art. 'The Argument from Desire' www.cslewisinstitute.org/Argument_from_Desire_Video.

Audio

Kreeft, Peter. 'Desire'
    www.peterkreeft.com/audio/23_desire.htm.

Online papers

Kreeft, Peter. 'The Argument from Desire'
    www.peterkreeft.com/topics/desire.htm.
— and Ronald K. Tacelli. 'Twenty Arguments for the Existence of God: The Argument from Desire' www.peterkreeft.com/topics-more/20_arguments-gods-existence.htm#16.
Last Seminary. 'The Argument from Desire'
    www.lastseminary.com/argument-from-desire/.
— 'Philosophy of Religion Articles'
    www.lastseminary.com/philosophy-of-religion-article/.
Plantinga, Alvin. 'Two Dozen or so Theistic Arguments' www.calvin.edu/academic/philosophy/virtual_library/articles/plantinga_alvin/two_dozen_or_so_theistic_arguments.pdf.

Books

Augustine. *Confessions* (Oxford University Press, 1992).

Barkman, Adam. *C.S. Lewis and Philosophy as a Way of Life* (Allentown, PA: Zossima, 2009).

Carnell, Corbin Scott. *Bright Shadow of Reality: Spiritual Longing in C.S. Lewis* (Cambridge: Eerdmans, 1999).

Craig, William Lane and J.P. Moreland, eds. *The Blackwell Companion to Natural Theology* (Oxford: Wiley-Blackwell, 2009).

Evans, C. Stephen. *Why Believe? Reason and Mystery as Pointers to God* (Downers Grove, IL: IVP, 1996).

Geisler, Norman L. and Winfried Corduan. *Philosophy of Religion* (Eugene, OR: Wipf & Stock, 2003).

Groothuis, Douglas. *On Pascal* (London: Thompson Wadsworth, 2003).

Kreeft, Peter. *Christianity for Modern Pagans: Pascal's Pensées Edited, Outlined and Explained* (San Francisco: Ignatius, 1993).

— *Heaven: The Heart's Deepest Longing* (San Francisco: Ignatius, 1989).

Küng, Hans. *Does God Exist? An Answer for Today* (London: Collins, 1980).

Morris, Thomas V. *Making Sense of It All: Pascal and the Meaning of Life* (Grand Rapids, MI: Eerdmans, 1998).

Pascall, Blaise. *Pensées* (trans. Honor Levi: Oxford University Press, 1995).

Purtill, Richard. *C.S. Lewis' Case for the Christian Faith* (San Francisco: Ignatius, 2004).

Walls, Jerry L. *Heaven: The Logic of Eternal Joy* (Oxford University Press, 2002).

Williams, Peter S. *The Case for God* (Crowborough: Monarch, 1999).

— *I Wish I Could Believe in Meaning: A Response to Nihilism* (Southampton: Authentic/Damaris, 2004).

— *A Sceptic's Guide to Atheism: God Is Not Dead* (Milton Keynes: Paternoster, 2009).

4.

The Argument from Reason

If thought is the undesigned and irrelevant product of
cerebral motions,what reason have we to trust it?
C.S. Lewis[1]

In 1924 C.S. Lewis noted in his diary that 'in [Bertrand Russell's
essay] "Worship of a Free Man" I found a very clear and noble
statement of what I myself believed a few years ago.'[2] According
to Russell: 'man is the product of causes which had no prevision
of the end they were achieving; that his origin, his growth, his
hopes and fears, his loves and his beliefs, are but the outcome of
accidental collocations of atoms . . . Only within the scaffolding
of these truths, only on the firm foundation of unyielding
despair, can the soul's habitation henceforth be safely built.'[3] As
Russell wrote elsewhere, it follows from naturalism that 'man is
a part of nature, not something contrasted with Nature. His
thoughts and his bodily movements follow the same laws that
describe the motions of stars and atoms . . . we are subordinated
to nature, the outcome of natural laws, and their victims in the
long run.'[4]

By the time of his diary entry, Lewis had come to view such
stoic statements of the naturalistic worldview with deep suspicion, for it seemed to him that Russell failed to face 'the real
difficulty – that our ideals are after all a natural product, facts
with a relation to all other facts, and cannot survive the condemnation of the fact as a whole. The Promethean attitude
would be tenable only if we were really members of some other
whole outside the real whole: [which on any monistic hypothe-
sis] we are not.'[5]

This suspicion of what Lewis came to call the 'Promethean fallacy' would eventually flourish in his acceptance of the moral argument for God (examined in chapter five). However, it was not the *moral*, but rather the *rational* consequences of viewing each and every one of our ideas (including, but not limited to, our ideals) as 'a natural product, facts with a relation to all other facts,'[6] which principally spurred Lewis into parting company with Russell's materialism. In *Surprised by Joy* Lewis recalls how his friend Owen Barfield:[7]

> convinced me that the positions we had hitherto held left no room
> for any satisfactory theory of knowledge. We had . . . accepted as
> rock-bottom reality the universe revealed to the senses. But at the
> same time, we continued to make for certain phenomena claims
> that went with a theistic or idealistic view. We maintained that
> abstract thought (if obedient to logical rules) gave indisputable
> truth, that our moral judgment was 'valid' and our aesthetic expe-
> rience was not just pleasing but 'valuable.' The view was, I think,
> common at the time; it runs though Bridges' *Testament of Beauty*
> and Lord Russell's' 'Worship of a Free Man.' Barfield convinced
> me that it was inconsistent. If thought were merely a subjective
> event, these claims for it would have to be abandoned. If we kept
> (as rock-bottom reality) the universe of the sense, aided by instru-
> ments co-ordinated to form 'science', then one would have to go
> further and accept a Behaviorist view of logic, ethics and aesthet-
> ics. But such a view was, and is, unbelievable to me.[8]

As Oxford philosopher C.E.M. Joad would warn in his 1933 *Guide to Modern Thought*:

> If the individual is all body . . . his behaviour will ultimately be
> explicable in terms of the same laws as those which determine the
> motions of other bodies . . . But in establishing this conclusion
> Behaviourism runs a considerable risk of destroying the founda-
> tion on which it is based . . . since the chains of reasoning which
> constitute their theories, like their blood pressures, are merely bod-
> ily functions, bearing relation not to the outside facts which they
> purport to describe, but to the bodily conditions of which they are
> a function. This kind of criticism is valid against any theory which

seeks to impugn the validity of reason by representing it either as a function of the body or as the tool of an unconscious and non-rational self.[9]

Like Barfield and Joad, Lewis became convinced that Russell's materialistic worldview couldn't accommodate the logically undeniable fact that Russell could reason about it.

Metaphysical Bias against Default Dualism

> C.S. Lewis would have been as skeptical of the modern reductionist Richard Dawkins today as he was of J.B.S. Haldane . . .
>
> *Henry F. Schaefer*[10]

Richard Dawkins' faith in naturalism prevents him from accepting any immaterial account of consciousness: 'spirit . . . is not an explanation, it's an evasion . . . The scientist may agree to use the word soul for that which we don't understand, but the scientist adds, "But we're working on it, and one day we hope we shall explain it [naturalistically]."'[11] Note that Dawkins' belief that the mind is nothing but the brain is not grounded in evidence. Rather, it's deduced from his prior commitment to a naturalistic worldview. Likewise, Peter Atkins no sooner admits that philosophers of mind 'have made little progress in understanding the nature of subjective experience, with *qualia* and the sense of I'[12] than he expresses his commitment to physicalism: 'I at least am confident that all such aspects of consciousness are rooted in the physical brain and one day will be fully illuminated [by science].'[13] The same *a priori* dialectic can be seen at work in Sam Harris's comments:

> While there is much to be said against the naïve conception of a soul that is independent of the brain, the place of consciousness in the natural world is very much open to question. The idea that brains *produce* consciousness is little more than an article of faith among scientists at present, and there are many reasons to believe that the methods of science will be insufficient to either prove or disprove it

. . . nothing about a brain, when surveyed as a physical system, declares it to be a bearer of that peculiar, interior dimension that each of us experiences as consciousness in his own case . . . And so, while we know many things about ourselves in anatomical, physiological and evolutionary terms, we currently have no idea why it is 'like something' to be what we are. The fact that the universe is illuminated where you stand, the fact that your thoughts and moods and sensations have a qualitative character, is an absolute mystery . . . The problem is that our experience *of* brains, as objects in the world, leaves us perfectly insensible to the reality of consciousness, while our experience *as* brains grants us knowledge of nothing else.[14]

Although there is much to be said against naïve concepts of the soul as wholly independent of the brain, it's nevertheless crystal clear that our experience *of* brains fails to justify Harris's claim that we have our experiences *as* brains *simpliciter*. Harris himself admits that such a claim is 'little more than an article of [blind] faith'! Indeed, its an article of blind faith held in the teeth of *prima facie* evidence to the contrary, as Harris admits when he acknowledges that 'for most of us, a dualism of this sort is more or less a matter of common sense.'[15]

The longstanding debate within the philosophy of mind between different versions of mind-body dualism on the one hand and different versions of physicalism on the other hand is a prime testing-ground for naturalism, because naturalism excludes dualism and entails physicalism. 'Unfortunately for naturalists,' observes J.P. Moreland, 'consciousness has stubbornly resisted treatment in physical terms.'[16] Consider these admissions from a dozen leading naturalists:

- Peter Atkins: 'It is certainly true that [philosophers] have made little progress in understanding the nature of subjective experience . . .'[17]
- Susan Blackmore: 'objects in the physical world and subjective experience of them seem to be two radically different things: so how can one give rise to the other? No one has an answer to this question . . .'[18]
- Ned Block: 'We have no conception of our physical or functional nature that allows us to understand how it could explain

our subjective experience . . . in the case of consciousness we have nothing – zilch – worthy of being called a research programme, nor are there any substantive proposals about how to go about starting one . . . Researchers are stumped.'[19]

- Francis Crick: 'There's no easy way of explaining consciousness in terms of known science . . . how can you explain the redness of red in terms of physics and chemistry?'[20]
- Richard Dawkins: 'In *How the Mind Works* Steven [Pinker] elegantly sets out the problem of subjective consciousness, and asks where it comes from and what's the explanation. Then he's honest enough to say, "Beats the heck out of me." That is an honest thing to say, and I echo it. We don't know. We don't understand it.'[21]
- Jerry Fodor: 'Nobody has the slightest idea how anything material could be conscious.'[22]
- A.C. Grayling: 'one of the greatest mysteries facing science and philosophy is the phenomenon of consciousness . . . How do we explain the existence of belief, memory, reason?'[23] Grayling admits: 'What has rightly been called "the hard problem" of consciousness – namely, how it arises from brain activity – has yet to be solved.'[24]
- Stuart Hameroff and Roger Penrose: 'The "hard problem" of incorporating the phenomenon of consciousness into a scientific worldview involves finding scientific explanations of . . . the subjective experience of mental states. On this subject, reductionist science is still at sea.'[25]
- Sam Harris: 'the ultimate relationship between consciousness and matter has not been settled . . .'[26]
- Steven Pinker: 'The Hard Problem is explaining how subjective experience arises from neural computation. The problem is hard because no one knows what a solution might look like or even whether it is a genuine scientific problem in the first place . . . No one knows what to do with the Hard Problem . . .'[27]
- Victor J. Stenger: 'neuroscientists do not yet have an established material model of mind . . . the main problem is our lack of understanding of what constitutes *consciousness*.'[28]

Agnostic James Le Fanu poses the question of 'how to reconcile what the brain is with what it *does*?',[29] asking: 'How can the electronic firing of those billions of neurons of the same monotonous physical structure of the brain be the entire causal basis of so vast a range of mental life, the near-infinite diversity of our individual selves, with our own unique thoughts, memories and beliefs?'[30] He concludes that the obvious answer 'would be that they cannot be reconciled.'[31] Belief in the duality of mind and matter (however closely integrated) remains the most obvious response to the apparent dissonance between mind and body, and should therefore be considered innocent until proven guilty by a sufficient weight of contrary evidence. Even Richard Dawkins allows that 'if scientists suspect that all aspects of the mind have a scientific [i.e. naturalistic] explanation but they can't actually say what that explanation is yet, then of course it's open to you to doubt whether the explanation ever will be forthcoming. That's a perfectly reasonable doubt.'[32] As David Chalmers writes:

> If it turns out that the facts about consciousness can't be derived from the fundamental physical properties we already have . . . the consistent thing to say is 'OK, then consciousness isn't to be reduced. It's irreducible. It's fundamental. It's a basic feature of the world.' So what we have to do when it comes to consciousness is admit it as a fundamental feature of the world – as irreducible as space and time.[33]

On the one hand, then, we have a traditional belief in the spiritual self. On the other hand we have a reductive, physicalist view of humanity. The former view is supported *prima facie* by the very 'within-ness' of all our experience, including our experience of the material world. Indeed, C.S. Lewis criticized naturalists for trying to explain everything in material categories when this approach a) depends upon a belief in something (i.e. matter) *that is only known through thinking* and b) is advanced to the metaphysical detriment of the fact of thinking itself, *which is immediately and certainly known*; for 'reason is given before Nature and upon reason our concept of Nature depends.'[34] Agnostic philosopher Antony O'Hear agrees: 'there are aspects of our experience and existence more fundamental than science, and on which science depends for its possibility. So science cannot be used, as it often is, to undermine those features of our natures.'[35] The idea that the mind is 'nothing but' the brain is ultimately a deduction from the assumption of naturalism. Since dualism is the common-sense, default view of humanity through the ages, one might well take the repeated failure of naturalism to account for the mind in purely physical terms as a predictable failure to rebut dualism, a failure that justifies sticking with the default mode of explanation and thus rejecting the naturalistic worldview.

The Waning of Materialism

It's not just the longstanding failure of physicalist attempts to explain the mind that's a problem for naturalism. A wide range of arguments within the philosophy of mind claim to show that, *in principle*, various aspects of consciousness can never be plausibly explained in purely physical terms. This two-pronged attack upon physicalism is making headway against the materialistic orthodoxy. Introducing *The Waning of Materialism* (Oxford University Press, 2010), philosophers Robert C. Koons and George Bealer state:

> materialism is waning in a number of significant respects – one of which is the ever-growing number of major philosophers who reject materialism or at least have strong sympathies with anti-materialist views . . . Over the last fifty or so years, materialism has been challenged by a daunting list of arguments . . . This seems to be reflected in the attitudes of many contemporary philosophers of mind. A growing number – among them prominent philosophers who once had strong materialist sympathies – have come to the conclusion that at least some of the arguments against materialism cannot be overcome.[36]

Moreland observes: 'there is a growing dissatisfaction with the various versions of strong physicalism, and more and more are breaking ranks by venturing into emergent property dualism (e.g. the evolution of Jaegwon Kim's thought in the last ten years) . . .'[37] As David Chalmers commented in 2005:

Jaegwon Kim's new book, *Physicalism or Something Near Enough*
. . . is especially notable for the fact that Kim, *often seem as an arch-
reductionist, comes out of the closet as a dualist* . . . this makes at least
three prominent materialists who have abandoned the view in the
last few years. Apart from Kim, there's Terry Horgan and Stephen
White . . . If I had to guess, I'd guess that the numbers within philosophy of mind are 50% materialist, 25% agnostic, 25% dualist.[38]

William Hasker believes that 'the prevalent materialisms concerning persons and consciousness are in a state of incipient crisis – a crisis to be sure, which as yet is inadequately recognized
and acknowledged.'[39] C. Stephen Evans confirms that 'a careful
look at recent work on the mind-body problem clearly shows that
materialism is in what could be called a state of crisis.'[40] Edward
Feser notes that 'today, critics of materialism constitute a large
and influential minority position within the field.'[41] Kevin
Corcoran simply states that 'dualism is making a comeback.'[42]
And it's not just dualists making this claim. For example, naturalistic philosopher of mind John Heil admits that 'in recent years,
dissatisfaction with materialist assumptions has led to a revival
of interest in forms of dualism.'[43]

Dawkins and Reductionism

The new atheist's view of reality goes by many names: metaphysical naturalism, materialism, etc. One of its most descriptive names
is 'ontological reductionism', because it seeks to explain everything by *reducing* it to naturalistically acceptable categories. On the
one hand, Dawkins writes as if reductionism is acknowledged by
all right-thinking people to be an unqualified good, one opposed
for purely sentimental reasons by misguided religious fundamentalists: 'Reductionist explanations are true explanations,' says
Dawkins: 'It's the only kind of explanation I find satisfying. I wish
I could persuade you that it's the only kind of explanation that is
satisfying.'[44] On the other hand, Dawkins complains: 'If you read
trendy intellectual magazines, you may have noticed that "reductionism" is one of those things, like sin, that is only mentioned by
people who are against it.'[45] Dawkins objects that 'reductionism is

one of those words that . . . means nothing. Or rather it means a whole lot of different things, but the only thing anybody knows about it is that it's bad, you're supposed to disapprove of it.'[46]

William Hasker affirms that 'no sensible person should want to avoid reductionism altogether. Many of the greatest successes of the sciences have come through reductive explanations.'[47] However, he points out that there are different kinds of reductionism, and 'the kind of reductionism to be avoided is the kind that gives reductive explanations which deny or ignore the reality and importance of that which is in fact real and important.'[48] The danger of reductionism is that the search for the simplest adequate unifying explanation of any given data-set will be pursued in such a way that the demand for simplicity will outweigh the primary explanatory demand *that explanations must be adequate to the nature of the data they are meant to explain.* If this happens, facts are *reduced* to fit a single, simplistic, inadequate explanation, rather than explanations being expanded to fit the facts. When the demand for simplicity outweighs the demand for adequacy, explanation becomes explaining-away and data is dismissed as 'only apparent' on the basis that it doesn't fit *the explanation!* Such a Procrustean approach to explanation is clearly base over apex, but it's an approach Dawkins takes repeatedly on a variety of subjects. Dawkins asserts *a priori* that 'the kind of explanation we come up with must not contradict the laws of physics. Indeed it will make use of the laws of *physics, and nothing more than the laws of physics.*'[49] Hence Dawkins is committed to the reduction of mind to matter *quite irrespective of the evidence*: 'consciousness must be a manifestation of the evolutionary process, presumably via brains . . . consciousness is ultimately a material phenomenon'.[50]

The Inflated Subject

> C.S. Lewis put it quite bluntly: Man is being abolished . . .
> What is being abolished is autonomous man . . . the man
> defended by literatures of freedom and dignity. His
> abolition has been long overdue . . . To man qua man we
> readily say good riddance.
> *B.F. Skinner,* Beyond Freedom and Dignity[51]

In a *New Humanist* article, Oxford-educated philosopher Mary Midgely bemoans the baleful influence of positivism on the philosophy of mind:

> Positivism got rid of . . . the twofold world of Spirit and Matter . . . by simply eliminating Spirit, leaving Matter to manage on its own. The main reason for doing this was undoubtedly the fear of religion. The whole concept of Spirit was seen as too dangerous . . . The unlucky consequence of this clash can be seen in what is now called the Problem of Consciousness, the desperate ongoing attempt by many scientists to find ways of talking about human experience in 'scientific' language – language that has been carefully designed to make all such talk impossible. This problem began to distress people during the 1970s because that was when the behaviourist veto on ever mentioning subjectivity finally lost its force. Behaviourists had been following positivist principles in dismissing the phenomena of consciousness as effectively unreal, since they could not be described in physical terms . . . Not surprisingly, this worked so badly that the theory was officially abandoned. Yet the general suspicion of talking about conscious experience remained very strong . . . The world, in fact, consisted solely of objects with no subjects to observe them . . . Thus our only source of information about the outer world was no longer available. Despite this ruling, however, the difficulty of discussing observation without an observer – the absurdity of enquirers trying to leave themselves out of their own enquiries – increasingly bothered scientists, especially ones concerned with evolution, where the role and origin of conscious experience needed to be considered. It is all very well to eliminate God from the intelligible universe but eliminating ourselves from it blocks all sorts of enquiries.[52]

C.S. Lewis rejected the march of reductionism during the behaviourist era:

> At the outset the universe appears packed with will, intelligence, life and positive qualities; every tree is a nymph and every planet a god . . . The advance of knowledge gradually empties this rich and genial universe: first of its gods, then of its colours, smells, sounds and tastes, finally of solidity itself as solidity was originally imagined. As

these items are taken from the world, they are transferred to the subjective side of the account: classified as our sensations, thoughts, images or emotions. The Subject becomes gorged, inflated, at the expense of the Object.[53]

However, observed Lewis, reductionism doesn't stop there: 'The same method which emptied the world now proceeds to empty ourselves. The masters of the method soon announce that we were just as mistaken (and mistaken in much the same way) when we attributed "souls" . . . to human organisms, as when we attributed Dryads to trees.'[54] The problem with taking reductionism to this, its logical extreme, is that it reduces away the reducers: 'While we were reducing the world to almost nothing we deceived ourselves with the fancy that all its lost qualities were being kept safe (if in a somewhat humbled condition) as "things in our own mind". Apparently we had no mind of the sort required. *The Subject is as empty as the Object.*'[55] Lewis thinks this ontological reductionism commits a common sort of mistake:

> We start with a view which contains a good deal of truth, though in confused or exaggerated form. Objections are then suggested and we withdraw it. But [then] we discover that we have emptied the baby out with the bathwater and that the original view must have contained certain truths for lack of which we are now entangled in absurdities. So here. In emptying out the Dryads and the gods (which, admittedly, 'would not do' just as they stood) we appear to have thrown out the whole universe, ourselves included.[56]

Not all progressions can be reasonably carried to zero:

> Consider the joke about the miserly farmer who fed his longsuffering cow less and less each day; but just when he thought that he had weaned the cow from eating altogether, the unfortunate animal died . . . showing that we do not need as many gods as early man believed does not show that we need no gods at all; that must be argued on its own merits.[57]

Indeed, if we consider belief in non-material realities *in general*, it would seem that following the logical progression of reductionism to zero is self-defeating. As Richard Purtill frames the conundrum: 'if the universe is purely material and has no intelligence or purpose, then our minds are the result of something with no intelligence or purpose. However, if this is true, then what confidence can we have in the workings of our minds?'[58]

The Argument from Reason

> Explaining reason in terms of unreason explains
> reason away . . .
> *Victor Reppert*[59]

The 'argument from reason' (AFR) is a family of arguments within the philosophy of mind that focuses upon acts of reasoning, for as Victor Reppert points out: 'Any genuinely naturalistic position requires that all instances of explanation in terms of reasons be further explained in terms of a non-purposive substratum. For if some purposive or intentional explanation can be given and no further analysis can be given in non-purposive and non-rational terms, then reason must be viewed as a fundamental cause in the universe.'[60]

The AFR can be formulated both as an argument *against* naturalism, and as an argument *for* theism (broadly construed). To argue that finite human minds transcend the categories of naturalism is to invite questions about which supernatural worldview best accounts for this transcendence, and to conclude that finite minds cannot be explained by wholly mindless causes implies the need to posit an un-designed intelligence. The core insight of the AFR can thus be stated as follows:

1) Naturalism reduces reasoning to a closed, mechanistic, deterministic system of physical cause and effect
2) This reduction is unable to accommodate acts of reasoning (including the naturalist's acts of reason)
3) Therefore, naturalism is self-contradictory and reason must be viewed as a fundamental cause

The first premise of this logically valid argument is, of necessity, accepted by the naturalist. As Paul M. Churchland writes: 'The important point about the standard [naturalistic] evolutionary story is that the human species and all of its features are the wholly physical outcome of a purely physical process . . .'[61] Therefore, if the second premise can be shown to be more plausible than its denial, the conclusion will be supported.

The Cardinal Difficulty of Naturalism

> There is a patent self-contradiction running through all attempts, however sophisticated they may appear, to derive rationality from irrationality.
> *John C. Lennox*[62]

In *Miracles: A Preliminary Study*, C.S. Lewis presented a particularly famous version of the AFR. He set the scene by arguing that 'if Naturalism is true, every finite thing or event must be (in principle) explicable in terms of the Total System [of material realities and relations] . . . If any one thing exists which is of such a kind that we see in advance the impossibility of ever giving *that kind* of explanation, then Naturalism would be in ruins.'[63] In particular, Lewis reasons that 'a theory which explained everything else in the whole universe but which made it impossible to believe that our thinking was valid, would be utterly out of court. For that theory would itself have been reached by thinking, and if thinking is not valid that theory would . . . have destroyed its own credentials.'[64] If naturalism excludes the reality of such necessary components of rationality as thinking that premises are true, or drawing a conclusion because it is seen to follow from premises that we think are true, then naturalism 'would be in ruins'. Indeed, as soon as a naturalist reasoned about anything, they would falsify their worldview!

The Argument from Logical Relations

> The presupposition of the uniformity of natural causes in a closed system seems to involve serious epistemological difficulties . . .
> *Thomas V. Morris*[65]

The easiest way to exhibit the fact that naturalism discredits reason, writes Lewis, is to begin by noting that there are two different senses of the word 'because', as in the statement 'I believe X because of Y.' One sense is the relation of *physical cause and effect*, as in: 'Grandfather is ill today *because* (cause-effect) he ate lobster yesterday.'[66] The other is the relation of *logical ground and consequent*, as in: 'Grandfather must be ill *because* (ground-consequent) he hasn't got up yet (and we know he is an invariably early riser when he is well).'[67] Grandpa's failure to get out of bed doesn't *cause* Grandfather to be ill, nor does it *cause* us to conclude he is ill; rather, it is our *grounds* for making the logical inference that he is ill. The cause-effect sense of because indicates 'a dynamic connection between events;'[68] the ground-consequent sense of *because* indicates 'a logical relation between beliefs or assertions'.[69] Now, as Thomas Nagel observes: 'if we can reason, it is because our thoughts can obey the order of logical relations among propositions . . .'[70] Lewis explains:

> a train of reasoning has no value as a means of finding truth unless each step in it is connected with what went before in the Ground-Consequent relation . . . If what we think at the end of our reasoning is to be [a valid conclusion], the correct answer to the question, 'Why do you think this?' must begin with the Ground-Consequent *because*. On the other hand, every event in Nature must be connected with previous events in the Cause and Effect relation. But [if Naturalism is true] our acts of thinking are events [in Nature]. Therefore the true answer to 'Why do you think this?' must begin with the Cause-Effect *because*.[71]

As soon as we reduce thinking to naturalistically acceptable categories, the ground-consequent sense of *because* gets pushed out of the picture by the cause-effect sense of *because*. This is a problem because:

> To be caused is not to be proved. Wishful thinkings, prejudices, and the delusions of madness, are all caused, but they are ungrounded . . . The implication is that if causes fully account for a belief [as they must do if naturalism is true], then, since causes work inevitably [naturalism entails determinism], the belief would have had to arise

whether it had grounds or not . . . If it is an event, it must be caused. It must in fact be simply one link in a causal chain which stretches back to the beginning and forward to the end of time. How could such a trifle as lack of logical grounds prevent the belief's occurrence or how could the existence of grounds promote it?[72]

Professor Henry Melvill Gwatkin had argued likewise in his Gifford Lecturers on *The Knowledge of God* that 'necessity reduces every belief to a necessary effect of past states of mind which have nothing to do with truth and untruth. No means is left for distinguishing them, and reason and science disappear in idle speculation.'[73] A.E. Taylor (an Oxford-educated philosopher contemporary with Lewis) deployed a similar train of thought in *Does God Exist?* (Fontana, 1945): 'it is clear from the very nature of knowledge that the event I call my knowledge . . . is something more than one item among others in the series of natural events; the knowing mind is something more than, or other than, "a part of nature" among other parts; if it were not, there could be no knowledge at all . . .'[74] Contemporary philosopher of mind William Hasker agrees that 'in a physicalist world, principles of sound reasoning have no relevance to determining what actually happens.'[75] If naturalism is true: 'our thoughts . . . are governed by biochemical laws; these, in turn, by physical laws which are themselves actuarial statements about the . . . movements of matter'.[76] Nowhere in this closed chain of physical cause and effect is there room for an efficacious relationship of ground and consequent to influence or explain our arrival at this or that conclusion:

> each mental event is [on the hypothesis of naturalism] either identical with or supervenient on a physical event. By hypothesis, the physical event in question has a complete causal explanation in terms of previous events with which it is connected according to the laws of physics . . . each such event has whatever causal powers it has solely in virtue of its physical characteristics . . . No causal role for the mental characteristics as such can be found . . . [Hence] on the assumption of the causal closure of the physical, no one ever accepts a belief because it is supported by good reasons. To say that this constitutes a serious problem for physicalism seems an understatement.[77]

If naturalism is true, humans don't believe anything *from reason* in the sense of believing things because (ground-consequent) they have good reason to believe them; rather, we hold whatever beliefs we have because (cause-effect) we are given them by nothing but a mechanistic sequence of physical causes.[78] As Karl Popper observed: 'physical determinism is a theory which . . . is not arguable, since it must explain all our reactions, including what appear to us as beliefs based on arguments, as due to purely physical conditions.'[79]

Calculating Moves in a Chinese Room

Daniel Dennett effectively concedes Lewis's distinction between the Cause-Effect and Ground-Consequent explanations, as well as the fact that naturalism privileges the Cause-Effect explanation at the expense of the Ground-Consequent explanation:

> It is true that every belief state is what it is, and locally causes whatever it causes, independently of whether it is true or false. As I have said, our brains are *syntactic engines*, not *semantic engines*, which, like perpetual motion machines, are [physically] impossible. But syntactic engines can be designed to track truth, and this is just what evolution has done. A useful comparison might be with a hand calculator.[80]

Alvin Plantinga points out that the ability of a purely physical, man-made computer to calculate the product of two numbers isn't a counterexample to the AFR: 'This seems to me an unfortunate analogy from Dennett's point of view. Calculators, of course, are designed and created by intelligent beings, namely us human beings. Calculators track the truth, and do so precisely because they are *designed* to do so.'[81] Chess computer Deep Blue's ability to defeat world chess champion Gary Kasparov in their notorious 1997 match 'was not the exclusive result of physical causation, unless the people on the programming team (such as Grandmaster Joel Benjamin) are entirely the result of physical causation. And that, precisely, is the point at issue.'[82] One can't point to computers as a counter-example to the argument from the distinction between physical and logical relations (a distinction Dennett himself draws) without begging the question.

Indeed, the issue here isn't whether reason can be *incarnated* in matter *by the action of rational agency*, but whether matter can *account for* rational agency per se *all by itself* in the first place. John Searle brings out this point with his famous 'Chinese room' thought experiment:

> Imagine that you are locked in a room, and in that room are several baskets full of Chinese symbols. Imagine that you (like me) do not understand a word of Chinese, but that you are given a rule book in English for manipulating Chinese symbols . . . Now suppose that some other Chinese symbols are passed into the room, and that you are given further rules for passing back Chinese symbols out of the room. Suppose that unknown to you the symbols passed into the room are called 'questions' by the people outside the room, and the symbols you pass back out of the room are called 'answers to questions'. Suppose, furthermore, that the programmers are so good at designing the programs and that you are so good at manipulating the symbols, that very soon your answers are indistinguishable from those of a native Chinese speaker . . . Now the point of the story is simply this: by virtue of implementing a formal computer program from the point of view of an outside observer, you behave exactly as if you understand Chinese, but all the same you don't understand a word of Chinese.[83]

The only understanding of Chinese in the story is located in the programmers and the questioners. According to Searle: 'You can expand the power all you want, hook up as many computers as you think you need, and they still won't be conscious, because all they'll ever do is shuffle symbols.'[84] Moreover, as Mark Baker points out: 'well-programmed computers are wonderful at deductive logic, telling us what conclusions follow because of the *form* of the premises. But they cannot reason abductively, telling us what conclusions follow because of the *meaning* of the premises . . . constructing and interpreting novel sentences that are appropriate is an intrinsically abductive process. Therefore, it is not a computational process.'[85]

In Dennett's terminology, a well-designed and programmed computer is a syntactic engine and not a semantic engine, because a semantic engine is a physical impossibility. Of course, one need only add the observation that the human mind functions semantically as well as syntactically, to prove that the human mind isn't explicable in terms of a purely physical mechanism.

The so-called 'systems reply' to Searle's argument – that although none of the individual elements that allow the room to imitate a Chinese speaker understands Chinese, nevertheless the room *as a whole* understands Chinese – is actually a *reductio ad absurdum* (reduction to absurdity) of the hypothesis that mind can be reduced to mechanistic function. This 'as a whole' reply puts the claim that 'conscious understanding is explicable in terms of nothing but neurons running computational routines' on a *par* with the claim that 'one can create an understanding of Chinese by giving a rule book and some pictograms to someone who doesn't speak a word of Chinese'! Are we *really* to believe that there is no substantive difference between a native Chinese speaker on the one hand and Searle's Chinese Room on the other (even considered as a whole)? Searle's thought experiment brings out the strong intuition that while the Chinese speaker *possesses a conscious understanding of Chinese*, the Chinese Room merely *imitates* such an understanding without *exemplifying* it (and even then, only because someone who *did* understand Chinese wrote a rule book, etc.).

Finally, the 'as a whole' rejoinder also commits a fallacy of composition akin to thinking that you *can* get blood out of stones, if only you have enough stones: 'Baskets of paper don't understand anything (including Chinese) and neither do rulebooks. So if *you* can't figure out what any of the symbols mean, then combining you with another non-understanding entity, or even a whole slew of non-understanding entities, is not going to bring about understanding.'[86] As Angus Menuge comments:

> the problem with the systems reply is that [proponents] do not say why connecting enough non-understanding entities in a certain way should suddenly produce understanding, and the analogy with networking computers is a good one: no-one thinks that all

the computers attached to the entire world-wide web understand anything, so it looks like understanding isn't a matter of complexity but of an entirely different ontological category.[87]

Searle argues that merely increasing the complexity of a physical system fails to provide any way of moving from syntax to semantics:

> why don't I understand Chinese? The answer is obvious: because I have no way to get from the syntax to the semantics; I have no way to get from the symbols to their meaning. But if I don't have any way of getting from the symbols to the meaning, neither does the room. Just imagine that I put the room inside me; imagine that I memorize the rule book and all the symbols . . . now get rid of the room, and I work outdoors in an open field and do all the calculations in my head; then there isn't anything in the system that isn't in me – and I still don't understand Chinese.[88]

Since Dennett admits that semantic engines, 'like perpetual motion machines, are impossible',[89] this is a point he must concede. Like a book, a computer *contains* knowledge, but *has* none itself. One cannot avoid the AFR by viewing the human mind as 'nothing but a biological computer'. As Aristotle put it: 'understanding is not an act of our brain. It is an act of our mind – an immaterial element in our makeup that may be related to, but is distinct from, the brain as a material organ.'[90]

Put that in your pipe and smoke it

According to C.S. Lewis:

> It would be impossible to accept naturalism itself if we really and consistently believed naturalism. For naturalism is a system of thought. But for naturalism all thoughts are mere events with irrational causes. It is, to me at any rate, impossible to regard the thoughts which make up naturalism in that way and, at the same time, to regard them as a real insight into external reality.[91]

To retain such an expectation would be 'like expecting that the accidental shape taken by the splash when you upset a milk jug should give you a correct account of how the jug was made and why it was upset.'[92] Lewis observed:

> To be the result of a series of mindless events is one thing: to be a kind of plan or true account of the laws according to which those mindless events happened is quite another. Thus the Gulf Stream produces all sorts of results: for instance, the temperature of the Irish Sea. What it does not produce is maps of the Gulf Stream. But if logic, as we find it operative in our own minds, is really a result of mindless nature, then it is a result as improbable as that. The laws whereby logic obliges us to think turn out to be the laws according to which every event in space and time must happen. The man who thinks this an ordinary or probable result does not really understand. It is . . . as if, when I knocked out my pipe, the ashes arranged themselves into letters which read: 'We are the ashes of a knocked-out pipe.' But if the validity of knowledge cannot be explained in that way, and if perpetual happy coincidence throughout the whole of recorded time is out of the question, then surely we must seek the real explanation elsewhere . . . Where thought is strictly rational it must be, in some odd sense, not ours, but cosmic or super-cosmic.[93]

Having ruled out *mindless* and/or *naturalistic* explanations for human acts of cognition, the only explanations left to us are *mindful* and *supernatural* in nature. By asking if it is coherent to regard human thinking as giving 'a real insight into external reality' if one explains it as the product of nothing but mindless (natural) forces, and by using the analogy of milk splashes or pipe ashes that not only result from but accurately describe their natural causes, Lewis prefigured a version of the AFR given by philosopher Richard Taylor.

Taylor begins with a thought experiment: Suppose that you are travelling by train and, glancing out of the window, you see some stones on a hillside spelling out the words 'Welcome to Wales'. Taylor points out that if, purely on the basis of this observation, you formed the belief that you are indeed entering Wales 'you would, in fact, be presupposing that they were arranged that way by an intelligent and purposeful being or beings for the purpose of conveying a certain message having nothing to do with the stones themselves'.[94] It would be unreasonable to base the belief that you are entering Wales on one's observation of these stones, argues Taylor, if you believed that the stones had *not* been arranged on purpose to give a real insight into a reality external to themselves, but had taken form as a result of nothing but natural causes: 'it would be *irrational* for you to regard the arrangement of the stones as evidence that you were entering Wales, *and at the same time to suppose that they might have come to that arrangement* . . . as the result of the ordinary interactions of natural or physical forces'.[95]

Taylor then argues that if you believe that *your own cognitive faculties* are the result of nothing but natural forces, it would be just as unreasonable to base this belief on one's experience of those faculties:

> It would be irrational for one to say *both* that his sensory and cognitive faculties had a . . . nonpurposeful origin and *also* that they reveal some truth with respect to something other than themselves . . . If, on the other hand, we do assume that they are guides to some truths having nothing to do with themselves, then it is difficult to see how we can, consistently with that supposition, believe them to have arisen . . . by the ordinary workings of purposeless forces, even over ages of time.[96]

If we trust the stone sign to give us an insight into reality beyond itself, reason demands that we must attribute it to design rather than to chance and/or necessity. Likewise, if our (inescapable) trust in our own cognitive faculties for insight into reality beyond those faculties themselves is to be coherent, then we must not explain those faculties in terms of nothing but chance and/or necessity (but must include an irreducible reference to intelligent design).

The Dawkins Evasion

After a 2011 lecture by Richard Dawkins, philosopher Paul Copan questioned him on 'how he could claim that the naturalist is rationally superior to the theist since, according to his book

River out of Eden, all of us are dancing to the music of our DNA.'[97]
Copan asked:

> It seems hard to differentiate between the arguments of the athe-
> ist, who believes himself to be more rational than the theist, when
> actually the same non-rational, physical, genetic forces are at work
> in both, so that even if the atheist is correct it seems to me that it
> would be completely by accident, rather than by any virtue of
> rationality that the atheist has. So I was curious as to what you
> would say in response to that: If the same forces are at work in
> both the atheist and the theist, why would we consider the atheist
> to be the more rational?[98]

In response, Dawkins admitted, 'I'm not sure that I've got this',
before affirming: 'I mean, the same forces are shaping both the
atheist and the theist and, indeed, everybody, yet we come to different conclusions.'[99] Then he asked: 'Is your problem how is it
that we come to different conclusions if our brains are shaped by
the same forces?'[100] Clearly, Dawkins had *not* 'got this' *at all*,
which indicates he had never before pondered the rational coherence of his own theory of knowledge! Copan repeated the question: 'My question is: Why should the atheist believe that he is
more rational than the theist if the same forces are at work in both
of them, forces beyond both their control?'[101] In reply, having
irrelevantly noted that one could 'ask the same question about
any difference of opinion',[102] Dawkins *changed the subject* by sub-
stituting a new question of his own: 'If you were to ask me why
I am confident that my scientific rationalism is, uh, is the right
answer, I mean, the answer is that it works.'[103] Dawkins' response
showed that a) he is ignorant about a major philosophical criticism of his naturalistic worldview, b) he illegitimately conflates
the naturalistic worldview with science and c) he begs the very
question Copan raised! As Copan commented afterwards:

> here's the problem: what 'works' is logically distinct from 'true' or
> 'matching up with reality' – since we may hold to a lot of *false* beliefs
> that help us survive and reproduce . . . To top off his answer to me
> (without addressing how to ground rationality), Dawkins dismis-
> sively quipped that *science flies rockets to the moon while religion* flies

planes into buildings . . . [But] how can Dawkins condemn 'religious' people who fly planes into buildings since they are just *dancing to their DNA – just like the naturalist is?* . . . Dawkins himself has elsewhere admitted that he doesn't know what to do with determinism, and he recognizes something hypocritical in his own emotional reaction to murder or rape . . . if he's right [about determinism], then his beliefs – on religion or biology – are just as determined by non-rational, material forces as anyone else's, including the theist's. They're *both* in the same non-rational camp . . .[104]

This is a *reductio ad absurdum* of naturalism, as E. Jonathan Lowe explains:

> To form a rational belief that we are not free to act in the light of reason, we should have to exercise rationality in action at the very least in directing our thoughts towards putative sources of evidence for that belief and in evaluating the deliverances of those sources of evidence . . . If we are not free to act in the light of reason, then we are not free to deploy our judgement in the light of reason in seeking out and assessing evidence and arguments for or against this or that belief. If, lacking freedom of rational action, we were to acquire the belief that we lack that freedom not through the free direction of our thoughts and the free use of our power of judgement, but rather as a consequence of prior causes determining the contents of our beliefs, then we would not have acquired that belief rationally and would not be rationally justified in holding it. There is a perfectly good sense, then, in which we simply cannot rationally believe that we lack freedom of rational action.[105]

Evolutionary Epistemology

It is, of course, true that if we were mere evolutionary products, then we should not be able to arrive at knowledge; we would merely have sentience linked by a multitude of routes to behaviour that would maximize the chances of our genetic material being replicated.
Raymond Tallis[106]

In Dawkins' view: 'We are jumped-up apes and our brains were only designed to understand the mundane details of how to survive in the Stone Age African savannah.'[107] Although he says that our brains were 'designed', Dawkins doesn't mean it literally. The 'Blind Watchmaker' of evolution mindlessly weeds out any sufficiently non-adaptive bodily behaviour, not false beliefs *per se*. Dawkins means that a combination of unintended natural laws and unguided contingent happenstance (i.e. chance) just happened to throw up an ape with a brain that tended to keep its gene-machine of a body alive long enough to reproduce in the conditions of Stone Age Africa; and that jumped-up ape is us. Of course, exactly insofar as Dawkins' description of humans as *nothing but* 'jumped-up apes' is *true*, so is it *self-defeating*. For isn't it unlikely that brains only 'designed' (i.e. evolved *without design*) to navigate 'the mundane details of how to survive in the Stone Age African savannah' should be capable of understanding the far from mundane details of our naturalistic evolutionary origins, or epistemology? Dawkins writes: 'Our mental burka window is narrow because it didn't need to be any wider in order to assist our ancestors to survive.'[108] Hasn't Dawkins thus laid claim to a position on a par with the man who trusts the 'Welcome to Wales' sign while simultaneously believing that it is the result of purely natural forces? As Leslie D. Weatherhead argued: 'If mind . . . has been selected and preserved . . . because it is a useful instrument in a struggle for survival which has no other purpose than to survive, then the validity has clearly vanished from the thinking of all men, including that of the scientist who so laboriously has come to his dismal conclusion.'[109] Arthur J. Balfour (whose lectures on this subject impressed Lewis) presses the point:

> At first sight we might suppose that, at the worst, the cognitive series and the causal series might be harmonised on the basis of natural selection if knowledge never aspired to rise above the level which promoted race survival, if no faculties of knowing were trusted beyond the point where they ceased effectively to foster the multiplication of the species . . . This scheme of thought, though narrowly constricted, is apparently coherent. Yet even this modest claim must be deemed excessive: for the speculation on which it rests does violence to its own principles. Manifestly we

cannot indulge ourselves in reflections upon the limits of the 'knowable' without using our intellect for a purpose never contemplated by selection. I do not allege that our intellect is therefore unequal to the task. I only say that, if it indeed be equal to it, we are in the presence of a very surprising coincidence. Why should faculties, 'designed' only to help primitive man, or his animal progenitors, successfully to breed and feed, be fitted to solve philosophic problems so useless and so remote? Why, indeed, do such problems occur to us? Why do we long for their solution? To such questions Naturalism can neither find an answer nor be content without one . . . No rational cure is, on naturalistic principles, within our reach.[110]

As G.K. Chesterton (another Christian thinker who had a major influence upon Lewis) argued:

It is an act of faith to assert that our thoughts have any relation to reality at all. If you are merely a sceptic, you must sooner or later ask yourself the question, 'Why should anything go right; even observation and deduction? Why should not good logic be as misleading as bad logic? They are both movements in the brain of a bewildered ape?' The young sceptic says 'I have a right to think for myself.' But the old sceptic, the complete sceptic, says 'I have no right to think for myself. I have no right to think at all.'[111]

Chesterton went on to warn that 'evolution is either an innocent scientific description of how certain earthly things came about; or, if it is anything more than this, it is an attack upon thought itself.'[112]

With Dawkins, one might suppose that an appeal to evolution – to what works – is the obvious rejoinder for the naturalist to make in the face of the AFR. However, leading naturalist Richard Rorty *agrees* with Chesterton, stating: 'The idea that one species of organism is, unlike all the others, oriented not just toward its own increased propensity but toward Truth, is as un-Darwinian as the idea that every human being has a built-in moral compass . . .'[113] Likewise, atheist John Gray argues that naturalists should *not* treat science as a quest for truth:

Now and then, perhaps, science can cut loose from our practical needs, and serve the pursuit of truth. But to think that it can ever embody that quest is pre-scientific – it is to detach science from human needs, and make of it something that is not natural but transcendental. To think of science as the search for truth is to renew a mystical faith, the faith of Plato and Augustine, that truth rules the world, that truth is divine . . . Modern humanism is the faith that through science humankind can know the truth – and so be set free. But if Darwin's theory of natural selection is true this is impossible. The human mind serves evolutionary success, not truth. To think otherwise is to resurrect the pre-Darwinian error that humans are different from all other animals . . . Darwinian theory tells us that an interest in truth is not needed for survival or reproduction . . . Truth has no systematic evolutionary advantage over error.[114]

As noted naturalistic philosopher of mind Patricia Churchland writes: 'Boiled down to essentials, a nervous system enables the organism to succeed in the four F's: feeding, fleeing, fighting, and reproducing. The principal chore of nervous systems is to get the body parts where they should be in order that the organism may survive . . . Truth . . . definitely takes the hindmost.'[115]

Victor J. Stenger's riposte to theologian John Haught's claim that naturalism 'logically undermines cognitional confidence'[116] is blatantly self-contradictory: 'The new atheists do not trust any minds, including their own. That's why we require the objective methods of science and reason.'[117] Of course, it's impossible even for a neo-atheist to employ 'the objective methods of science and reason' *without trusting their own mind*! French atheist André Comte-Sponville's recognition that 'cognitional confidence' entails theism likewise drives him to embrace a self-contradiction (and to beg the question against arguments for theism): 'Why shouldn't reason – our reason – get lost in the universe, if the latter is too big, too deep, too complex, too dark or too bright for it? Indeed, how can we be certain our reason is perfectly rational? Only a God could guarantee us that . . .'[118] Indeed.

Darwin's Doubt and the Evolutionary Anti-Naturalism Argument

> Our logical, mathematical, and physical intuitions have not
> been designed by natural selection to track the Truth.
> *Sam Harris*[119]

In an argument that he notes bears some similarity with that of
Lewis, Alvin Plantinga has developed what he calls an 'evolutionary anti-naturalism argument'. If one assumes the conjunction of naturalism and evolution:

> What our minds are *for* is not the production of true beliefs, but the
> production of adaptive behavior. That our species has survived
> and evolved at most guarantees that our behavior is adaptive; it
> does not guarantee or even suggest that our belief-producing
> processes are for the most part reliable, or that our beliefs are for
> the most part true. That is because, obviously, our behavior could
> be adaptive, but our beliefs mainly false.[120]

Since naturalistic evolution is 'interested' only in what *works* and
not what's *true*, a belief in naturalistic evolution eliminates any
rational grounds for confidence in the truth of our beliefs, including belief in naturalism (note that Plantinga doesn't advance this
as an argument against evolution, but as an argument against
belief in the conjunction of evolution with metaphysical naturalism).

Having distinguished between the neurophysiological properties (NP) of a *syntactic* structure in the brain and the *semantic* content of a 'belief that p', Plantinga points out that *on the naturalistic
account* of mind our beliefs are either 'nothing but' syntactic
neurophysiology (reductive materialism), or else the conjunction
of syntactic neurophysiology with causally impotent semantic content wholly dependent upon and determined by our syntactic
neurophysiology (semantic epiphenomenalism). The explanation
of a belief's being adaptive *on the naturalistic view of things* 'is that
having the NP properties . . . of the belief causes adaptive behavior, not that the belief is [or determines content that is] true. And,
of course, having those NP properties can cause adaptive behavior

whether or not the content they constitute [or determine] is true.'[121] Hence Plantinga both endorses and points out the obvious problem with the claims about human cognition made from the naturalistic perspective of Churchland, Dawkins, Gray, Harris, Rorty, etc., namely that *in undermining reason the conjunction of naturalism and evolution undermines itself.*

Plantinga dubs the self-defeating conjunction of naturalism and evolution 'Darwin's Doubt', because Darwin himself admitted: 'the horrid doubt always arises whether the convictions of man's mind, which has been developed from the mind of the lower animals, are of any value or at all trustworthy'.[122]

The Deniable Dennett

> There are major problems to be overcome by those who
> think that evolutionary considerations impose interesting
> limits on irrationality.
> *Stephen Stitch*[123]

In a significant debate with Alvin Plantinga, Daniel Dennett responded to the evolutionary anti-naturalism argument by simply *asserting* that 'evolution by natural selection, with its naturalistic presuppositions, *explains* why . . . eyes are highly reliable distal-information acquirers, and the beliefs that are provoked by those eyes (and other senses) are highly reliable truth trackers.'[124] But as Plantinga replied, on the naturalistic theory of evolution, the *semantic* reliability of an organism's beliefs just doesn't follow from the reliability of its information-acquiring *syntactic* apparatus:

> NP properties are *physical* properties; the property of having such and such a content is a *mental* property. Materialists hold that mental properties are identical with physical properties (reductive materialism) or that mental properties are determined by physical properties . . . Now the NP properties of a belief can cause behavior . . . Natural selection selects for adaptive behavior and against maladaptive behavior. In so doing, it also selects for adaptive neuro-physiology . . . [But] what about the *truth* of those beliefs?

. . . What evolution selects for is adaptive behavior and adaptive NP properties; but . . . Evolution just has to put up with the content that is determined by the particular NP properties in question. And the point is, it doesn't matter to the adaptivity of those NP properties, whether the content they determine is true or false. Those NP properties cause adaptive behavior; they also determine belief content, but we have no reason to think the belief content is true. If it's true, fine; but if it's false, that's equally fine.[125]

Plantinga knocks Dennett's backfiring appeal to naturalistic evolution and the possibility of truth-tracking machines for six:

Think about a frog sitting on a lily pad: A fly buzzes past, the frog's tongue flicks out and nails the fly. Does it matter what the frog then believes, if indeed frogs have beliefs? Clearly not: What matters is the frog's behavior and the neurophysiology that causes that behavior. Of course *something* in the frog registers or indicates the approach of the fly, the distance from fly to frog, the velocity of the fly, and so on; and those somethings are part of the cause of the frog's capturing the fly. Call those structures *indicators*. For the frog's behavior to be adaptive, for it to capture the fly, it is necessary that there be indicators, and necessary that they indicate accurately. But none of that need involve *belief* . . . We don't need to posit true beliefs in the frog to account for its adaptive behavior: what is required is only accurate indication; and accurate indication need not be accompanied by true belief. As long as the indication is accurate, the belief content can be anything whatsoever.[126]

There are two significant consequences of the evolutionary anti-naturalism argument:

The first is that . . . one can't rationally accept the conjunction of naturalism with evolution . . . Second, if naturalism is true, then so, in all probability, is evolution; evolution is the only game in town, for the naturalist, with respect to the question how all this variety of flora and fauna has arisen. If *that* is so . . . then naturalism *simpliciter* is self-defeating and cannot be rationally accepted . . .[127]

The Epistemological Irrelevance of Evolution

William Hasker agrees that 'if we accept the physicalist premise of causal closure and the supervenience of the mental, Darwinist epistemology . . . has no ability whatever to explain how any of our conscious mental states have even the most tenuous hold on objective reality'.[128] Given physicalist assumptions about the causal closure of the physical domain:

> the occurrence and content of conscious mental states such as belief and desire are irrelevant to behaviour and are not subject to selection pressures. On this assumption, natural selection gives us no reason to assume that the experiential content of my mental states corresponds in any way whatever to objective *reality*. And since on the physicalist scenario Darwinist epistemology is the *only* available explanation for the reliability of our epistemic faculties, the conclusion to be drawn is that physicalism not only *has not given* any explanation for such reliability, but it is *in principle unable to give* any such explanation. And that, it seems to me, is about as devastating an objection to physicalism as anyone could hope to find.[129]

Lewis was clearly thinking along the same lines:

> natural selection could operate only by eliminating responses that were biologically hurtful and multiplying those which tended to survival. But it is not conceivable that any improvement of responses could ever turn them into acts of insight [i.e. syntax cannot produce semantics] . . . The Naturalist [gives] a history of the evolution of reason which is inconsistent with the claims that he and I both have to make for inference as we actually practise it. For his history is . . . an account, in Cause and Effect terms, of how people came to think the way they do. And this of course leaves in the air the quite different question of how they could possibly be justified in so thinking. This imposes on him the very embarrassing task of trying to show how the evolutionary product which he has described could also be a power of 'seeing' truths. But the very attempt is absurd.[130]

Truth and Intentionality

> The directedness, or 'about-ness' of thought is a basic fact
> of experience, and there appears nothing to which it could
> possibly be reduced in analysis.
> *Geoffrey Madell*[131]

In *Some Problems in Ethics* (Oxford University Press, 1931), H.W.B. Joseph argued against the view that knowledge can be accounted for in terms of matter in motion: 'All movements of bodies are equally necessary, but they cannot be discriminated as true or false. It seems as nonsensical to call a movement true as a flavour purple or a sound avaricious.'[132] As C.E.M. Joad argued in his 1936 *Guide to Philosophy*:

> it would be meaningless to ask whether a bodily event, for example, the state of my blood pressure or the temperature of my skin, was true. These are things which occur and are real; they are facts. But they are not and cannot be true, because they do not assert anything other than themselves. It is, then, on this basis equally meaningless [given Materialism] to say of a thought that it is true; we can say only that it occurs . . . Thus in so far as it establishes its conclusion, Materialism destroys its case.[133]

In the same tradition, C.S. Lewis argued that 'acts of thinking are no doubt events; but they are a very special sort of events. They are "about" something other than themselves and can be true or false.'[134] However, '[physical events] are not about anything and cannot be true or false'.[135] Hence thinking 'events' in our minds cannot be reduced to physical 'events' in our brains. A thought – e.g. 'The AFR is a sound argument' – cannot be a merely physical event, because the former possess qualities that the latter cannot: the quality of being *about* something, and the quality of being *true*. As Lewis observed:

> We are compelled to admit between the thoughts of a terrestrial astronomer and the behaviour of matter several light-years away that particular relation which we call truth. But this relation has no meaning at all if we try to make it exist between the matter of the

star and the astronomer's brain, considered as a lump of matter. The brain may be in all sorts of relations to the star no doubt: it is in a spatial relation, and a time relation . . . But to talk of one bit of matter as being true about another bit of matter seems to me to be nonsense.[136]

'We experience,' says Lewis, 'thoughts, which are "about" or "refer to" something other than themselves . . . but physical events, as such, cannot in any intelligible sense be said to be "about" or to "refer to" anything.'[137] Philosopher Howard Robinson notes that 'this feature of the mind's meaning, pointing or intending something beyond itself, is something which many philosophers have thought cannot be numbered among or reduced to normal physical relations.'[138] As Raymond Tallis acknowledges: 'Intentionality . . . tears the seamless fabric of the causally closed material universe . . . it points in the direction opposite to causation . . . it is incapable of being accommodated in the materialistic world picture as it is currently constructed.'[139] Electrical activity in a computer chip or a brain has all sorts of physical qualities and stands in all sorts of physical relations to other physical realities, but an exhaustive list of such qualities and relations would not include the quality of 'being about' anything. According to Dallas Willard: 'no such property or combination of properties constitutes a representation of anything, or qualifies their bearer as being of or about anything'.[140] John Searle concludes that 'any attempt to reduce intentionality to something non-mental will always fail because it leaves out intentionality.'[141]

Naturalism is 'nonsensical' as a worldview, as J.P. Moreland argues, because it 'denies intentionality by reducing it to a physical relation . . . thereby denying that the mind is genuinely capable of having thoughts about the world'.[142] And if thoughts cannot be about anything, then they can't be true or false; and if thoughts can't be true or false, then the claim that naturalism is true is self-contradictory. Since many things are known to be true, observes Willard: 'naturalism must be false. It cannot accommodate the ontological structure of knowing and knowledge.'[143]

Naturalism and the End of Reason

> When we hear of some new attempt to explain reasoning
> . . . naturalistically, we ought to react as if we were told
> that someone had squared the circle. . .
> *Peter Geach*[144]

Lewis was right: there are several independent arguments showing that while 'naturalism . . . offers what professes to be a full account of our mental behaviour', this account 'leaves no room for the acts of knowing . . . on which the whole value of our thinking, as a means to truth, depends.'[145] The failure of reductionistic physical explanations of rationality entails the failure of naturalism, for 'in order to avoid this kind of reductionism, one must abandon a cornerstone of contemporary naturalism, namely the causal closure of the physical domain.'[146] Instead, one must accept that 'human beings possess rational powers that are impossible for beings whose actions are governed entirely by the laws of physics . . .'[147]

The Rationality Argument for a Supernatural Reason

> The essential spiritual selfhood of man has its only
> adequate ground in the transcendent spiritual Selfhood
> of God as Absolute Mind.
> *Stuart C. Hackett*[148]

C.S. Lewis turned the conclusion of the anti-naturalism argument from reason into the first premise of an argument for the existence of a transcendent Reason at the heart of reality:

> It is . . . an open question whether each man's reason exists absolutely on its own or whether it is the result of some (rational) cause – in fact, of some other Reason. That other Reason might conceivably be found to depend on a third, and so on; it would not matter how far this process was carried provided you found reason coming from reason at each stage. It is only when you are asked to believe in Reason coming from non-reason that you must

cry Halt, for if you don't, all thought is discredited. It is therefore obvious that sooner or later you must admit a Reason which exists absolutely on its own. The problem is whether you or I can be such a self-existent Reason.[149]

Lewis thought not:

> This question almost answers itself the moment we remember what existence 'on one's own' means. It means that kind of existence which Naturalists attribute to 'the whole show' and Supernaturalists attribute to God . . . Now it is clear that my reason has grown up gradually since my birth and is interrupted for several hours each night. I therefore cannot be that eternal self-existent Reason . . . yet if any thought is valid, such a Reason must exist and must be the source of my own imperfect and intermittent rationality.[150]

He concluded: 'Human minds . . . are not the only supernatural entities that exist. They do not come from nowhere . . . each has its tap-root in an eternal, self-existent, rational Being, whom we call God.'[151] Hence, as Keith Ward argues: 'To believe in God is not to take a leap of blind faith beyond reason. It is to take a leap of faith in reason as the ultimate principle of reality.'[152] This 'Reason' with a capital 'R' may or may not be the 'God' with a capital 'G' of Christianity, but at the very least it exhibits certain qualities of the kind of deity acknowledged within the great monotheistic traditions.

Thomas Nagel concedes that 'the reliance we put on reason implies a belief that . . . the basic methods of reasoning we employ are not merely human but belong to a more general category of *mind*.'[153] Nagel concludes that 'the idea of a natural sympathy between the deepest truths of nature and the deepest truths of the human mind . . . makes us more at home in the universe than is secularly comfortable.'[154] Antony O'Hear likewise admits that 'in a contest between materialistic atheism and some kind of religious-cum-theistic view, the materialistic conclusion leaves even more mysteries than a view which sees reason and consciousness as part of the essence of the universe'.[155] As atheist Peter Cave writes: 'No convincing explanation yet exists of how our experiences relate to the physical world and their evolutionary value. It may be that the development of psychological features – of consciousness, desires, beliefs, sensations – cannot be accounted for in concepts of current scientific and causal laws, but require teleological laws of some kind.'[156]

Cave denies that this line of thought 'suggests that a reference to God will pop up in the future scientific explanations';[157] however (debates about the definition of science aside), appeals to teleology clearly lend themselves to the thought that there must be an ultimate purposer with a capital 'P' behind finite examples of purposive consciousness. As Menuge argues: 'if human personality cannot arise from the impersonal matter of the universe, its source surely has to be a supernatural being; and on pain of regress, this being must be supposed to be a necessary . . . being'.[158] Moreland concludes: 'Mind appears to be a basic feature of the cosmos and its origin at a finite level of persons is best explained by postulating a fundamental Mind who gave finite minds being and design.'[159]

Conclusion

> I have consciousness: but it is impossible that consciousness
> could emerge from the action of the unconscious. Therefore
> the original Being was conscious.
> C.S. Lewis[160]

Contra Russell's belief that human thoughts are 'subordinated to nature, the outcome of natural laws',[161] the various arguments from reason show that humans are *not* wholly subordinated to nature, and that 'nature' (i.e. material reality) is *not* all there is to reality:

> acts of reasoning are not interlocked with the total interlocking system of Nature as all other items are interlocked with one another. They are connected with it in a different way; as the understanding of a machine is certainly connected with the machine but not in the way the parts of the machine are connected with each other. The knowledge of a thing is not one of the thing's parts. In this sense something beyond Nature operates whenever we reason.[162]

Naturalism insists on putting the material cart before the thinking horse, and the result is self-defeating: 'Naturalists have been engaged in thinking about Nature. They have not attended to the fact that they were *thinking*. The moment one attends to this it is obvious that one's own thinking cannot be a merely natural event, and that therefore something other than Nature exists.'[163] Hence Lewis affirmed: 'The validity of rational thought, accepted in an utterly non-naturalistic, transcendental (if you will), supernatural sense, is the necessary presupposition of all other theorizing . . . By thinking at all we have claimed that our thoughts are more than mere natural events. All other propositions must be fitted in as best they can round that primary claim.'[164]

When we ask which worldview makes the best sense out of the irreducible nature of rationality, the matter-first view of naturalism is revealed as a complete non-starter, whereas the mind-first view of theism provides a coherent explanatory context for our rational capacities.

* * *

Recommended Resources

By C.S. Lewis:
Miracles (London: HarperCollins, 2002), especially 'The Cardinal Difficulty of Naturalism' www.lastseminary.com/argument-from-reason/The%20Cardinal%20Difficulty%20of%20Naturalism%20in%20Chapter%203%20of%20Miracles.pdf.
'Religion without Dogma?', in *C.S. Lewis Essay Collection: Faith, Christianity and the Church* (ed. Lesley Walmsley; London: HarperCollins, 2002)

Video

Moreland, J.P. 'Arguing God from Consciousness' www.closertotruth.com/video-profile/Arguing-God-from-Consciousness-J-P-Moreland-/1168.

Audio

Menuge, Angus J. 'Agents under Fire: Part One' http://intelligentdesign.podomatic.com/entry/eg/2008-08-18T17_44_24-07_00.
— 'Apologist Interview' http://j.mp/Apologetics315-InterviewAngusMenuge.
Plantinga, Alvin. 'The Evolutionary Argument against Naturalism (2007 Norton Lectures)' www.sbts.edu/media/audio/Norton/20071025plantinga.mp3.
— vs Daniel Dennett. 'Science and Religion: Are They Compatible?' www.apologetics315.com/2009/02/alvin-plantinga-daniel-dennett-debate.html.
— vs Stephen Law. 'Evolutionary Argument against Naturalism: The Debate' www.youtube.com/watch?v=JyQ5cFIoKts.

Online papers

Budziszewski, J. 'Escape from Nihilism' www.leaderu.com/real/ri9801/budziszewski.html.
Copan, Paul. 'My Recent Interaction with Richard Dawkins' www.reclaimingthemind.org/blog/2011/03/my-recent-inter-action-with-richard-dawkins/.
Goetz, Stewart. 'Naturalism and Libertarian Agency' www.lastseminary.com/against-naturalism/Naturalism%20and%20Libertarian%20Agency.pdf.
— and Charles Taliaferro, 'An Argument from Consciousness and Free Will' www.infidels.org/library/modern/stewart_goetz/dualism.html.
William Hasker, 'Emergent Dualism' www.lastseminary.com/dualism/Emergent%20Dualism.pdf.
— 'How Not to Be A Reductionist' www.lastseminary.com/dualism/How%20Not%20To%20Be%20A%20Reductivist.pdf.

Johnson, Phillip E. 'The Robot Rebellion of Richard Dawkins'
www.arn.org/docs/johnson/pj_robotrebellion.htm.
Koons, Robert C. 'The Incompatibility of Naturalism and
Scientific Realism'
www.leaderu.com/offices/koons/docs/natreal.html.
Lovell, Steven. 'C.S. Lewis' Argument against Naturalism'
www.lastseminary.com/argument-from-reason/
C.S.%20Lewiss%20Case%20Against%20Naturalism.pdf.
Lucas, J.R. 'The Godelian Argument'
www.leaderu.com/truth/2truth08.html.
Meilaender, Gilbert. 'The Last Word'
www.firstthings.com/article/2007/01/the-last-word-40.
Menuge, Angus J. 'Dennett Denied: A Critique of Dennett's
Evolutionary Account of Intentionality'
www.lastseminary.com/dualism/A%20Critique%20of%20-
Dennetts%20Evolutionary%20Account%20of%20Intentionalit
y.pdf.
— 'The Role of Agency in Science'
www.4truth.net/fourtruthpbscience.aspx?pageid=
8589952943&terms=angus%20menuge.
Moreland, J.P. 'Does the Argument from Mind Provide Evidence
of God?'
www.lastseminary.com/argument-from-
mind/Does%20the%20Argument%20from%20Mind%20Provi
de%20Evidence%20for%20God.pdf.
— 'If You Can't Reduce, You Must Eliminate: Why Kim's Version
of Physicalism Isn't Close Enough'
www.lastseminary.com/dualism/Why%20Kims%20-
Version%20of%20Physicalism%20Isnt%20Close%20Enough.
pdf.
Plantinga, Alvin. 'Against Materialism'
http://philosophy.nd.edu/people/all/profiles/plantinga-
alvin/documents/AGAINSTMATERIALISM.pdf.
— 'Against Naturalism' (from *Knowledge of God*)
www.thedivineconspiracy.org/Z5223A.pdf.
— 'Content and Natural Selection'
http://philosophy.nd.edu/people/all/profiles/plantinga-
alvin/documents/CONTENTANDNATURALSELECTION
.pdf.

— 'An Evolutionary Argument against Naturalism'
www.lastseminary.com/argument-fromreason/An%20
Evolutionary%20Argument%20Against%20Naturalism.pdf.

Reppert, Victor. 'The Argument from Reason'
www.lastseminary.com/argument-from-reason/Reppert%20-
%20The%20Argument%20from%20Reason.pdf.

— 'Interview on the Argument from Reason'
www.lastseminary.com/argumentfromreason/QCI%
20Interview%20-%20Dr.%20Victor%20Reppert%20on%20the%
20Argument%20from%20Reason.pdf.

— 'Taking Lewis Seriously: Apologetics and the Personal Heresy'
www.ivpress.com/title/exc/2732-1.pdf.

West, John G. 'C.S. Lewis and the Materialist Menace'
www.independent.org/newsroom/article.asp?id=1565.

Willard, Dallas. 'Knowledge and Naturalism'
www.lastseminary.com/againstnaturalism/Knowledge%
20and%20Naturalism.pdf.

Williams, Peter S. 'Nothing More Than Blood and Bones?
Consciousness, Artificial Intelligence and God'
www.arn.org/docs/williams/pw_bloodandbone.htm.

— 'Why Naturalists Should Mind about Physicalism'
www.lastseminary.com/argument-frommind/Why%
20Naturalists%20Should%20Mind%20about%20Physicalism%
20and%20Vice%20Versa.pdf.

Books

Balfour, Arthur J. *Theism and Humanism* (Seattle: Inkling Books, 2000).

Beauregard, Mario and Denyse O'Leary. *The Spiritual Brain: A Neuroscientist's Case for the Existence of the Soul* (New York: HarperOne, 2008).

Corcoran, Kevin. *Soul, Body and Survival: Essays on the Metaphysics of Human Persons* (London: Cornell University Press, 2001).

Craig, William Lane, ed. *Philosophy of Religion: A Reader and Guide* (Edinburgh University Press, 2002).

— and J.P. Moreland. *Naturalism: A Critical Analysis* (London: Routledge, 2000).

Feser, Edward. *Philosophy of Mind: A Beginner's Guide* (Oxford: OneWorld, 2006).

Goetz, Stewart and Mark C. Baker, eds. *The Soul Hypothesis: Investigations into the Existence of the Soul* (New York: Continuum, 2011).

— and Charles Taliaferro. *Naturalism* (Boston: Eerdmans, 2008).

Gordon, Bruce L. and William A. Dembski, eds. *The Nature of Nature: Examining the Role of Naturalism in Science* (Wilmington, DE: ISI, 2011).

Hasker, William. *The Emergent Self* (Cornell University Press, 2001).

Koons, Robert C. and George Bealer, eds. *The Waning of Materialism* (Oxford University Press, 2010).

Lucas, J.R. *Freedom of the Will* (Oxford University Press, 1970).

Menuge, Angus. *Agents under Fire: Materialism and the Rationality of Science* (New York: Rowman & Littlefield, 2004).

Moreland, J.P. *Consciousness and the Existence of God: A Theistic Argument* (London: Routledge, 2009).

— *The Recalcitrant Imago Dei: Human Persons and the Failure of Naturalism* (London: SCM Press, 2009).

— 'The Argument from Consciousness.' Pages 282–343 in *The Blackwell Companion to Natural Theology* (ed. William Lane Craig and J.P. Moreland; Oxford: Wiley-Blackwell, 2009).

— 'The Argument from Consciousness.' Pages 204–20 in *The Rationality of Theism* (ed. Paul Copan and Paul K. Moser; London: Routledge, 2003).

— 'Hume and the Argument from Consciousness.' Pages 271–96 in *In Defense of Natural Theology: A Post-Humean Assessment* (ed. James F. Sennett and Douglas Groothuis; Downers Grove, IL: IVP, 2005).

Nagel Thomas. *Mind & Cosmos: Why the Materialistic Neo-Darwinian Conception of Nature Is Almost Certainly False* (Oxford University Press, 2012).

Nash, Ronald H. 'Miracles and Conceptual Systems.' Pages 115–31 in *In Defense of Miracles: A Comprehensive Case for God's Action in History* (ed. R. Douglas Geivett and Gary R. Habermas; Leicester: Apollos, 1997).

Plantinga, Alvin. *Where the Conflict Really Lies: Science, Religion, and Naturalism* (Oxford University Press, 2011).

– and Michael Tooley. *Knowledge of God* (Oxford: Blackwell, 2008).

Reppert, Victor. *C. S. Lewis's Dangerous Idea: In Defense of the Argument from Reason* (Downers Grove, IL; IVP Academic, 2003).

– 'The Argument from Reason.' Pages 344–90 in *The Blackwell Companion to Natural Theology* (ed. William Lane Craig and J.P. Moreland; Oxford: Wiley-Blackwell, 2009).

– 'The Argument from Reason and Hume's Legacy.' Pages 253–70 in *In Defense of Natural Theology: A Post-Humean Assessment* (ed. James F. Sennett and Douglas Groothuis; Downers Grove, IL: IVP, 2005).

Sterba, James P, ed. *Alvin Plantinga vs Daniel Dennett, Science and Religion: Are They Compatible?* (Oxford University Press, 2011).

Taliaferro, Charles. *Consciousness and the Mind of God* (Cambridge University Press, 1994).

Tallis, Raymond. *Aping Mankind: Neuromania, Darwinitis and the Misrepresentation of Humanity* (Durham: Acumen, 2011).

Taylor, A.E. *Does God Exist?* (London: Fontana, 1945).

Ward, Keith. *More Than Matter: Is Matter All We Really Are?* (Oxford: Lion, 2010).

Williams, Peter S. *The Case for Angels* (Carlisle: Paternoster, 2002).

– *I Wish I Could Believe in Meaning: A Response to Nihilism* (Southampton: Damaris, 2004).

5.

The Problem of Goodness

C.S. Lewis tried to prove too much by opining that the presence of a
conscience indicated the divine spark.
Christopher Hitchens[1]

C.S. Lewis was well acquainted with pain and suffering: 'the man
never enjoyed the kind of cloistered, protective and safe academic life often assumed and at times wrongly depicted.'[2] For example, Lewis's mother died of cancer when he was nine, his prayers
for her recovery unanswered. Cancer also took Lewis's father
and ended his brief marriage to American writer Joy Davidman.
Lewis's stepson recalls how:

> When I began, as ignorant young men will, to speak of war and
> warriors with words of admiration and began to show I had
> some idea that there was something glorious about it all, Jack
> told me about a lot of his experiences in World War I. Many of
> the things that happened to him, and to thousands of others,
> were absolutely horrible, like the times when he and his men
> would advance across the land between the trenches of the two
> armies, 'no-man's-land' as they called it, and on the way, some of
> the men would become bogged down in waist-deep mud. Jack
> and the platoon couldn't stop to pull them out but had to keep
> on advancing according to their orders, so they left the men
> where they were. After the attack was over and they were return-
> ing to their own trenches, they would often find these men again,
> physically unharmed but completely mindless, as if the horrors
> of spending a day trapped in the vile stinking morass and seeing
> the battle go on all around them while they were unable even to

move simply snapped their minds and reduced them to nothing-ness.[3]

In *Surprised by Joy* Lewis tells how the 'Great War' gave him a 'familiarity both with the very old and the very recent dead'[4] and he vividly recalls 'the cold, the smell of H.E. [high explosive], the horribly smashed men still moving like half-crushed beetles, the sitting or standing corpses, the landscape of sheer earth without a blade of grass, the boots worn day and night till they seemed to grow to your feet . . .'[5] He comments: 'Through the winter, weariness and water were our chief enemies. I have gone to sleep marching and woken again and found myself marching still. One walked in the trenches in thigh gum boots with water above the knee; one remembers the icy stream welling up inside the boot when you punctured it on concealed barbed wire.'[6]

Lewis spent his nineteenth birthday in the front-line trenches of World War I, before being wounded during the Battle of Arras when a British creeping barrage crept the wrong way:

as they advanced with bayonets at the ready, the barrage stopped advancing and began to come back towards them. Soon Jack and his men were being bombarded by their own artillery from far behind them, and to his helpless fury Jack watched his men being blown to pieces in the constant roar of their own artillery support. Suddenly Jack saw a blinding light, everything went completely silent, and then the ground came up slowly and hit him in the face. Jack had been hit by both the concussion and shrapnel from a British shell. His trusted sergeant had been between Jack and the shell when it exploded and was blown to bits.[7]

Although his wounds weren't life-threatening, they were bad enough to render him unfit for service: 'The piece of shrapnel in Jack's chest was considered to be too close to his heart to be safely removed, so it was left in place, which was not uncommon medical practice in those days, and he carried it with him for the rest of his life.'[8]

Not Positive about the Problem of Evil

According to logical positivism, since moral judgements are neither tautological nor reducible to empirically verifiable propositions, they are neither true nor false. Lewis observes that 'on this view, the world of facts, without one trace of value, and the world of feelings, without one trace of truth or falsehood, justice or injustice, confront one another, and no rapprochement is possible.'[9] Positivism is thus allied to moral subjectivism, the view 'that moral judgements are not objectively true or false and thus that different individuals or societies can hold conflicting moral judgements without any of them being mistaken.'[10] As Lewis explains: 'It is widely believed that scientific thought does put us in touch with reality, whereas moral or metaphysical thought does not. On this view, when we say that the universe is a space-time continuum we are saying something about reality, whereas if we say that . . . men ought to have a living wage, we are only describing our own subjective feelings.'[11]

The parallel problem of beauty

In *The Abolition of Man* C.S. Lewis relates how the authors of an English textbook, whom he names 'Gaius' and 'Titus', comment upon a story about the poet Coleridge and a waterfall.[12] Two tourists were present besides Coleridge: one called the waterfall 'sublime',[13] the other 'pretty'. Coleridge 'mentally endorsed the first judgement and rejected the second with disgust'.[14] Gaius and Titus assert: 'When the man said *This is sublime*, he appeared to be making a remark about the waterfall . . . Actually . . . he was not making a remark about the waterfall, but a remark about his own feelings. What he was saying was really *I have feelings* associated in my mind with the word 'Sublime', or shortly, I have sublime feelings.'[15]

According to Gaius and Titus, this supposed confusion is common: 'We appear to be saying something very important about something: and actually we are only saying something about our own feelings.'[16] This subjective reduction of 'beauty' parallels the subjectivist reduction of 'goodness'; in attacking the former, Lewis implicitly attacks the latter. Lewis points out that 'the man who says *This is sublime* cannot mean *I have sublime feelings* . . . The feelings which make a man call an object sublime are not sublime feelings, but feelings of veneration.'[17] The correct translation of the tourist's assertion, if a translation must be made, would be I have humble feelings.[18] Otherwise we'd end up translating moral assertions such as 'You are contemptible' as 'I have contemptible feelings', which is ludicrous. As W.D. Ross observed in *The Right and the Good* (Oxford University Press, 1930):

> When a man thinks an object to be beautiful . . . the judgement is a judgement about the object, not about the judger's state of mind. And [when we judge something to be beautiful], we judge that it was beautiful before we were thrilled by it, and will be beautiful when we have ceased to be thrilled by it. The judgement, while it is not a judgement about the judger's state of mind, is one in which, on the strength of his knowledge of (or opinion about) his state of mind, he ascribes an attribute to an object.[19]

Lewis points out that if a humble feeling of veneration prompts Coleridge to judge that the waterfall is sublimely beautiful, we may ask *whether that feeling was an appropriate response* relative *not to the person* expressing appreciation (i.e. Coleridge), but *to the intrinsic nature of the object* being thus appreciated. Picking up on this line of thought, atheist Russ Shafer-Landau poses the question:

> is it possible to value something that is unworthy of your affection? The subjectivist must return a negative answer. If value is in the eye of the beholder, then so long as you like something, it is valuable. It is valuable *because* you like it, rather than the other way around. To suppose that the object of your affections doesn't deserve such flattering treatment, you must first suppose that the object possesses a degree of value independently of your attitude towards it. But that is impossible if subjectivism is true.[20]

Lewis notes that:

> Until quite modern times all . . . men believed the universe to be such that certain emotional reactions on our part could be congruous or incongruous to it – believed, in fact, that objects did not

merely receive, but could merit, our approval or disapproval . . .
The reason why Coleridge agreed with the tourist who called the
cataract sublime and disagreed with the one who called it pretty
was of course that he believed inanimate nature to be such that
certain responses could be more 'just' or 'appropriate' to it than
others . . . the man who called the cataract sublime was not intending simply to describe his own emotions about it: he was also
claiming that the object was one which merited those emotions.[21]

Lewis grounds his account of beauty in Augustine's definition of
moral virtue as *ordo amoris* or 'appropriate love', that is: 'the ordi-
nate condition of the affections in which every object is accorded
that kind and degree of love which is appropriate to it'.[22] On this
basis Lewis argues that 'because our approvals and disapprovals
are thus recognitions of objective value or responses to an objective order, therefore emotional states can be in harmony with reason . . . or out of harmony with reason . . .'[23] As contemporary
Oxford aesthetician Roger Scruton argues:

> Beauty . . . is a real and universal value . . . The judgement of taste
> is about the beautiful object, not about the subject's state of mind
> . . . When I describe something as beautiful I am describing *it*, not
> my feelings towards it – I am making a claim, and that seems to
> imply that others, if they see things aright, would agree with me.[24]

Lewis saw that if positivism/subjectivism were correct, if value
were purely 'in the eye of the beholder', then the problem of evil
couldn't be coherently raised as an argument against God:

> Unless we judge this waste and cruelty to be real evils we can-
> not of course condemn the universe for exhibiting them. Unless
> we take our own standard of goodness to be valid in principle
> (however fallible our particular applications of it) we cannot
> mean anything by calling waste and cruelty evils. And unless
> we take our own standards to be something more than ours, to
> be in fact an objective principle to which we are responding, we
> cannot regard that standard as valid. In a word, unless we
> allow ultimate reality to be moral, we cannot morally condemn
> it.[25]

The Problem of Evil

Lewis wasn't taken in by the self-contradictory philosophy of positivism: 'the distinction thus made between scientific and non-scientific thoughts will not easily bear the weight we are attempting to put on it.'[26] Hence Lewis was free to believe that it really was *true* to say that the suffering and inhumanity he experienced was *objectively* evil. As Arthur F. Holmes argues:

> *Right* and *wrong* are not empirical terms denoting empirically observable qualities, but neither are they just emotivisms. They are evaluative, interpretive terms that refer to nonempirical concepts of rightness or wrongness. The positivist could never admit that because of his theory of meaning. But if that theory is mistaken, then we can admit nonempirical concepts, and ethical judgements may be cognitive [i.e. true or false] after all.[27]

For Lewis, evil *was* an objective fact: 'a real thing – a thing that is really there, not made up by ourselves.'[28] In addition to believing that evil was an objective reality, Lewis believed that evil was something any God worth the name objectively *ought not* to permit. Hence, for Lewis the atheist, the evident existence of evil justified his atheism: 'Several years before I read Lucretius I felt the force of his argument (and it is surely the strongest of all) for atheism . . . *Had God designed the world, it would not be A world so frail and faulty as we see* . . .'[29] As Lewis explained in *The Problem of Pain*:

> Not many years ago when I was an atheist, if anyone had asked me, 'Why do you not believe in God?' my reply would have run something like this . . . if you ask me to believe that this [universe] is the work of a benevolent and omnipotent spirit, I reply that the evidence points in the opposite direction. Either there is no spirit behind the universe, or else a spirit indifferent to good and evil, or else an evil spirit.[30]

Sorley Tested by the Problem of Goodness

> If nothing is certainly right, then of course it follows that
> nothing is certainly wrong. And that is the snag about what
> I call Heroic Pessimism . . .
>
> C.S. *Lewis*[31]

Lewis came to believe that his central argument against God contained the seed of its own subversion:

> My argument against God was that the universe seemed so cruel and unjust. But how had I got this idea of *just* and *unjust?* A man does not call a line crooked unless he has some idea of a straight line. What was I comparing this universe with when I called it unjust? If the whole show was bad and senseless from A to Z, so to speak, why did I, who was supposed to be part of the show, find myself in such violent reaction to it? A man feels wet when he falls into water, because man is not a water animal: a fish would not feel wet. Of course I could have given up my idea of justice by saying it was nothing but a private idea of my own. But if I did that, then my argument against God collapsed too – for the argument depended on saying that the world was really unjust, not simply that it did not happen to please my fancies. Thus in the very act of trying to prove that God did not exist – in other words, that the whole of reality was senseless – I found I was forced to assume that one part of reality – namely my idea of justice – was full of sense. Consequently atheism turns out to be too simple. If the whole universe has no meaning, we should never have found out that it has no meaning: just as, if there were no light in the universe and therefore no creatures with eyes, we should never know it was dark. *Dark* would be a word without meaning.[32]

Likewise, *evil* would be a word without an objective referent in a materialistic universe devoid of any *objective* meaning, purpose or metaphysical standard of goodness. To make a moral judgement about the material cosmos while holding that only the material cosmos was real, such that one's moral judgement was just another part of that cosmos, is what Lewis came to dub the Promethean fallacy: 'the real difficulty [with Bertrand Russell's

Promethean attitude towards reality is] that our ideals are [on Russell's own worldview] after all a natural product, facts with a relation to all other facts, and cannot survive the condemnation of the fact as a whole. The Promethean attitude would be tenable only if we were really members of some other whole outside the real *whole* . . .'[33] Hence Lewis came to believe that Russell's condemnation of the material world pointed towards the existence of something besides the material world:

> if . . . nature – the space-time-matter system – is the only thing in existence, then of course there can be no other source for our standards. They must, like everything else, be the unintended and meaningless outcome of blind forces . . . All that we say about 'Nature red in tooth and claw' . . . is quite inexplicable on the theory that we are simply natural creatures. If this world is the only world, how did we come to find its laws either so dreadful or so comic? If there is no straight line elsewhere, how did we discover that Nature's line is crooked?[34]

One might put Lewis's realization like this:

Premise 1:   If metaphysical naturalism is true, then nothing is objectively evil
Premise 2:   Something is objectively evil
Conclusion: Therefore, metaphysical naturalism is false

Lewis became convinced that once we allow our *knowledge* of evil to trump the self-contradictory *theory* of positivism/subjectivism, so that we can reason about the problem of evil (something we can only do if naturalism is false – cf. chapter four), we are faced with an even deeper 'problem of goodness':

> The defiance of the good atheist hurled at an apparently ruthless and idiotic cosmos is really an unconscious homage to something in or behind that cosmos which he recognizes as infinitely valuable and authoritative: for if mercy and justice were really only private whims of his own . . . he could not go on being indignant. The fact that he arraigns heaven itself for disregarding them means that at some level of his mind he knows they are enthroned in a higher heaven still.[35]

Lewis's advocacy of the moral argument in *Mere Christianity* is basically a popularization of W.R. Sorley's Gifford Lectures on *Moral Values and the Idea of God*; lectures we know Lewis read and later owned in book form.[36] Sorley pointed out that to recognize the objective validity of moral values is to recognize that 'their validity could not be verified in external phenomena; they cannot be established by observation of the course of nature. They hold good for persons only: and their peculiarity consists of the fact that their validity is not in any way dependent upon their being manifested in the character or conduct of persons, or even on their being recognised in the thoughts of persons.'[37] Indeed, 'We acknowledge the good and its objective claim upon us when we are conscious that our will has not yielded to the claim; and we admit that its validity existed before we recognised it.'[38] Furthermore, 'the perfect moral ideal does not exist in the volitional, or even in the intellectual, consciousness of [finite] persons; they have not achieved agreement with it in their lives, and even their understanding of it is incomplete.'[39] Having made these observations, Sorley asks a significant question concerning where in our account of reality (our ontology) we are to locate objective moral values:

> Seeing then that [the moral ideal] is not manifested by finite [personal] existents, how are we to conceive of its validity? Other truths are displayed in the order of the existing world; but this is not so with moral values. And yet the system of moral values has been acknowledged to be an aspect of the real universe to which existing things belong. How are we to conceive its relation to them? A particular instance of goodness can exist only in the character of an individual person or groups of persons; an ideal of goodness such as we have is found only in minds such as ours. But the ideal of goodness does not exist in finite minds or in their material environment. What then is its status in the system of reality?[40]

Sorley argued that 'the question is answered if we regard the moral order as the order of a Supreme Mind and the ideal of goodness as belonging to this Mind.'[41] In other words, since objectively correct moral value judgements are possible and require an objective moral standard, and as no *moral standard* can exist in matter, and yet no *objective* moral standard can exist in a finite immaterial mind or minds, an *objective moral standard* must exist *in an infinite immaterial mind*:

> Persons are conscious of values and of an ideal of goodness, which they recognise as having undoubted authority for the direction of their activity; the validity of these values or laws and of this ideal, however, does not depend upon their recognition: it is objective and eternal; and how could this eternal validity stand alone, not embodied in matter and neither seen nor realised by finite minds, unless there were an eternal mind whose thought and will were therein expressed? God must therefore exist and his nature be goodness.[42]

One might phrase Sorley's argument as follows:

Premise 1:   If a wholly good personal god doesn't exist, then objective moral values can't exist
Premise 2:   Objective moral values exist
Conclusion: Therefore, a wholly good personal god exists

This type of moral argument, concerning the ontological basis for objective moral values, continues to be the most discussed of moral arguments for God's existence in contemporary philosophy of religion (interestingly enough, although consistent atheists cannot afford to endorse both premises of this argument, it's easy enough to find atheists who argue for either premise). Let's examine the premises of this argument in reverse order.

Objective Values

> The ideal of absolute value is at the heart of human experience.
> *Bruce Sheiman*[43]

As William Lane Craig explains, moral objectivism is the view that:

moral values . . . are valid and binding whether anybody believes in them or not. Thus, to say, for example, that the Holocaust was objectively wrong is to say that it was wrong even though the Nazis who carried it out thought that it was right and that it would still have been wrong even if the Nazis had won World War II and succeeded in exterminating or brain-washing everyone who disagreed with them.[44]

Atheists are perfectly able to recognize and defend the existence of the objective reality of good and evil. Indeed, as John Cottingham observes: 'the increasing consensus among philosophers today is that some kind of objectivism of truth and of value is correct . . .'[45] For example, together with many other contemporary philosophers, atheist Peter Cave defends moral objectivism by appealing to moral intuitions: 'whatever sceptical arguments may be brought against our belief that killing the innocent is morally wrong, we are more certain that the killing is morally wrong than that the argument is sound . . . Torturing an innocent child for the sheer fun of it is morally wrong. Full stop.'[46] Although it means abandoning the scientistic theory of knowledge he relies upon elsewhere, Sam Harris recognizes the legitimacy of appealing to properly basic moral intuitions:

'intuition' . . . denotes the most basic constituent of our faculty of understanding. While this is true in matters of ethics, it is no less true in science. When we can break our knowledge of a thing down no further, the irreducible leap that remains is intuitively taken. Thus, the traditional opposition between reason and intuition is a false one: reason is itself intuitive to the core, as any judgement that a proposition is 'reasonable' or 'logical' relies on intuition to find its feet . . . we cannot step out of the darkness without taking a *first* step. And reason, without knowing how, understands this axiom if it would understand anything at all. The reliance on intuition, therefore, should be no more discomforting for the ethicist than it has been for the physicist.[47]

Likewise, C.S. Lewis observes how 'the philosopher's or theologian's theory of ethics arises out of the practical ethics he already holds and attempts to obey . . .'[48] In other words, in debating different systems of normative ethics, and in the underlying meta-ethical debate between objectivism and sub-jectivism, the only data we have to hand is our moral intuitions. These intuitions can be divided into various 'particular' intu-itions and one 'universal' intuition. The former are intuitions about *particular specific or general things* being objectively right or wrong. The latter intuition is about *whether anything at all is objectively right or wrong.*

For a paradigm case study of a particular moral intuition, con-sider the atrocities perpetrated by the Nazis during World War II. As C.S. Lewis asked: 'What was the sense in saying the enemy were in the wrong unless Right is a real thing which the Nazis . . . ought to have practised?'[49] Adolf Hitler declared: 'I have freed Germany from the stupid and degrading fallacies of conscience and morality . . . We will train young people before whom the world will tremble.'[50] But as Oxford philosopher Richard Swinburne says: 'One is inclined to say that the man who says that there was nothing morally evil in Hitler's exterminating the Jews is saying something false.'[51] If moral subjectivism is true, the Holocaust was not objectively wrong. However, the Holocaust was objectively wrong (this is a particular moral intuition). Therefore, moral subjectivism is false.

In another paradigm example of a particular moral intuition, I find myself with the properly basic belief that torturing a baby for fun is wrong. Such torture isn't *merely* something that stops the baby functioning as it otherwise would (an empirical obser-vation), or something I feel bad about because of my species' evo-lutionary history, or something my society has decided not to endorse. Rather, torturing a baby for fun is *something that is objec-tively wrong.* So *at least one thing is objectively wrong.* Therefore, *moral subjectivism is false.*

I have a number of particular moral intuitions, some of which are specific (e.g. the Holocaust was wrong; torturing a baby for fun is wrong) and some of which are general (e.g. it's always right to choose the lesser of two evils, whatever they might be). Of course, as a fallible being I *could* be mistaken in these intu-itions (although I don't think I am); but note that *this very admis-sion* of particular moral fallibility contains and endorses the *uni-versal* intuition that *moral claims are either objectively true or false,* for if moral subjectivism were true, then none of my moral intuitions could be false! The intuition that it's possible to have false moral opinions entails the truth of moral objectivism. As atheist Russ Shafer-Landau argues: 'subjectivism's or relativism's picture of ethics as a wholly conventional enterprise entails a kind of moral infallibility for individuals or societies . . . This sort of infallibility is hard to swallow.'[52] Just try swallowing 'this sort of infallibility' in the face of these words from Italian fascist Mussolini:

> [moral subjectivism] is simply a fact . . . Everything I have said and done in these last years is relativism by intuition . . . If relativism signifies contempt for fixed categories and men who claim to be the bearers of an objective and immortal truth . . . then there is nothing more relativistic than Fascist attitudes and activity . . . From the fact that all ideologies are of equal value, that all ideologies are mere fictions, the modern relativist infers that everybody has the right to create for himself his own ideology and to attempt to enforce it with all the energy of which he is capable.[53]

Moreover, *it is self-contradictory to argue for moral subjectivism*. If there are no objective moral values then it can't be objectively true that I morally *ought* to consider the relativist's arguments, or that I *ought* to consider them fairly, or that I *ought* to value truth over falsehood such that I *should* accept the subjectivist's conclusion if I find their arguments persuasive: 'Why should you,' asked Friedrich Nietzsche, 'pay attention to the truth?'[54] Indeed, since the subjectivist cannot say that we objectively *ought* to reject beliefs we have sufficient reason to doubt, why shouldn't I believe that objectivism is true *even if I were given sufficient reason to doubt it*? For the subjectivist there's no possible *objective* moral 'shouldn't' about it! Knowing this, how could I view any argument against objectivism as sufficient? To take any such argument seriously would be to embrace the self-contradictory position that a) there are no objective moral values, and that b) one objectively *ought* to accept subjectivism. As philosopher Margarita Rosa Levin comments in a related context:

> Even the enemies of objectivity rely on it . . . the skeptic states a position that cannot possibly be sustained or rationally believed

[because] he is in effect asking you not to apply his assertion to his own position, without giving any reason for exempting his own words from his own general claim. His position is futile and self-refuting; it can be stated, but it cannot convince anyone who recognizes its implications.[55]

Hence, as Lewis concluded, humans simply 'find themselves under a moral law, which they did not make, and cannot quite forget even when they try, and which they know they ought to obey.'[56]

Obfuscating the Question of Moral Ontology

As Craig J. Hazen warns:

> The primary technique the new atheists have adopted for dealing with the issue of the origin or grounding of the moral law is obfuscation. The new atheists are very fond of saying, 'We don't need God to be good.' Indeed, they often say that atheists, agnostics and skeptics often lead more wholesome lives than lifelong professing Christians. Now, theists should not be fooled by this. Our response should be, 'Of course you don't need God to be good – we've never claimed that you do.' You see, it is not knowledge (epistemology) of the moral law that is a problem – after all, the Bible teaches that this law is written on every human heart. Rather, the daunting problem for the new atheist is the nature and source (ontology) of the moral law.[57]

Ontology, not *epistemology*

The New Atheists *are* absolutely correct that we don't need
to believe in God or follow the Bible to have a general
knowledge of what's right and wrong.
Paul Copan[58]

Sam Harris evinces a serious confusion when he complains: 'the pervasive idea that religion is somehow the *source* of our deepest ethical intuitions is absurd.'[59] As C.S. Lewis comments:

> The idea . . . that Christianity brought a new ethical code into the world is a grave error. If it had done so, then we should have to

conclude that all who first preached it wholly misunderstood their own message: for all of them, its Founder, His precursor, His apostles, came demanding repentance and offering forgiveness, a demand and an offer both meaningless except on the assumption of a moral law already known and already broken. It is far from my intention to deny that we find in Christian ethics a deepening, an internalisation, a few changes of emphasis, in the moral code. But only serious ignorance of Jewish and Pagan culture would lead anyone to the conclusion that it is a radically new thing. Essentially, Christianity is not the promulgation of a moral discovery. It is addressed only to . . . those who admit their disobedience of the known moral law . . . A Christian who understands his own religion laughs when unbelievers expect to trouble him by the assertion that Jesus uttered no command which had not been anticipated by the Rabbis – few, indeed, which cannot be paralleled in classical, ancient Egyptian, Ninevite, Babylonian, or Chinese texts. We have long recognised that truth with rejoicing. Our faith is not pinned on a crank.[60]

Lewis argued that the unity of human moral opinion is more significant than the admitted diversity. In the appendix of *The Abolition of Man* Lewis collected parallel statements of basic moral precepts from classical, ancient Egyptian, Babylonian, Norse and Chinese texts, among others. As early and significant a Christian writer as the apostle Paul clearly agrees with Lewis on this point: 'when Gentiles, who do not have the law, do by nature things required by the law, they are a law for themselves, even though they do not have the law, since they show that *the requirements of the law are written on their hearts, their consciences also bearing witness, and their thoughts now accusing, now even defending them*' (Romans 2:14–15, my italics).

Contemporary moral philosopher and atheist Peter Singer affirms:

ethics is *not* a meaningless series of different things to different people in different times and places. Rather, against a background of historically and culturally diverse approaches to the question of how we ought to live, the degree of convergence is striking . . . what is recognized as a virtue in one society or religious tradition is very likely to be recognized as a virtue in the others; certainly, the set of virtues praised in one major tradition never makes up a substantial part of the set of vices of another major tradition (exceptions tend to be short-lived, societies in the process of decay or self-destruction).[61]

Oxford atheist J.L. Mackie acknowledged that such moral variation as does exist 'is in itself merely . . . a fact of anthropology which entails neither first order nor second order ethical views.'[62] That is, observations about moral *knowledge* and moral *action* are completely beside the point when it comes to the argument about moral *ontology* with which Lewis wrestled. Hence, whether or not Sam Harris is right about 'our ethical intuitions [having] their roots in biology',[63] he is wrong to think that this assumption 'reveals our efforts to ground ethics in religious conceptions of "moral duty" are misguided.'[64] The moral argument doesn't claim that atheists can't *know the difference* between good and evil. Nor does it make any claims about *how* anyone knows the difference between good and evil. It certainly doesn't claim that atheists can't *do the right thing* without *belief* in God. Rather, the moral argument claims that there couldn't *be* such a thing as an objective moral value if 'god' didn't exist to ground it.

Ontology, not psychology

We simply do not need religious ideas to motivate us to
live ethical lives.
Sam Harris[65]

A.C. Grayling inaccurately reduces the 'debate about the basis and nature of ethics' to 'the claim by theists that there can be no morality unless there is an invisible police force in the sky that will give you a bad time after death if you sin, and reward you if you behave as your religion instructs you.'[66] Richard Dawkins' discussion of the moral argument gets sidetracked by the same red herring: 'Many religious people find it hard to imagine how, without religion, one can be good, or would even want to be good.'[67] However, as we've already seen, neither C.S. Lewis nor the apostle Paul would count among Dawkins' 'many'. Both would agree with Dawkins that 'we do not need [to believe in] God in order to be good – or evil.'[68]

In trying to cash-out the supposed connection between belief in God and the ability to behave morally, Dawkins poses a rhetorical question:

> Do you really mean to tell me the only reason you try to be good is to gain God's approval and reward, or to avoid his disapproval and punishment? That's not morality, that's just sucking up, apple-polishing, looking over your shoulder at the great surveillance camera in the sky, or the still small wiretap in your head, monitoring your every move, even your every base thought . . . It seems to me to require quite a low self-regard to think that, should belief in God suddenly vanish from the world, we would all become callous and selfish hedonists, with no kindness, no charity, no generosity, nothing that would deserve the name of goodness.[69]

A.C. Grayling portrays Christian ethics in similarly coercive terms: 'For anyone who does not accept the simple-minded idea that doing good is a response to threats of punishment and promise of reward by a supernatural being in an afterlife, the question is how to treat others humanely and with respect, and recognize principles that are worth observing in the conduct of life, independently of the ancient threat-reward myths.'[70]

In the same vein Christopher Hitchens complains: 'Ordinary conscience will do, without any heavenly wrath behind it.'[71] Of course, C.S. Lewis was just as emphatic in rejecting the 'great surveillance camera in the sky' model of moral motivation: 'God is to be obeyed because of what He is in Himself. If you ask why we should obey God, in the last resort the answer is "I am." To know God is to know that our obedience is due to Him.'[72] Lewis observed:

> People often think of Christian morality as a kind of bargain in which God says, 'If you keep a lot of rules I'll reward you, and if you don't I'll do the other thing.' I don't think that is the best way of looking at it. I would much rather say that every time you make a choice you are turning the central part of you, the part of you that chooses, into something a little different from what it was

before. And taking your life as a whole, with all your innumerable choices, all your life long you are slowly turning this central thing either into a heavenly creature or into a hellish creature: either into a creature that is in harmony with God, and with other creatures, and with itself, or else into one that is in a state of war and hatred with God, and with its fellow creatures, and with itself.[73]

For Lewis, the good and bad consequences of good and bad behaviour are *intrinsic* rather than *extrinsic*.

As atheist Bruce Sheiman acknowledges: 'Religious people do not strive to be good because they want to avoid punishment and earn bonus points in the heavenly sweepstakes; they strive to behave consistent with God's love and grace in much the same way we naturally strive to be good for anyone we love.'[74] After all, the central point of the Christian 'gospel' (a Greek term that means 'good news') is that although a) it is impossible for humans to earn their way to heaven by behaving well, b) heaven is offered as a freely available gift to everyone who will acknowledge their need for the divine forgiveness displayed in the cross and resurrection of Jesus. Whatever one makes of this 'gospel', it clearly offers no grounds for treating morality as a matter of pragmatic submission to a system of divine punishments and rewards. Christianity isn't analogous to a loyalty reward scheme. As J.P. Moreland and William Lane Craig caution:

> The question is *not*: Must we believe in God in order to live moral lives? There is no reason to think that atheists and theists alike may not live what we normally characterize as good and decent lives. Similarly, the question is *not*: Can we formulate a system of ethics without reference to God? If the non-theist grants that human beings do have objective value, then there is no reason to think that he cannot work out a system of ethics with which the theist would largely agree. Or again, the question is *not*: Can we recognize the existence of objective moral values without reference to God? The theist will typically maintain that a person need not believe in God in order to recognize, say, that we should love our children.[75]

Rather, as Paul Copan explains, the moral argument urges that although '*belief* in God isn't a requirement for being moral . . . the *existence* of a personal God is crucial for a coherent understanding of objective morality.'[76] Although the non-theist can do the right thing because they *know* what the objectively right thing to do is, their worldview can't cogently provide *an adequate ontological account* of the objective moral values they know and obey. As Lewis saw, 'an objective standard of goodness' just isn't the sort of thing that fits into the naturalistic worldview; rather, it is the sort of thing best explained by a theistic worldview. Writing in *Scientific American*, Dawkins agrees with Lewis that if a personal god doesn't exist, then objective moral values don't exist: 'The universe that we observe has precisely the properties we should expect if there is, at bottom, no design, no purpose [that is, no god], *no evil, no good*, nothing but pitiless indifference.'[77]

Biting the Bullet

> If there is no God, there is no universally-obligatory moral law and no absolute objective values.
> F.C. Copleston[78]

> It is our attitudes to things that give them their value, whether good or bad, or indifferent.
> A.C. Grayling, The Good Book *(Wisdom 12:3)*

Joel Marks, Professor Emeritus of Philosophy at the University of New Haven, explains why his commitment to atheism leads him to reject moral objectivism:

> the religious fundamentalists are correct: without God, there is no morality. But they are incorrect, I still believe, about there being a God. Hence, I believe, there is no morality . . . In sum, while theists take the obvious existence of moral commands to be a kind of proof of the existence of a Commander, i.e., God, I now take the non-existence of a Commander as a kind of proof that there are no Commands, i.e., morality.[79]

Richard Dawkins likewise evades the conclusion of the moral argument at the terribly high price of denying premise two (i.e.

the existence of objective moral values). Thus Dawkins asserts that there is a distinction 'between ideas that are false or true about the real world (factual matters, in the broad sense) and ideas about what we ought to do . . . for which the words "true" and "false" have no meaning.'[80] As Christopher Hitchens warns, 'an atheist can easily be a nihilist . . .'[81] – at least, *if they are willing to retain their atheism at the expense of embracing moral subjectivism.* For which option is really most plausible: that it's false to say 'There is a god', or that it's false to say 'It is objectively wrong to torture a small child for fun'? Hitchens may ask his audience: 'are you willing to pay the price of a permanent supervisor? Are you willing to pay the price of believing in things that are supernatural?'[82] Atheists should ask themselves if they're really willing to pay the price of believing that the Holocaust wasn't objectively wrong just to avoid belief in a supernatural ground of value.

A nihilistic denial of objective moral value renders the moral critique of religion beloved by neo-atheists either self-contradictory (if it assumes objective values) or toothless (if not). It also removes any basis for the evident expectation that we *should* attend carefully to neo-atheist arguments and that we *ought* to change our views if we find them convincing! How can anyone be convinced to adopt a worldview that denies that anyone *should* ever be convinced of anything? Hence Stephen Unwin's complaint that 'Dawkins' assertion . . . that morality doesn't need faith [misses] the more fundamental question of why we have moral or aesthetic values at all – such as the ones by which Dawkins, myself and others venerate rational analysis.'[83] Anyone who isn't prepared to bite the self-defeating bullet of moral subjectivism faces the dilemma summarized by H.P. Owen: 'On the one hand [objective moral] claims transcend every human person . . . On the other hand . . . it is contradictory to assert that impersonal claims are entitled to the allegiance of our wills. The only solution to this paradox is to suppose that the order of [objective moral] claims . . . is in fact rooted in the personality of God.'[84]

Can Science Ground Objective Morality?

> Every attempt to reduce ethics to scientific formulae
> must fail.
>
> *Albert Einstein*[85]

In *The Moral Landscape* (Bantam, 2010) Sam Harris claims to resolve Owen's paradox *without abandoning metaphysical naturalism*. Against received philosophical wisdom, Harris argues that naturalism can accommodate moral objectivism because objective moral values 'translate into facts that can be scientifically understood.'[86] Even most neo-atheists think that Harris is wrong about this.

In *The God Delusion* (Bantam, 2006) Richard Dawkins assumes 'we can all agree that science's entitlement to advise us on moral values is problematic, to say the least.'[87] On the back cover of *The Moral Landscape* Dawkins writes: 'I was one of those who had unthinkingly bought into the hectoring myth that science can say nothing about morals. *The Moral Landscape* has changed all that for me.' However, Dawkins has qualified his support for Harris's project with the devastating observation that before translating morality into facts that can be scientifically understood, 'you do have to make the *assumption* that what matters is suffering.'[88] Just to be clear, that's *a moral assumption* brought *into* the science lab and not justified by the work *of* the science lab!

Moreover, the ontological status of this assumed value is an open question. Indeed, in *The Magic of Reality* (Bantam, 2011) Dawkins continues to treat values as subjective opinions relative to 'our point of view',[89] and he reduces questions about good and evil to questions about physical causation in an amoral material cosmos:

> what is a bad thing for one person may be a good thing for another . . . There is no special reason to ask 'Why do bad things happen?' Or, for that matter, 'Why do good things happen?' The real question underlying both is the more general question: 'Why does *anything* happen?' . . . The universe has no mind, no feelings and no personality; so it doesn't do things in order to either hurt or please you. Bad things happen because things happen. Whether they are bad or

good from our point of view doesn't influence how likely it is that they will happen . . . Unfortunately, the universe doesn't care what people prefer.[90]

Finally, while Dawkins' observation that 'neuroscience really can tell you when people suffer'[91] falsifies the 'myth that science can say nothing about morals' (if one takes this to mean that science has nothing to say *of relevance to* ethics), it clearly doesn't entail the conclusion that science can say everything about ethics.

A.C. Grayling observes that 'when science . . . addresses itself directly to morality, it does not do so to solve moral problems, but to investigate the nature and sources of moral sentiments and attitudes. This is an empirical proceeding, aimed at discovering and describing [empirical] facts, not a "normative" proceeding, aimed at telling us what we should think and do.'[92]

Grayling elaborates upon the distinction between the *descriptions* of science and the *prescriptions* of moral values:

> prudential guidance . . . can typically be framed as a 'hypothetical imperative': 'If you wish to maximise profits, ensure that . . .' Morality, by contrast with these sorts of considerations, is 'categorical' as opposed to hypothetical; it is about intrinsic questions of right and wrong, the good and the bad, obligation and duty, consequences and intentions, as these apply to our conduct . . . where the right and the good are under consideration in themselves and not merely as instrumental or some non-moral goal such as profit . . .[93]

To assert that the categorical *prescriptions* of objective morality can be translated into scientific *descriptions* means riding roughshod over David Hume's 'distinction between the *is* and the *ought*', a distinction C.S. Lewis endorsed as having 'great merit'.[94] The relationship between 'is' and 'ought' is asymmetrical, in that while every statement about a moral 'ought' is necessarily a description of something that 'is' the case (i.e. 'It is the case that one ought to X'), statements about what 'is' the case do not necessarily carry any prescriptive content concerning what 'ought' to be the case. Thus Hume noted the logical impossibility of validly arguing for any conclusion about what morally 'ought' to be the case on the exclusive basis of 'is' propositions lacking prescriptive content. As Lewis argued: 'You can shuffle "I want" and "I am forced" and "I shall be well advised" and "I dare not" as long as you please without getting out of them the slightest hint of "I ought" and "ought not".'[95] That is, however many purely descriptive propositions one has, and however one arranges them, questions of a categorical, prescriptive, moral nature will always remain separate, open questions. Hence, as Sam Harris observes: 'philosopher G.E. Moore declared that any attempt to locate moral truths in the natural world was to commit a "naturalistic fallacy" . . . because it would always be appropriate to ask whether the property on offer was itself [intrinsically morally] *good*.'[96] As Bertrand Russell argued:

> We judge, for example, that happiness is more desirable than misery . . . goodwill than hatred, and so on. Such judgements must, in part at least, be immediate and *a priori* . . . they may be *elicited* by [empirical] experience . . . But it is fairly obvious that they cannot be proved by [empirical] experience; for the fact that a thing exists or does not exist cannot prove either that it is good that it should exist or that it is bad. The pursuit of this subject belongs to ethics . . .[97]

Thus Kenan Malik takes Harris to task for committing the naturalistic fallacy: 'Science . . . may be able to develop machines that can predict whether an individual is lying or not. But it cannot tell us whether it is a good thing that all our thoughts be monitored. That is a moral, not a scientific, judgement.'[98]

In his 2011 debate with William Lane Craig on the grounding of objective moral values, Sam Harris tried and failed to erase the distinctions drawn by Hume and Moore:

> We simply cannot speak of facts without resorting to values. Consider the simplest statement of scientific fact: Water is two parts hydrogen and one part oxygen. This seems as value-free an utterance as human beings ever make. But what do we do when someone doubts the truth of this proposition? OK, all we can do is appeal to scientific values. The value of understanding the world. The value of evidence. The value of logical consistency.[99]

The problem with Harris's claim that 'values translate into facts that can be scientifically understood'[100] is that when we invoke objective values in support of science (as we must), we are appealing to facts of a type that science simply cannot grasp (i.e. categorical imperatives) because they are accessed via properly basic intuitions that *cannot be scientifically justified*. It's worth reiterating the fact that *Harris himself recognizes the legitimacy of this point*:

> 'intuition' . . . denotes the most basic constituent of our faculty of understanding. While this is true in matters of ethics, it is no less true in science. When we can break our knowledge of a thing down no further, the irreducible leap that remains is intuitively taken. Thus, the traditional opposition between reason and intuition is a false one: reason is itself intuitive to the core, as any judgement that a proposition is 'reasonable' or 'logical' relies on intuition to find its feet . . . The point, I trust, is obvious: we cannot step out of the darkness without taking a *first* step. And reason, without knowing how, understands this axiom if it would understand anything at all. The reliance on intuition, therefore, should be no more discomforting for the ethicist than it has been for the physicist.[101]

Understanding, evidence and logical consistency are only 'scientific values' *in the sense that they are values that must be assumed by the scientific enterprise*. They aren't the type of facts that can be *discovered by* the scientific enterprise (as if 'You ought to strive for logical consistency' were the same kind of fact as 'Water is two parts hydrogen and one part oxygen')!

Harris's argument for naturalizing ethics

Sam Harris summarizes his case for a naturalistic account of objective moral values:

> So here's my argument, for moral truth in the context of science. Questions of right and wrong, and good and evil, depend upon minds. They depend upon the possibility of experience. Minds are natural phenomena. They depend upon the laws of nature in some way. Morality and human values, therefore, can be understood

through science, because in talking about these things, we are talking about all of the facts that influence the well-being of conscious creatures.[102]

If Harris only means to claim that questions of right and wrong 'depend upon minds' in the sense that the existence of minds is a *necessary* condition of there being questions about moral behaviour, then his conclusion simply doesn't follow (making his argument logically invalid). In charity, then, we should take Harris to be claiming that questions of right and wrong 'depend upon minds' in the sense that the existence of minds is a *sufficient* condition of there being questions about morality. This sufficiency claim certainly seems to be what Harris has in mind when he states that 'questions about values . . . are really questions about the well-being of conscious creatures. Values, therefore, translate into facts that can be scientifically understood'[103] and that 'values reduce to the well-being of conscious creatures . . .'[104] Harris is therefore arguing as follows:

1) The existence of mind (i.e. of conscious creatures capable of experiencing suffering and well-being) is a sufficient condition of there being questions about morality
2) Mind is a wholly natural phenomenon (i.e. physicalism is true) that can therefore, at least in principle, be understood wholly through naturalistic science
3) Therefore, at least in principle, all questions about morality can be dealt with wholly through naturalistic science

However, the existence of conscious creatures capable of experiencing suffering and well-being *cannot* be a sufficient condition of there being questions about morality, since the purely descriptive proposition that a mind exists (in some conscious state or other) simply isn't identical to any proposition about the existence of mind being a good or bad thing, or to any proposition about the conscious state in question being something it would be categorically right or wrong to promote. In other words, values can't 'reduce to the well-being of conscious creatures'[105] since 'the well-being of conscious creatures' is itself a reality that requires moral evaluation. Thus Harris fails to escape from his own summary of

Moore's 'naturalistic fallacy'. As C.S. Lewis argued: 'If we ask: "Why ought I to be unselfish?" and you reply "Because it is good for society," we may then ask, "Why should I care what's good for society . . ?" and then you will have to say, "Because you ought to be unselfish" – which simply brings us back to where we started.'[106]

When Harris says that 'if we define "good" as that which supports well-being . . . the regress initiated by Moore's "open question argument" really does stop,'[107] he's really only observing that *if* we ignore Moore's 'open question argument' *then* we will have ignored Moore's 'open question argument'! Harris doesn't furnish us with any *reason* to ignore Moore's 'open question' argument; he simply begs the 'open' question of whether or not 'well-being' is an objectively good thing; and science simply can't answer this question.

The fact that (all things being equal) 'the well-being of conscious creatures' is a good thing doesn't mean that goodness *is* 'the well-being of conscious creatures', and in thinking so Sam Harris fallaciously confuses the 'is' of predication (as in 'The grass is green') and the 'is' of identity (as in 'The morning star is the evening star'). It's as if Harris were arguing that because grass is green, therefore greenness is identical to being grass!

Harris *implicitly contradicts* his fallacious reduction of moral values to the well-being of conscious creatures when he states: 'I think it's pretty clear that right and wrong relate to human well-being . . .'[108] Well, if right and wrong *relate to* human (conscious) well-being, they cannot *be the same thing as* human (conscious) well-being. Harris *explicitly contradicts* his assertion that 'values translate into facts that can be scientifically understood'[109] when he admits:

> Science cannot tell us why, scientifically, we should value health . . . It is essential to see that the demand for radical justification levelled by the moral skeptic could not be met by any branch of science. Science is defined with reference to the goal of understanding the processes at work in the universe. Can we justify this goal scientifically? Of course not . . . What evidence could prove that we should value evidence?[110]

Once again, to invoke objective values to support the scientific project is to appeal to facts that transcend the domain and methodology of science. Harris poses the rhetorical question: 'Does this make science itself *unscientific?*'[111] Of course not.[112] However, it does prove that *scientism* is false. Science *can't* be the only (or best) way to know anything because science rests upon a host of philosophical assumptions (including assumptions about moral values) with which science *per se* cannot grapple. Harris's 'science of morality' is a scientistic oxymoron that only goes to prove the wisdom of A.E. Taylor's warning that 'the type of scientific man who is most eloquent in denouncing all metaphysics is himself perpetually talking bad metaphysics under the impression that it is "science".'[113] As Craig comments:

> The purpose of Dr. Harris's book *The Moral Landscape* is to explain the basis, on atheism, of the existence of objective moral values . . . how does Sam Harris propose to solve the value problem? The trick he proposes is simply to redefine what he means by 'good' and 'evil', in non-moral terms. He says, 'We should define "good" as that which supports the well-being of conscious creatures. So,' he says, 'questions about value are really questions about the well-being of conscious creatures. And therefore,' he concludes, 'it makes no sense to ask whether maximizing well-being is good.' Why not? Because, he's redefined the word 'good' to mean 'the well-being of conscious creatures.' So, to ask, 'Why is maximizing creatures' well-being good?' is, on his definition, the same as asking 'Why does maximizing creatures' well-being maximize creatures' well-being?' It's just a tautology. It's just talking in circles. So, Dr. Harris has quote-unquote 'solved' the value problem just by redefining his terms. It's nothing but wordplay . . . Thus Dr. Harris has failed to solve the value problem. He hasn't provided any justification or explanation for why, on atheism, moral values would objectively exist at all.[114]

Moreover, Harris's argument assumes that mind is a wholly natural phenomenon that can therefore (in principle) be understood through science alone. On the one hand, as C.S. Lewis argued, this assumption isn't true (cf. chapter four). On the other hand, Harris acknowledges that *if* mind were a wholly natural phenomena *then* no one would have the freedom of will that is surely a necessary pre-requisite of genuine moral responsibility. Indeed, Harris himself asks: 'If we view people as neuronal weather patterns, how can we coherently speak about morality?'[115] Given the truth of naturalism, Harris affirms that 'every action is clearly reducible to a totality of impersonal events merely propagating their influence: genes are transcribed, neurotransmitters bind to their receptors, muscle fibres contract, and John Doe pulls the trigger on his gun.'[116] Thus Harris concludes that 'free will is nowhere to be found.'[117] (Dawkins comes to the same conclusion.)[118] But as Craig argued in debate with Harris:

> A person is not morally responsible for an action which he is unable to avoid. For example, if somebody shoves you into another person, you're not responsible for bumping into him; you had no choice. But Sam Harris believes that all of our actions are causally determined, and that there is no free will . . . But, if there is no free will, then no one is morally responsible for anything! In the end, Dr. Harris admits this . . . Moral responsibility, he says, and I quote, 'is a social construct', not an objective reality . . . His thoroughgoing determinism spells the end of any hope or possibility of objective moral duties, because on his worldview, we have no control over what we do.[119]

While C.S. Lewis would agree with Harris that 'the world of measurement and the world of meaning must eventually be reconciled',[120] he'd point out that the correct way to remove the false 'firewall between facts and values'[121] so as to effect such a reconciliation cannot be through *reducing* the world of meaningful values and choices to the world of valueless measurement and unintentional physical forces, but rather though *subsuming* the world of valueless measurement and unintentional physical forces into the world of meaningful values and free choices. And the only way to do *that* is to abandon metaphysical naturalism.

Bipartisan Agreement about the Grounding Issue

> Atheists and theists alike usually agree that if God does not
> exist, objective moral values do not exist.
> *Michael Licona*[122]

Plenty of atheists (of both the 'new' and traditional varieties) concur with Lewis that the existence of objective moral values finds no ontological home within a naturalistic, atheistic universe. For example:

- Julian Baggini: 'If there is no single moral authority [i.e. no God] we have to in some sense "create" values for ourselves . . . [and] that means that moral claims are not true or false . . . you may disagree with me but you cannot say I have made a factual error.'[123]
- Richard Dawkins: 'In a universe of blind physical forces and genetic replication some people are going to get hurt, other people are going to get lucky, and you won't find any rhyme or reason in it, nor any justice. The universe we observe has precisely the properties we should expect if there is, at bottom, no design, no purpose, no evil and no good, nothing but blind, pitiless indifference.'[124]
- Paul Kurtz: 'The central question about moral and ethical principles concerns their ontological foundation. If they are neither derived from God nor anchored in some transcendent ground, they are purely ephemeral.'[125]
- In a paper familiar to Lewis,[126] Jean-Paul Sartre wrote: 'The existentialist is strongly opposed to a certain type of secular moralism which seeks to suppress God at the least possible expense. Towards 1880, when the French professors endeavoured to formulate a secular morality, they said . . . nothing will be changed if God does not exist; we shall rediscover the same norms of honesty, progress and humanity, and we shall have disposed of God as an out-of-date hypothesis which will die away quietly of itself. The existentialist, on the contrary, finds it extremely embarrassing that God does not exist, for there disappears with Him all possibility of finding values in an intelligible heaven. There can no longer be any good *a priori*, since there is no infinite and perfect consciousness to think it. It is nowhere written that "the good" exists, that one must be honest or must not lie, since we are now upon the plane where there are only men. Dostoevsky once wrote: "If God did not exist, everything would be permitted"; and that, for existentialism, is the starting point. Everything is indeed permitted

if God does not exist, and man is in consequence forlorn, for he cannot find anything to depend upon either within or outside himself.'[127]

- Bruce Sheiman: 'while it is true that without religion people can certainly have a morality, it is problematic if that morality is not felt to be rooted in something objective and absolute . . . With no transcendent and objective claim to moral standards, scientific materialism has no claim to the moral high ground.'[128]

Euthyphro *Non Sequitur*

> There are alternatives in addition to the two that the
> Euthyphro argument considers. The argument would suc-
> ceed only if there were not.
> *Keith E. Yandell*[129]

Sam Harris objects to the conclusion of the moral argument by assuming that if there were a relationship between God and moral values it would be that which exists between an arbitrary rule-maker to his arbitrary rules: 'once we abandon our belief in a rule-making God, the question of *why* a given action is good or bad becomes a matter of debate.'[130] This is an issue raised in Plato's *Euthyphro* dialogue, where Socrates asks: 'Is what is holy holy because the gods approve it, or do they approve it because it is holy?'[131] Today, this question is often taken by atheists to show that 'God' is a redundant explanation for the objectivity of moral values: On the one hand, if we ground morality in God's commands, morality becomes arbitrary (if something is good simply because God commands it, he could just have easily commanded the opposite). On the other hand, if we don't ground morality in God's commands, morality must be *independent of God's commands*, and thus (so it is frequently but mistakenly urged) *independent of God*. As Bertrand Russell argued:

> if you are quite sure there is a difference between right and wrong, you are then in this situation: is that difference due to God's fiat or is it not? If it is due to God's fiat, then for God himself there is no difference between right and wrong, and it is no longer a significant

statement to say that God is good. If you are going to say, as the-ologians do, that God is good, you must then say that right and wrong have some meaning which is independent of God's fiat, because God's fiats are good and not bad independently of the mere fact that He made them. If you are going to say that, you will then have to say that it is not only through God that right and wrong came into being, but that they are in their essence logically anterior to God.[132]

Russ Shafer-Landau uses the Euthyphro dilemma to argue that 'ethical objectivists – even the theists among them – should insist on the existence of a realm of moral truths that have not been cre-ated by God.'[133] I agree. To say that God is 'a rule-making God' who 'creates' moral truths by merely issuing *contingent* prescrip-tions would entail the self-contradictory claim that *objective* moral truths are *contingent* and *arbitrary*. However, Shafer-Landau jumps from the need to reject the 'arbitrary' horn of the Euthy-phro dilemma to the conclusion that 'even if you believe in God, you should have serious reservations about tying the objectivity of morality to God's existence.'[134] Here we have a *non sequitur* (a conclusion that doesn't follow), one that equivocates between a) the conclusion that the objectivity of moral values is not grounded in God's *commands* and b) the conclusion that the objectivity of moral values is not grounded in God's *nature*.

We must distinguish between positing a transcendent moral prescriber *as an explanation for the prescriptive nature of objective moral values*, and positing a transcendent person *as an explanation of the objective existence of moral values*. While the moral argument posits *a personal God* to account for the existence of objective moral values *per se*, it does not employ the concept of God *qua* moral prescriber for *this* purpose. Rather: 'God's commands are good, not because God commands them, but because God is *good*. Thus, God is not subject to a moral order outside of himself, and neither are God's moral commands arbitrary. God's commands are issued by a perfect being who is the source of all goodness.'[135]

The Euthyphro dilemma destroys the 'Divine Command Theory' according to which 'actions are right because (and only because) God commands them.'[136] Shafer-Landau is therefore right to say that 'the best option for theists is to reject the Divine

Command Theory';[137] however, he is wrong to conclude from this that the moral argument is therefore unsound, because the moral argument simply doesn't depend upon the Divine Command Theory. As Lewis (who knew his Plato) cautioned:

> saying that God 'made' the [moral law] . . . might suggest that it was an arbitrary creation . . . whereas I believe it to be the necessary expression . . . of what God of his own righteous nature necessarily is . . . I think (with Hooker) *not* that certain things are right because God commands them, but that God commanded them because they are right.[138]

As A.E. Taylor argued:

> were there no will in existence except the wills of human beings, who are so often ignorant of the law of right and so often defy it, it is not apparent what the validity of the law could mean. Recognition of the validity of the law thus seems to carry with it a reference to an intelligence which has not, like our own, to make acquaintance with it piecemeal, slowly and with difficulty, but has always been in full and clear possession of it, and a will which does not, like our own, often set it at nought, but is guided by it in all its operations.[139]

Conclusion

> That is what we need above all else, to feel that what is right
> is rooted in an absolute good that transcends human will.
> *Bruce Sheiman*[140]

As John Cottingham writes: 'truth, goodness and beauty appear to be objective properties . . . They seem to presuppose an objective order or value that is logically independent of the beliefs and desires human beings may happen to have at any given time.'[141] All three values are bound by a sense of objective *worthiness*: 'The true is that which is worthy of belief . . . the beautiful is that which is worthy of admiration; and the good is that which is worthy of choice.'[142] The naturalistic worldview is unable to explain the existence of such objective worthiness; it can only explain it away. Paradoxically, then, it was his personal and intellectual engagement with the problem of evil that played a major role in bringing C.S. Lewis to the point of belief in God. 'I am not yet within a hundred miles of the God of Christian theology,' observed Lewis:

> All I have got to is a Something which is directing the universe, and which appears to me as a law urging me to do right and making me feel responsible and uncomfortable when I do wrong. I think we have to assume it is more like a mind than it is like anything else we know – because after all the only other thing we know is matter and you can hardly imagine a bit of matter giving instructions.[143]

The only coherent explanation of the *worthy prescriptions* and *obligations* presented to our consciences in the 'moral law' is that they are grounded in the essential character of a transcendent, necessary and personal being 'intensely interested in right conduct . . . an absolute goodness.'[144]

* * *

Recommended Resources

By C.S. Lewis:
The Abolition of Man
   www.columbia.edu/cu/augustine/arch/lewis/abolition1.htm#1.
Mere Christianity (London: HarperCollins, 2001) – cf. C.S. Lewis, 'Right and Wrong as a Clue to the Heart of the Universe' http://afterall.net/papers/491366
The Problem of Pain (London: Fount, 2002)
'De Futilitate', in *Christian Reflections* (ed. Walter Hooper; London: Fount, 1991)
'On Ethics', in *C.S. Lewis Essay Collection: Faith, Christianity and the Church* (ed. Lesley Walmsley; London: HarperCollins, 2002)

Video

Craig, William Lane. 'The Euthyphro Dilemma'
www.youtube.com/user/oneminuteapologist#p/u/129/
IgGB4Oxs5VU.
— vs Sam Harris. 'Is the Foundation of Morality Natural or
Supernatural?' (2011)
www.rfmedia.org/av/video/craig-vs-harris-foundation-of-
morality/.
Koukl, Greg. 'Relativism: Feet Firmly Planted in Mid-Air'
www.youtube.com/watch?feature=endscreen&NR=1&v=
bWe2Agj5nw8.
Williams, Peter S. and William Lane Craig vs Andrew Copson
and Arif Ahmed. 'Cambridge Union Debate: This House
Believes That God Is Not a Delusion'
http://idpluspeterswilliams.blogspot.com/2012/01/cam-
bridge-union-debate-this-house.html.

Audio

Craig, William Lane. 'The Problem of Evil'
www.rfmedia.org/av/audio/gracepoint-the-problem-of-evil-
and-suffering/.
Geivett, Douglas. 'Problems of Evil'
www.brianauten.com/Apologetics/problems-of-evil
.mp3.
Kreeft, Peter. 'A Refutation of Moral Relativism'
www.peterkreeft.com/audio/05_relativism.htm.
Williams, Peter S. 'Living with Evil: Three Problems of Evil'
www.damaris.org/cm/podcasts/559.
— 'Meta-Ethics and God'
www.damaris.org/cm/podcasts/528.

Online papers

Adams, Marylin McCord. 'Horrendous Evil and the Goodness of
God'
www.lastseminary.com/problem-of-evil/Horrendous%
20Evil%20and%20the%20Goodness%20of%20God.pdf.
Adams, Robert M. 'Moral Arguments for God'
www.lastseminary.com/moral-argument/Moral%20Argum
ents%20for%20Theistic%20Belief.pdf.

Beckwith, Francis J. 'Why I Am Not a Moral Relativist' www.lastseminary.com/moral-argument/Why%20I%20am% 20Not% 20a%20Moral%20Relativist.pdf.

Budziszewski, J. 'Can We Be Good without God?' www.boundless.org/2005/articles/a0000054.cfm.

Clark, Kelly James. 'I Believe in God the Father, Almighty' www.calvin.edu/academic/philosophy/writings/ibig.htm.

Copan, Paul. 'Can Michael Martin Be a Moral Realist? Sic Et Non' www.paulcopan.com/articles/pdf/Michael-Martin-a-moral-realist.pdf.

— 'God Can't Possibly Exist Given the Evil and Pain I See in the World!' www.bethinking.org/resource.php?ID=30&TopicID=3&-CategoryID=3.

— 'God, Naturalism and the Foundations of Morality' www.paulcopan.com/articles/pdf/God-naturalism-morality.pdf.

— 'The Moral Argument for God's Existence' www.4truth.net/fourtruthpbgod.aspx?pageid=8589952712.

— 'Morality and Meaning without God: Another Failed Attempt' www.paulcopan.com/articles/pdf/morality-meaning.pdf.

Copleston, F.C. vs Bertrand Russell. 'A Debate on the Existence of God' www.philvaz.com/apologetics/p20.htm.

Cowan, Steven B. 'Peering through a Glass Darkly: Responding to the Philosophical Problem of Evil' www.arcapologetics.org/articles/article09.htm.

Craig, William Lane. 'The Indispensability of Theological Meta-Ethical Foundations for Morality' www.reasonablefaith.org/site/News2?page=NewsArticle& id=5175.

— 'The Problem of Evil' www.bethinking.org/resource.php?ID=60&TopicID=3&-CategoryID=3.

— vs Richard Taylor. 'Is the Foundation for Morality Natural or Supernatural?' www.reasonablefaith.org/site/News2?page=NewsArticle&-id=5305.

Habermas, Gary R. 'Atheism and Evil: A Fatal Dilemma' www.garyhabermas.com/books/why_believe/whybelieve .htm.

Koukl, Gregory and Francis Beckwith, 'What Is Moral Relativism?' www.bethinking.org/resource.php?ID=229&TopicID=10&-CategoryID=9.

Lindville, Mark D. 'The Moral Argument' http://commonsenseatheism.com/wp-content/uploads/2009/11/Linville-The-Moral-Argument.pdf.

Lovell, Steven. 'God as the Grounding of Moral Objectivity: Defending against Euthyphro' http://myweb.tiscali.co.uk/annotations/euthyphro.html.

Moreland, J.P. 'The Ethical Inadequacy of Naturalism' http://afterall.net/papers/24.

Rea, Michael C. 'Naturalism and Moral Realism' www.lastseminary.com/moral-argument/Naturalism%20and%20Moral%20Realism.pdf.

Snyder, Daniel Howard. 'God, Evil and Suffering' http://faculty.wwu.edu/howardd/god,evil,andsuffering.pdf.

Swinburne, Richard. 'The Problem of Evil' http://mind.ucsd.edu/syllabi/02-03/01w/readings/swinburne-evil.pdf.

Williams, Peter S. 'The Abolition of Man: Reflections on Reductionism with Special Reference to Eugenics' www.lewissociety.org/abolition.php.

— 'Can Moral Objectivism Do without God?' www.bethinking.org/right-wrong/advanced/can-moral-objectivism-do-without-god.htm.

— vs Carl Stetcher. 'Morality and the Biblical God' www.bethinking.org/who-are-you-god/advanced/god-questions-1-morality-and-the-biblical-god.htm.

Books

Baggett, David, Gary R. Habermas and Jerry L. Walls. *C.S. Lewis as Philosopher: Truth, Goodness and Beauty* (Downers Grove, IL: IVP, 2008).

Baggett, David and Jerry L. Walls. *Good God: The Theistic Foundations of Morality* (Oxford University Press, 2011).

Beckwith, Francis J. 'Moral Law, the Mormon Universe, and the Nature of the Right We Ought to Choose.' Pages 219–42 in *The New Mormon Challenge* (ed. Francis J. Beckwith et al; Jonathan Ball Publishers, 2002).

— 'Why I Am Not a Moral Relativist.' Pages 17–32 in *Why I Am a Christian: Leading Thinkers Explain Why They Believe* (ed. Norman L. Geisler and Paul K. Hoffman; Grand Rapids, MI: Baker, rev. and expanded edn, 2006).

— and Gregory Koukl. *Relativism: Feet Firmly Planted in Mid-Air* (Grand Rapids, MI: Baker, 1998).

Copan, Paul. *Is God a Moral Monster? Making Sense of the Old Testament God* (Grand Rapids, MI: Baker, 2011).

— *True for You, but Not for Me* (Minneapolis, MN: Bethany House, 1998).

— 'A Moral Argument.' Pages 108–23 in *To Everyone an Answer: A Case for the Christian Worldview* (ed. Francis J. Beckwith, William Lane Craig and J.P. Moreland; Downers Grove, IL; IVP, 2004).

Craig, William Lane. *On Guard: Defending Your Faith with Reason and Precision* (David C. Cook, 2010).

Farrer, Austin. *Love Almighty and Ills Unlimited* (London: Collins, 1962).

Garcia, Robert K. and Nathan L. King, eds. *Is Goodness without God Good Enough? A Debate on Faith, Secularism, and Ethics* (Lanham, MD: Rowman & Littlefield, 2009).

Joad, C.E.M. *The Recovery of Belief* (London: Faber, 1952).

Lennox, John C. *Gunning for God: Why the New Atheists Are Missing the Target* (Oxford: Lion, 2011).

McGinn, Colin. *Ethics, Evil and Fiction* (Oxford: Clarendon Press, 1999).

Moreland, J.P. and William Lane Craig. *Philosophical Foundations for a Christian Worldview* (Downers Grove, IL; IVP, 2003).

Murray, Michael J. *Nature Red in Tooth and Claw: Theism and the Problem of Animal Suffering* (Oxford University Press, 2011).

Nash, Ronald H. 'The Problem of Evil.' Pages 203–23 in *To Everyone an Answer: A Case for the Christian Worldview* (ed. Francis J. Beckwith, William Lane Craig and J.P. Moreland; Downers Grove, IL; IVP, 2004).

Owen, H.P. 'Why Morality Implies the Existence of God.' Pages 646–58 in *Philosophy of Religion: A Guide and Anthology* (ed. Brian Davies; Oxford University Press, 2000).

Ross, W.D. *The Right and the Good* (Oxford: Clarendon Press, 1930).

Sorley, W.R. *Moral Values and the Idea of God* (Cambridge University Press, 3rd edn, 1919).

Taylor, A.E. *Does God Exist?* (London: Fontana, 1945).

6.

Jesus in the Dock

The first real work of the Gospels on a fresh reader is . . . to
raise very acutely the question, 'Who or what is this?' For
there is a good deal in the character which, unless He really
is what He says He is, is not lovable or even tolerable.
C.S. Lewis[1]

In a diary entry dated 15 January 1927 Lewis records: 'Was thinking about . . . the unholy muddle I am in . . . And all the time (with
me) there's the danger of falling back into most childish supersti-
tions, or of running into dogmatic materialism to escape them.'[2]
Owen Barfield had introduced Lewis to the 'argument from reason'; and although the various strands of this argument were
principally defeaters for naturalism, Lewis saw they had the secondary effect of arguing positively that the fundamental fact of
existence was 'an eternal, self-existent, rational Being . . .'[3] Not
that Lewis immediately became a theist, as he recalls in his autobiography:

> I had been trying to defend [naturalism] ever since I began read-
> ing philosophy . . . But now it seemed to me, I had to give that up.
> Unless I were to accept an unbelievable alternative, I must admit
> that mind was no late-come epiphenomenon . . . that our logic was
> participation in a cosmic *Logos* . . . it is astonishing (at this time of
> day) that I could regard this position as something quite distinct
> from Theism . . . But there were in those days all sorts of blankets,
> insulators, and insurances which enabled one to get all the con-
> veniences of Theism, without believing in God. The English
> Hegelians, writers like T.H. Green, Bradley, and Bosanquet (then

mighty names), dealt in precisely such wares . . . the Absolute Mind – better still, the Absolute – was impersonal, or it knew itself (but not us?) only in us, and it was so absolute that it wasn't really much more like mind than anything else. And anyway, the more muddled one got about it and the more contradictions one committed, the more this proved that our discursive thought moved only at the level of 'Appearance,' and 'Reality' must be somewhere else . . . The emotion that went with all this was certainly religious. But this was a religion that cost nothing. We could talk religiously about the Absolute; but there was no danger of Its doing anything about us . . . There was nothing to fear; better still, nothing to obey.[4]

Lewis's principal *argument* against the existence of any being worthy of the name 'God' was the classical problem of evil. While Lewis's rejection of scientism allowed him to acknowledge the objective reality of evil, it also forced him to grapple with the problem of objective goodness:

A man does not call a line crooked unless he has some idea of a straight line. What was I comparing this universe with when I called it unjust? . . . Of course I could have given up my idea of justice by saying it was nothing but a private idea of my own. But if I did that, then my argument against God collapsed too . . . Thus in the very act of trying to prove that God did not exist – in other words, that the whole of reality was senseless – I found I was forced to assume that one part of reality – namely my idea of justice – was full of sense. Consequently atheism turns out to be too simple.[5]

Hence Lewis came to agree with philosophers like W.R. Sorley that the problem of goodness entailed the existence of:

Something which is directing the universe, and which appears to me as a law urging me to do right and making me feel responsible and uncomfortable when I do wrong. I think we have to assume it is more like a mind than it is like anything else we know – because after all the only other thing we know is matter and you can hardly imagine a bit of matter giving instructions.[6]

If the *logos* was also the ground of the moral law (an identification encouraged by Occam's razor) then there was a clearly defined, rational and wholly good 'someone' for Lewis to 'fear' and 'obey'. This conclusion was reinforced by Lewis's experience as a philosophy tutor:

> my watered down Hegelianism wouldn't serve for tutorial purposes. A tutor must make things clear. Now the Absolute cannot be made clear. Do you mean Nobody-knows-what, or do you mean a superhuman mind and therefore (we may as well admit) a Person? After all, did Hegel and Bradley and all the rest of them ever do more than add mystifications to the simple, workable, theistic idealism of Berkeley?[7]

Lewis was ahead of the academic trend: 'The dynasty of Green, Bradley, and Bosanquet fell, and the world inhabited by philosophy students of my own generation became as alien to our successors as if not years but centuries had intervened.'[8] Lewis thought the collapse of Absolute Idealism a salutary lesson in the importance of following arguments rather than arguers:

> McTaggart, Green, Bosanquet, Bradley seemed enthroned forever; they went down as suddenly as the Bastille. And the interesting thing is that while I lived under that dynasty I felt various difficulties and objections which I never dared to express. They were so frightfully obvious that I felt sure they must be mere misunderstandings: the great men could not have made such very elementary mistakes as those which my objections implied. But very similar objections . . . were among the criticisms which finally prevailed.[9]

And all the while, Lewis pursued the mystery of the 'Romantic' desire he called 'Joy', a search that prodded him, by a process of elimination, ever closer to its divine satisfaction.

From 'Absolute' to the Great 'I Am'

C.S. Lewis didn't want to believe in God. In 1921 he wrote to his brother about responding to an examination question concerning

God's existence that 'to admit that person's existence would have upset my whole applecart.'[10] As Humphrey Carpenter recounts, Lewis:

> resorted to referring to fundamental truth as 'the Spirit', distinguishing this (though not really explaining how) from 'the God of popular religion', and emphasising that there was no possibility of being in a personal relationship with this Spirit. Meanwhile he adopted a benevolent but condescending attitude to Christianity, which he said was a myth conveying as much of the truth as simple minds could grasp. This was all very well, but among those 'simple minds' were men whose thinking he profoundly admired in other respects: Malory, Spencer, Milton, Donne and Herbert . . . Moreover, many of his friends were Christians. Tolkien was a Catholic, and Greeves and Coghill were Anglicans . . .[11]

Lewis explains:

> I must have been as blind as a bat not to have seen, long before, the ludicrous contradiction between my theory of life and my actual experiences as a reader. George MacDonald had done more to me than any other writer; of course it was a pity he had that bee in his bonnet about Christianity . . . Chesterton had more sense than all the other moderns put together; bating, of course, his Christianity. Johnson was one of the few authors whom I felt I could trust utterly; curiously enough, he had the same kink. Spencer and Milton by a strange coincidence had it too . . . The natural step would have been to inquire a little more closely whether the Christians were, after all, wrong. But I did not take it . . . I thought that 'the Christian myth' conveyed to unphilosophic minds as much of the truth, that is of Absolute Idealism, as they were capable of grasping . . . The implication – that something which I and most other undergraduates could master without extraordinary pains would have been too hard for Plato, Dante, Hooker, and Pascal – did not yet strike me as absurd. I hope this is because I never looked it squarely in the face.[12]

However, as he looked the cumulative conspiracy of arguments we have examined thus far 'squarely in the face', Lewis gradually came to believe in the existence of a supernatural Absolute that looked ever more like the Judeo-Christian God: 'I went from materialism to idealism, idealism to pantheism, from pantheism to theism . . .'[13]

The issue of personal relationship with 'the Spirit' came to a head for Lewis in a religious experience on the top of a bus going up Headington Hill:

> Without words and (I think) almost without images, a fact about myself was somehow presented to me. I became aware that I was holding something at bay, or shutting something out . . . I felt myself being, there and then, given a free choice. I could open the door or keep it shut; I could unbuckle the armour or keep it on. Neither choice was presented as a duty; no threat or promise was attached to either, though I knew that to open the door . . . meant the incalculable . . . Even if my own philosophy [i.e. Absolute Idealism] were true, how could the initiative lie on my side? . . . if Shakespeare and Hamlet could ever meet, it must be Shakespeare's doing . . . The real terror was that if you seriously believed in even such a 'God' or 'Spirit' as I admitted, a wholly new situation developed . . . a philosophical theorum, cerebrally entertained . . . became a living presence. I was to be allowed to play at philosophy no longer. It might, as I say, still be true that my 'Spirit' differed in some way from 'the God of popular religion'. My Adversary waived the point. It sank into utter unimportance. He would not argue about it. He only said, 'I am the Lord'; 'I am that I am'; 'I am'.[14]

Lewis recounts how he passed from merely believing *that* 'God' existed to believing *in* him:

> You must picture me alone in that room at Magdalen, night after night, feeling, whenever my mind lifted even for a second from my work, the steady, unrelenting approach of Him whom I so earnestly desired not to meet. That which I greatly feared had at last come upon me. In the Trinity Term of 1929 I gave in, and admitted that God was God, and knelt and prayed: perhaps, that night, the most dejected and reluctant convert in all England.[15]

The Myth of God, Incarnate?

> We are obligated both morally and intellectually to come to
> grips with Jesus Christ; if we refuse to do so we are guilty
> of being bad philosophers and bad thinkers.
>   *C.S. Lewis*[16]

C.S. Lewis now believed in a God, and was 'ready to hear more of
Him from any source . . .'[17] His 'conversion [was] to Theism, pure
and simple, not to Christianity. I knew nothing yet about the
Incarnation . . . My conversion involved as yet no belief in a future
life.'[18] Lewis was 'not yet within a hundred miles of the God of
Christian theology.'[19] Indeed, he didn't *want* to get within a hundred
miles of that particular deity. Given his previous experience of religion, one can see why. Moreover, as Lewis candidly admitted:

> Christianity placed at the centre what then seemed to me a tran-
> scendental Interferer. If its picture was true . . . There was no
> region even in the innermost depth of one's soul . . . which one
> could surround with a barbed wire fence and guard with a notice
> No Admittance. And that was what I wanted; some area, how-
> ever small, of which I could say to all other beings, 'This is my
> business and mine alone.'[20]

However, the fact that Lewis now believed in God meant he had
to admit the possibility of miraculous revelation. As Lewis said of
sceptics like Bultmann: 'The canon "If miraculous, unhistorical"
is one they bring to their study of the texts, not one they have
learned from it.'[21] Despite his admiration for David Hume, Lewis
pointed out that his notorious argument against belief in miracles
was deeply flawed:

> we must agree with Hume that if there is absolutely 'uniform
> experience' against miracles, if in other words they have never
> happened, why then they never have. Unfortunately we know the
> experience against them to be uniform only if we know that all
> reports of them are false. And we can know all the reports to be
> false only if we know already that miracles have never occurred.
> In fact, we are arguing in a circle.[22]

Lewis provided a much better definition of a miracle than Hume's rhetorically loaded talk of God 'violating' nature: 'When an agent is empowered by God to do that of which its own *kind* or *nature* would never have made it capable, it is said to act super-naturally, above its *nature*.'[23]

In 1926 Lewis read G.K. Chesterton's recently published, now classic book, *The Everlasting Man*:

> I read Chesterton's *Everlasting Man* and for the first time saw the whole Christian outline of history set out in a form that seemed to me to make sense. Somehow I contrived not to be too badly shaken. You will remember that I already thought Chesterton the most sensible man alive 'apart from his Christianity'. Now, I veritably believe, I thought . . . that Christianity itself was very sensible 'apart from its Christianity'.[24]

Nevertheless, it was through investigating Jesus that Lewis found his prejudices and his fears about God's claim upon his whole self being resolved; for Jesus revealed a deity who so loved the creatures he'd designed for personal relationship with Himself that He reached out to them with forgiveness through the crucified man from Nazareth, a man who humbly claimed to be the only way to quench the thirst that Lewis had called Joy: 'those who drink the water I give them will never thirst. Indeed, the water I give them will become in them a spring of water welling up to eternal life' (John 4:14).

Surprised by Jesus

Lewis described his Christian faith as flowing from multiple streams of evidence that met in the same sea:

> Faith . . . does not flow from philosophical arguments alone; nor from experience of the Numinous alone; nor from moral experience alone; nor from history alone; but from historical events which at once fulfil and transcend the moral category, which link themselves with the most numinous elements in paganism, and which (as it seems to me) demand at their presupposition the existence of

a Being who is more, but not less, than the God whom many reputable philosophers think they can establish.[25]

It was the resonances between the theological content of the Judeo-Christian scriptures and his personal philosophical pilgrimage that drew Lewis to examine Jesus. It seemed to Lewis that 'in all developed religion we find three strands or elements, and in Christianity one more.'[26] Lewis listed first 'what Professor Otto calls the experience of the *Numinous*.'[27] Second 'is the consciousness not merely of a moral law, but of a moral order at once approved and disobeyed. This consciousness is neither a logical, nor an illogical, inference from the facts of experience; if we did not bring it to our experience we could not find it there. It is either inexplicable illusion, or else revelation.'[28] Lewis observes:

> The moral experience and the numinous experience are so far from being the same that they may exist for quite long periods without establishing a mutual contact. In many forms of Paganism the worship of gods and the ethical discussions of the philosophers have very little to do with each other. The third stage in religious development arises when men identify them – when the Numinous Power to which they feel awe is made the guardian of the morality to which they feel obligation.[29]

Lewis comments:

> Perhaps only a single people, as a people, took the new step with perfect decision – I mean the Jews: but great individuals in all times and places have taken it also . . . it may be madness – a madness congenital to man and oddly fortunate in its results – or it may be revelation. And if revelation [as the moral argument suggests], then it is most really and truly in Abraham that all people shall be blessed, for it was the Jews who fully and unambiguously identified the awful Presence haunting black mountain-tops and thunderclouds with 'the *righteous* Lord' who 'loveth righteousness'.[30]

Lewis held that this third element of the developing religious consciousness was absolutely crucial to a clear understanding of the human condition:

If the universe is not governed by an absolute goodness, then all our efforts are in the long run hopeless [recall Bertrand Russell's 'scaffolding of despair']. But if it is, then we are making ourselves enemies to that goodness every day, and are not in the least likely to do any better tomorrow, and so our case is hopeless again. We cannot do without it, and we cannot do with it. God is the only comfort, He is also the supreme terror: the thing we most need and the thing we most want to hide from . . . Christianity simply does not make sense until you have faced the sort of facts I have been describing. Christianity tells people to repent and promises them forgiveness. It therefore has nothing (as far as I know) to say to people who do not know that they need forgiveness. It is after you have realised that there is a real Moral Law, and a Power behind the law, and that you have broken the law and put yourself wrong with that Power – it is after all this, and not a moment sooner, that Christianity begins to talk. When you know you are sick, you will listen to the doctor. When you have realised that our position is nearly desperate you will begin to understand what the Christians are talking about . . . how God Himself becomes a man to save man from the disapproval of God.[31]

Thus the numinous experience of 'Joy', the objective reality of the 'moral law' and the recognition that the moral law is grounded in the essential goodness of an Absolute Mind were all aspects of Lewis's own philosophical pilgrimage that he saw reflected in the Jewish scriptures, and which set the stage for his fascination with Jesus:

The fourth strand or element is a historical event. There was a man born among these Jews who claimed to be, or to be the son of . . . the Something which is at once the awful haunter of nature and the giver of the moral law. The claim is so shocking – a paradox, and even a horror, which we may easily be lulled into taking too lightly – that [given the sincerity of his claim] only two views of this man are possible. Either he was a raving lunatic of an unusually abominable type, or else He was, and is, precisely what He said. There is no middle way. If the records make the first hypothesis unacceptable, you must submit to the second. And if you do that, all else that is claimed by Christians becomes credible – that this Man, having been killed, was yet alive, and that His death, in some manner incomprehensible to human thought, has effected a real change in our relations to the 'awful' and 'righteous' Lord, and a change in our favour.[32]

Atonement

Christopher Hitchens expresses his aversion to 'the idea of *vicarious* atonement, of the sort that so much troubled even C.S. Lewis . . . [As in the story of Abraham] we have a father demonstrating love by subjecting a son to death by torture, but this time the father is not trying to impress God. He is god, and he is trying to impress humans.'[33] Hitchens fails to factor in the idea that the crucified son *is God incarnate*, such that the atonement is an act of divine *self-sacrifice*. As philosopher C. Stephen Evans observes: 'When Jesus gives his life for us, it is not God punishing an innocent victim, but God giving himself for us.'[34] Perhaps a similar recognition led Lewis to comment in *Mere Christianity* that vicarious atonement 'does not seem to me quite so immoral and so silly as it used to . . .'[35] Nevertheless, Lewis surely speaks for many when he muses:

> What I couldn't see was how the life and death of Someone Else (whoever he was) two thousand years ago could help us here and now – except in so far as his *example* helped us. And the example business, tho' true and important, is not Christianity: right in the centre of Christianity . . . you keep getting something quite different and very mysterious expressed in those phrases I have so often ridiculed ('propitiation' – 'sacrifice' – 'the blood of the lamb') – expressions [which] I [could] only interpret in senses that seemed to me either silly or shocking.[36]

Later in life, Lewis insightfully commented that 'if you take "paying the penalty", not in the sense of being punished, but in the more general sense of "standing the racket" or "footing the bill", then, of course, it is a matter of common experience that, when one person has got himself into a hole, the trouble of getting him out usually falls on a friend.'[37] After all, Isaiah 53 doesn't predict that the Messiah would suffer the punishment due to our sin, but that he would *suffer our sin* (cf. Isaiah 53:6, 12). Jesus' death certainly doesn't force or even enable God to love us, as theologians Joel B. Green and Mark D. Baker affirm: 'Whatever meaning atonement might have, it would be a grave error to imagine that it focused on assuaging God's anger or winning God's merciful attention.'[38] Rather, according to the New Testament, Jesus died for us *because* God already loved us: 'This is love: not that we loved God, but that he loved us and sent his Son as an atoning sacrifice for our sins' (1 John 4:10). Keith Ward follows Lewis's line of thought about God 'standing the racket' for us:

> Sin, we might well say, causes a change in the divine nature – the realization of anger, even when transformed by compassion, the frustration of divine purpose, and the frustration of joy. These are costs that God [freely] bears whenever sin impairs a possible divine-creaturely relationship. The crucifixion of Jesus, in so far as it is an act of God as well as the self-offering of a human life, is the particular and definitive historical expression of the universal sacrifice of God in bearing the cost of sin [cf. 2 Timothy 1:9–10; Revelation 13:8]. Sin is a harm done to God, inasmuch as it causes God to know, and to share, the suffering and reality of evil. The 'ransom' God pays is to accept this cost, to bear with evil, in order that it should be redeemed, transfigured, in God . . . The patience of God, bearing the cost of sin, takes the life and death and resurrection of Jesus as its own self-manifestation, and makes it the means by which the liberating life of God is made available in its essential form to the world.[39]

Lewis's own speculation about exactly *how* Jesus stands the racket to get us out of the hole we're in – that the incarnation enables God to experience a total surrender to God that he can then help us to imitate contrary to our fallen natures – isn't persuasive. Omniscience surely encompasses a sufficient 'knowledge by description' of how human beings can and should surrender themselves to God quite apart from the first-hand 'knowledge by aquaintance' involved in the incarnation. Lewis himself added the caveat: 'Such is my own way of looking at what Christians call the Atonement. But remember this is only one more picture.

Do not mistake it for the thing itself: and if it does not help you, drop it.'[40] Here Lewis's wisdom shines through in the insight that the metaphysical mechanics of the atonement (the how) are secondary to the fact of atonement (the what):

> Before I became a Christian I was under the impression that the first thing Christians had to believe was one particular theory as to what the point of [Jesus] dying was . . . What I came to see later on was that neither [the theory of penal substitution] nor any other is Christianity. The central Christian belief is that Christ's death has somehow put us right with God and given us a fresh start. Theories as to how it did this are another matter. A good many different theories have been held as to how it works; what all Christians are agreed on is that it does work . . . A man can eat his dinner without understanding exactly how food nourishes him. A man can accept what Christ has done without knowing how it works . . .[41]

C. Stephen Evans concurs that 'it is the *fact* of atonement that Christians are asked to believe, not any particular *theory* as to how this is achieved by Christ's death and resurrection. Indeed, Christians have over the centuries held a variety of theories about how this occurred.'[42] Thus Lewis makes a significant point of lasting value when he draws a parallel between theological models of the supernatural fact of atonement and scientific models of the facts of nature:

> What [scientists] do when they want to explain the atom, or something of that sort, is to give you a description out of which you can make a mental picture. But then they warn you that this picture is not what the scientists actually believe. What the scientists believe is a mathematical formula. The pictures are there only to help you to understand the formula. They are not really true in the way the formula is; they do not give you the real thing but only something more or less like it. They are only meant to help, and if they do not help you can drop them. The thing itself cannot be pictured, it can only be expressed mathematically. We are in the same boat here.[43]

Drawing upon his philosophy of language, Lewis came to believe that the 'myth become fact' of Jesus' death and resurrection was

itself the most adequate 'picture' of the atonement, and that theological models thereof, while they may help us to understand this
or that facet of the underlying reality, are necessarily *more abstract*
and therefore *less real* than the mythopoeic reality, which is thus
most adequately grasped through a sympathetic imagination
applied to Jesus' passion. As Lewis explained in a letter to Arthur
Greeves dated 18 October 1931:

> what Dyson and Tolkien showed me was this: that if I met the
> idea of sacrifice in a Pagan story I didn't mind it at all; again, that
> if I met the idea of a god sacrificing himself to himself, I liked it
> very much and was mysteriously moved by it: again, that the
> idea of the dying and reviving god (Baldar, Adonis, Bacchus)
> similarly moved me provided I met it anywhere *except* in the
> Gospels. The reason was that in Pagan stories I was prepared to
> feel the myth as profound and suggestive of meanings beyond
> my grasp even tho' I could not say in cold prose 'what it meant'.
> Now the story of Christ is simply a true myth: a myth working on
> us in the same way as the others, but with this tremendous dif-
> ference that it really happened: and one must be content to accept
> it in the same way, remembering that it is God's myth, where the
> others are men's myth: i.e. the Pagan stories are God expressing
> Himself through the minds of poets, using such images as He
> found there, while Christianity is God expressing Himself
> through what we call 'real things'. Therefore it is true, not in the
> sense of being a 'description' of God (that no finite mind could
> take in) but in the sense of being the way in which God chooses
> to (or can) appear to our faculties. The 'doctrines' we get out of
> the true myth are of course less true: they are translations into our
> concepts and ideas of that [which] God has already expressed in
> a language more adequate, namely the actual incarnation, cruci-
> fixion, and resurrection. Does this amount to a belief in
> Christianity? At any rate I am now certain (a) That this Christian
> story is to be approached, in a sense, as I approach the other
> myths. (b) That it is the most important and full of meaning. I am
> also *nearly* certain that it really happened . . .[44]

Aut Deus Aut Malus Homo

> Someone who claims to be God is either evil or crazy or
> exactly who he said he was.
>
> *Francis S. Collins*[45]

If his written apologetics are any guide, the argument that did the most to convince C.S. Lewis that the Christian myth 'really happened' was 'the old *aut deus aut malus homo*'[46] argument for the divinity of Jesus. As Peter Kreeft explains, *aut deus aut malus homo* is Latin for 'either God or a bad man':

> The first premise is that Christ must be either God, as he claims to be, or a bad man, if he wasn't who he claims to be. The second premise is that he isn't a bad man. The conclusion is that he is God ... You see, he either believes his claim to be God, or he doesn't. If he does [and the claim is false], then he is intellectually bad – very bad, in fact, because that's a pretty large confusion! And if he does not believe his claim [and it is false], then he is morally bad: a deceiver and a terrible blasphemer.[47]

Scotsman John Duncan (1796–1870) applied the term 'trilemma' to this ancient argument, when he observed: 'Christ either deceived mankind by conscious fraud, or He was Himself deluded and self-deceived, or He was Divine. There is no getting out of this trilemma. It is inexorable.'[48] As Chesterton mused in *The Everlasting Man*:

> Stark staring incredulity is a far more loyal tribute to that truth than a modernist metaphysic that would make it merely a matter of degree. It were better to rend our robes with a great cry against blasphemy, like Caiaphas in the judgment, or to lay hold of the man as a maniac possessed of devils like the kinsmen and the crowd, rather than to stand stupidly debating ... in the presence of so catastrophic a claim. There is more of the wisdom that is one with surprise in any simple person, full of the sensitiveness of simplicity, who should expect the grass to wither and the birds to drop dead out of the air, when a strolling carpenter's apprentice said calmly and almost carelessly, like one looking over his shoulder: 'Before Abraham was, I am.'[49]

Jesus' appropriation of God's self-description, given to Moses in Exodus 3:14, referenced by Chesterton, enjoys independent source attestation from John 8:58 (cf. John 18:5–6) and Mark 14:62. C.S. Lewis famously rephrased this argument in *Mere Christianity*:

> Among these Jews there suddenly turns up a man who goes about talking as if He was God. He claims to forgive sins . . . He says He is coming to judge the world at the end of time . . . I am trying here to prevent anyone saying the really foolish thing that people often say about Him: 'I'm ready to accept Jesus as a great moral teacher, but I don't accept his claim to be God.' That is the one thing we must not say. A man who was merely a man and said the sort of thing Jesus said would be either a lunatic – on a level with the man who says he is a poached egg – or else he would be the Devil of Hell. You must make your choice. Either this man was, and is, the Son of God: or else a madman or something worse [i.e. a blaspheming liar]. You can shut Him up for a fool, you can spit at Him and kill Him as a demon or you can fall at His feet and call Him Lord and God, but let us not come with any patronising nonsense about His being a great human teacher. He has not left that open to us. He did not intend to . . . Now it seems to me obvious that He was neither a lunatic nor a fiend: and consequently, however strange or terrifying or unlikely it may seem, I have to accept the view that He was and is God.[50]

Of all Lewis's arguments, this has received the most attention from the new atheists.

What Are We to Make of Jesus?

Writing in the *New York Times*, Christopher Hitchens contrasts two views of Jesus. On the one hand, he quotes deist Thomas Jefferson, who thought that Jesus was merely human despite promulgating 'the most sublime and benevolent code of morals which has ever been offered to man.'[51] Likewise, Ernest Renan 'also repudiated the idea that Jesus was the Son of God while affirming the beauty of his teachings.'[52] On the other hand, Hitchens references 'in rather striking contrast, C.S. Lewis',[53] who 'maintained in his classic statement *Mere Christianity*'[54] that 'a man who was merely a man and said the sort of things Jesus said would not be a great moral teacher . . . Either this man was, and is, the Son of God; or else a madman or something worse.'[55] Hitchens finds himself in agreement with Lewis: 'As an admirer of Jefferson and Renan and a strong non-admirer of Lewis, I am bound to say that Lewis is more honest here.'[56] In *God Is Not Great* Hitchens hails Lewis's argument as a 'stinging riposte'[57] to 'those who argue that Jesus may have been a great moral teacher without being divine',[58] and writes that 'Lewis . . . deserves some credit for accepting the logic and morality of what he has just stated.'[59] As Hitchens said in a 2009 interview: 'so many times you come up against the Jefferson line, that Jesus may not have been divine, but that his morality was divine. No. It's a wicked doctrine if it isn't fed by the force of revelation . . . the stuff is, as Lewis quite rightly said, wicked gibberish.'[60]

So, Hitchens agrees with Lewis that *if* Jesus falsely claimed to be divine, *then* Jesus was either insane or wicked. In *God Is Not Great* Hitchens does briefly try to evade the horns of the trilemma, asserting that Lewis 'takes his two false alternatives as exclusive antitheses, and then uses them to fashion a crude non-sequitur . . .',[61] but he doesn't substantiate this charge by elaborating any fourth thesis concerning Jesus' person (given his claim to divinity) to which one might appeal.

Sometimes Hitchens grasps at one non-Christian horn of the trilemma, as when he asserts that 'there were many *deranged* prophets roaming Palestine at the time, but this one reportedly believed himself, at least some of the time, to be god or the son of god. And that has made all the difference.'[62] Of course, this hypothesis sits just as ill with the moral lucidity of Jesus' teaching as does the alternative non-Christian horn of the trilemma, to which Hitchens leaps when he says that Jesus' teaching is '*a wicked doctrine* if it isn't fed by the force of revelation.'[63] However, branding Jesus a wicked, blaspheming liar, 'an exorcist on the make',[64] simply doesn't square with Richard Dawkins' acknowledgement of 'the moral superiority of Jesus.'[65] Dawkins states: 'Jesus . . . was surely one of the great ethical innovators of history. The Sermon on the Mount is way ahead of its time. His "turn the other cheek" anticipated Gandhi and Martin Luther King by two thousand years. It was not for nothing that I wrote an article called "Atheists for Jesus" (and was later delighted to be presented with a T-shirt bearing the legend).'[66] Dawkins describes Jesus as 'a charismatic young preacher who advocated generous forgiveness',[67] and praises Jesus for 'his genuinely original and radical ethics', saying that 'he publicly advocated niceness and was one of the first to do so'.[68]

In sum, although Hitchens can't decide which non-Christian horn of the trilemma he believes, he implicitly concedes that these are the only alternatives to the Christian understanding of Jesus *given that Jesus made the kind of claims repeatedly attributed to him by his earliest followers and biographers*. It comes as no surprise, therefore, to find Hitchens rejecting the very foundation of Lewis's argument, the proposition that Jesus did indeed claim to be divine: 'the Gospels are most certainly not literal truth . . . many of the "sayings" and teachings of Jesus are hearsay upon hearsay.'[69]

Hitchens seeks to bolster his assertion about the gospels being hearsay with reference to one of a very few gospel passages (i.e. John 8:3–11) widely believed to be a later addition. However, this particular passage is believed by some scholars to be based upon earlier reports, rather than fabricated out of whole cloth as implied by Hitchens.[70] Interestingly, it was concerning this very incident from the Gospel of John that C.S. Lewis argued:

> Of this text there are only two possible views. Either this is reportage – though it may no doubt contain errors – pretty close up to the facts; nearly as close as Boswell. Or else, some unknown writer . . . without known predecessors or successors, suddenly anticipated the whole technique of modern, novelistic, realistic narrative. If it is untrue, it must be narrative of that kind. The reader who doesn't see this has simply not learned to read.[71]

Even if we concede for the sake of argument that John 8:3–11 is unreliable hearsay, to draw the conclusion that the gospels are therefore *in general* 'not literal truth' would be like pointing to a few instances of scientific fraud to discredit the entire scientific enterprise! Besides, Hitchens explicitly admits Lewis's general point by writing that 'either the Gospels are in some sense literal truth, or the whole thing is essentially a fraud and perhaps an immoral one at that.'[72] In other words, the same kind of trilemma attaches *to the gospels and to their writers as to the person of Jesus* – either the gospel writer's claims about Jesus are true, or else they are false; if false then either sincere or insincere; if sincerely false then massively deluded; if insincere then brazenly fraudulent. Hence, to the extent to which one thinks the evidence is against delusion or fraud, so to that extent the truth of the proposition that Jesus claimed divinity becomes more plausible; all of which lands us back with 'the old *aut deus aut malus homo*'[73] argument for the divinity of Jesus. In this context, it's worth recording French neo-atheist Michel Onfray's concession that 'Mark, Matthew, Luke and John did not knowingly deceive. Neither did Paul . . . they said what they believed was true and believed that what they said was true . . . Clearly they believed what they wrote.'[74]

The Dawkins Alternative

In an interview on Canadian TV Richard Dawkins objected that the 'Lunatic, Liar or Lord' argument unfairly constrains the explanatory options:

> **Fanny Kiefer:** When you read some of C.S. Lewis' work . . . a Christian communicator with a fertile mind and a great intellect, why do you think someone who is a scholar . . . is grabbed by faith?
> **Richard Dawkins:** Well, you could pick a much better target than C.S. Lewis . . . He, after all, was a professor of English, and no doubt a very good one. But when you read some of his arguments, they are just pathetic. Things like: Well, Jesus claimed to be the Son of God, so either Jesus was mad, or bad, or He really was the Son of God. It did not seem to occur to him that Jesus could simply be mistaken, sincerely and honestly mistaken. I mean, what a pathetic argument.[75]

As Dawkins wrote in *The God Delusion*: 'A fourth possibility, almost too obvious to need mentioning, is that Jesus was honestly mistaken. Plenty of people are.'[76]

Leaving aside Dawkins' patronizing half-truth about Lewis being a professor of English, people can of course be honestly mistaken about plenty of things, but surely *not about their sharing in the divinity of Yahweh*! With philosopher Stephen T. Davis, I think 'it is not easy to see how any sane religious first-century Jew could sincerely but mistakenly hold the belief, *I am divine.*'[77] As Nicky Gumbel wittily comments: 'The irony of *The God Delusion* is that Dawkins . . . says that all Christians are deluded because they believe there is a God, but Jesus was not deluded even though he thought he was God.'[78] Mike King's response to Dawkins hits the nail on the head: 'anyone "honestly mistaken" in such a way would inevitably be considered insane. But why should Dawkins *et al.* not be content to simply dismiss Jesus as mad or bad? Quite clearly, it is because even a rudimentary flick through Jesus' life demonstrates both of these possibilities to be untenable.'[79] Thus, as Richard Purtill affirms: 'the old dilemma still holds: if Christ claimed to be God, he was speaking the truth, or was lying, or was insane. If common sense and available evidence rule out the last two hypotheses, the first must be true.'[80]

Did Jesus Exist?

> There is more evidence that Jesus of Nazareth certainly
> lived than for
> most famous figures of the ancient past.
> *Dr Paul L. Maier*[81]

According to Michel Onfray, 'Jesus' existence has not been historically established.'[82] Victor J. Stenger goes even further when he asserts: 'A number of scholars have made the case for the non-historicity of Jesus, and their conclusions are convincing.'[83] Christopher Hitchens, with only a pinch more caution, ponders 'the highly questionable existence of Jesus . . .'[84] and elsewhere states that he doesn't 'really believe'[85] in Jesus' existence. Richard Dawkins isn't willing to place himself quite so far out on the academic fringe and acknowledges that 'Jesus probably existed . . .'[86] Nevertheless, the admission is so begrudging it seems calculated to plant doubt in the uninformed reader's mind; doubt that

Dawkins isn't exactly keen to discourage: 'it is even possible to mount a serious, though not widely supported, historical case that Jesus never lived at all, as has been done by, among others, Professor G.A. Wells of the University of London . . .'[87]

Dawkins conveniently fails to inform readers that Professor Wells – to whom he passes the evidential ball – isn't a historian, but Professor Emeritus *of German* at Birkbeck College, London! As agnostic Bart Ehrman comments: 'There are a lot of people who want to write sensational books and make a lot of money who say Jesus didn't exist, but I don't know any serious scholar who doubts the existence of Jesus . . .'[88] Historian Michael Grant observes that 'if we apply to the New Testament, as we should, the same sort of criteria as we should apply to other ancient writings containing historical material, we can no more reject Jesus' existence than we can reject the existence of a mass of pagan personages whose reality as historical figures is never questioned.'[89] Michael Licona points out that:

> There are as many non-Christian sources who mention Jesus within 150 years of his life as there are within 150 years of the life of the Roman Emperor Tiberius who ruled during the ministry of Jesus. In addition, there are four biographies of Jesus, all of which were written within 70 years of his life, which is amazing compared to what we have for most other ancient figures.[90]

That's not even to mention extra-biblical writings by 'early church fathers' such as Clement and Ignatius. Particularly well evidenced (being mentioned by twelve ancient *non-Christian* sources as well as many first and second-century Christian sources) is Jesus' death by crucifixion; hence atheist New Testament scholar Gerd Ludemann states that 'Jesus' death as a consequence of crucifixion is indisputable',[91] and Jesus Seminar co-founder John Dominic Crossan affirms: 'That he was crucified is as sure as anything historical can ever be.'[92] Ehrman calls Jesus' crucifixion 'one of the most certain facts of history.'[93] Now, if Jesus' *crucifixion* is an indisputable fact of history, his *existence* can hardly be less certain! Little wonder Geza Vermes (Professor Emeritus of Jewish Studies and Emeritus Fellow of Wolfson College, Oxford) rejects the neo-atheist's hyper-scepticism: 'Jesus was a real historical person. In my opinion, the difficulties arising from the denial of his existence, still vociferously maintained in small circles of rationalist "dogmatists", far exceed those deriving from its acceptance.'[94] Mark Allan Powell, Associate Professor of New Testament at Trinity Lutheran Seminary, pulls no punches here: 'A hundred and fifty years ago a fairly well respected scholar named Bruno Bauer maintained that the historical person Jesus never existed. Anyone who says that today – in the academic world at least – gets grouped with . . . the scientific holdouts who want to believe the world is flat.'[95]

Getting at the Historical Jesus

While admitting that Jesus existed, Richard Dawkins advocates an extreme form of scepticism about what can be historically known about him:

> Ever since the nineteenth century, scholarly theologians have made an overwhelming case that the gospels are not reliable accounts of what happened in the history of the real world. All were written long after the death of Jesus, and also after the epistles of Paul, which mention almost none of the alleged facts of Jesus' life. All were then copied and recopied, through many different 'Chinese Whisper generations' . . . The four gospels that made it into the official canon were chosen, more or less arbitrarily, out of a larger sample of at least a dozen . . . Nobody knows who the four evangelists were, but they almost certainly never met Jesus personally. Much of what they wrote was in no sense an honest attempt at history but was simply rehashed from the Old Testament, because the gospel makers were devoutly convinced that the life of Jesus must fulfil Old Testament prophecies . . . Although Jesus probably existed, reputable Bible scholars do not in general regard the New Testament (and obviously not the Old Testament) as reliable records of what actually happened in history . . . The only difference between *The Da Vinci Code* and the gospels is that the gospels are ancient fiction while *The Da Vinci Code* is modern fiction.[96]

In reality, scholarly theologians would laugh Dawkins' assertion that the gospels are works of 'ancient fiction' out of court. While Dawkins says that the four gospels are 'pure fiction',[97] theologian N.T. Wright comments that 'one of the great gains of New Testament scholarship in the last generation has been to re-establish that the canonical gospels certainly were intended, and certainly are to be read, within the framework of ancient biographical writing.'[98] Richard Bauckham (Emeritus Professor of New Testament at the University of St Andrews) confirms that 'the best way of categorizing the Gospels as literature is to see them as biographies, more precisely biographies of a contemporary person, based (as such biographies were expected to be) on eyewitness testimony.'[99] Indeed, as Professor Craig A. Evans concludes: 'There is credible, early testimony to the effect that the material in the four New Testament Gospels reaches back to the original followers of Jesus and that this material circulated and took shape during the lifetime of eyewitnesses.'[100]

Dawkins' scepticism about Jesus is stuck in what scholarly theologians call the early twentieth-century 'no quest' period of historical Jesus research, a period associated with Albert Schweitzer and Rudolf Bultmann (both of whom, it should be noted, believed in the existence of Jesus). Dawkins is ignorant about the current standing among New Testament scholars of his scepticism about Jesus; but as Darrell L. Bock (Research Professor in New Testament Studies at Dallas Theological Seminary) reports: 'those who participate in the third quest have tended to see far more historicity in the Gospels than either of the previous quests, showing a renewed respect for the general historical character of the Gospels.'[101] This doesn't mean that 'the third quest has reached a consensus or that it is fundamentally conservative',[102] but it certainly puts the neo-atheist 'no quest' stance in perspective.

The Textual Reliability of the New Testament

> If we have doubts about what the original New Testament said, those doubts would have to be multiplied a hundredfold for the average classical author.
> *Daniel B. Wallace*[103]

It's worth noting in this context that Sam Harris's concern about the currently available text of the New Testament being 'evidenced by discrepant and fragmentary copies of copies of copies of ancient Greek manuscripts'[104] is tendentious. The fact of the matter is that 'no other ancient document equals the New Testament when it comes to the preservation of manuscripts, both in terms of number and closeness in time to the original autographs.'[105] Darrell L. Bock and Daniel B. Wallace confirm: 'The New Testament manuscripts stand closer to the original and are more plentiful than probably any other literature of that era. The New Testament is far and away the best-attested work of Greek or Latin literature from the ancient world.'[106] As Mark D. Roberts explains:

> the abundance of manuscripts and the antiquity of manuscripts, when run through the mill of text-critical methodology, allows us to know with a very high level of probability what the evangelists and other New Testament authors wrote . . . We can have confidence that the critical Greek texts of Matthew, Mark, Luke, and John represent, with a very high degree of probability, what the autographs of the Gospels actually contained.[107]

According to Bart Ehrman: 'scholars are convinced that we can reconstruct the original words of the New Testament with reasonable (although probably not 100 percent) accuracy.'[108] Even as an atheist, Antony Flew was forced to acknowledge that 'the textual authority, the earliness and the number of manuscripts for most of the Christian documents, is unusually great.'[109] Hence N.T. Wright concludes that 'the New Testament we have printed in our Bibles does indeed go back to what the very early Christians wrote.'[110]

The Mythical Gospel Myth

> For we did not follow cleverly devised stories when we
> told you about the coming of our Lord Jesus Christ in
> power, but we were eyewitnesses of his majesty.
> 2 Peter 1:16 TNIV

The time will come when people will not put up with
sound doctrine. Instead, to suit their own desires . . . They
will turn their ears away from the truth and turn aside
to myths.

2 Timothy 4:3–4 TNIV

The new atheists' Jesus-centric hyper-scepticism is a precondition
of their view that the Christian understanding of Jesus is, as Sam
Harris claims, 'a gratuitous, and rather gruesome, fairy tale';[111]
that is, a late accretion upon the original facts (whatever they
may have been). However, as J.P. Moreland observes: 'The idea of
a fully divine, miracle-working Jesus who rose from the dead was
present during the first decade of Christianity. Such a view was
not a legend which arose several decades after the crucifixion.'[112]
It is thus upon a foundation of sand that Dawkins opines: 'all the
essential features of the Jesus legend . . . are borrowed – every last
one of them – from other religions already in existence in the
Mediterranean and Near East region.'[113] A.C. Grayling likewise
asserts that 'there is nothing particularly original about the core
Christian stories. Think about the many other versions of what
appears in the Christian story, versions long antedating it in
Middle Eastern mythology or in Greek mythology . . .'[114] Not that
one wants to put too much faith in anything Grayling (or any
other neo-atheist[115]) has to say about ancient history. After all,
Grayling asserts: 'The first canonical gospel, the one according to
Mark, was written in Rome about AD 60 *soon after Jerusalem was
sacked*.'[116] However, leaving aside the date of Mark's gospel,[117] the
historical facts are that 'the Jewish revolt against Rome . . . began
in AD 66 and led to the destruction of Jerusalem and its Temple in
AD 70.'[118]

That Christianity was 'just another ancient mystery religion'
was an opinion C.S. Lewis held as an atheist: 'after the death of a
Hebrew philosopher Yeshua (whose name we have corrupted
into Jesus) he became regarded as a god, a cult sprang up, which
was afterwards connected with the ancient Hebrew Jahweh-
worship . . . one mythology among many . . .'[119] Unlike today's
neo-atheists, Lewis had the excuse that this theory of Christian
origins had only recently been advanced, concurrent with the
then dominant 'no quest' views of Schweitzer and Bultmann, and

had yet to be subjected to the academic scrutiny that led to its demise. 'Such a reliance on legends was a popular thesis in times past,' notes Gary R. Habermas, 'but has been dismissed today by most researchers.'[120] New Testament scholar Michael Green explains:

> The idea of a copycat religion really arose in Germany at the end of the nineteenth and the start of the twentieth century. It was put forward by the 'History of Religions' school. It was popularised by Sir James Frazer in Britain when he published his readable, but unreliable, *The Golden Bough* in 1906 – the first book in English to compare Christianity to the mystery religions . . . This seemed an attractive hypothesis for a while, but subsequent scholarship has examined this hypothesis and found it wanting, for a number of reasons. Nowadays it is regarded as a dead issue by almost all scholars.[121]

Edwin M. Yamauchi (Professor Emeritus of History at Miami University) recounts that 'by the mid-twentieth century, scholars had established that the sources used in these writings were far from satisfactory and the parallels were much too superficial.'[122] Moreover, as Green observes:

> The really special thing [about Jesus] was this: nobody had ever attributed divinity and a virgin birth, resurrection and ascension to a *historical person* whom lots of people knew. And certainly nobody claimed that the one and only God, the creator and judge of the whole earth, had embodied himself in Apollo, Hercules, Augustus, and the rest . . . Augustus had temples erected to him as *divus Augustus* in the East (whilst being more circumspect in the Roman West), but of course neither he nor anybody else imagined that by so doing he laid claim to embody the Godhead . . . Vesputin, dying in the seventies, quipped 'Alas, I fear I am becoming a god!' It is very difficult to see the Christian conviction about Jesus springing from such roots. But no better ones have been put forward. Analogies from the Hermetic literature, the Gnostic Redeemer myth or the Mandean literature are all post-Christian and therefore quite unable to account for the rise of the Christian belief; they may all also be influenced (two of them certainly are) by Christian beliefs.[123]

Alister McGrath comments with respect to Jesus' resurrection:

> Bultmann was among many scholars who . . . proceeded to take the logically questionable step of arguing that such parallels discredited the historicity of the resurrection of Jesus. Since then, however, scholarship has moved on considerably. The parallels between the pagan myths of dying and rising gods and the New Testament accounts of the resurrection of Jesus are now regarded as remote, to say the least . . . Furthermore, there are no known instances of the myth being applied to any *specific historical figure* in pagan literature . . . It is at this point that the wisdom of C.S. Lewis – who actually knew something about myths – must be acknowledged. Lewis intuitively realized that the New Testament accounts of the resurrection of Jesus bore no relation to 'real' mythology . . . Perhaps most important, however, was the realization that the gnostic redeemer myths – which the New Testament writers allegedly took over and applied to Jesus – were to be dated later than the New Testament. The challenge posed to the historicity of the resurrection by these theories has thus passed into textbooks of the history of ideas.[124]

Licona points out that, unlike anything in the mystery religions, Jesus' resurrection 'isn't repeated, isn't related to changes in the seasons, and was sincerely believed to be an actual historical event by those who lived in the same generation of the historical Jesus.'[125] As Lewis commented: 'A *myth* is . . . not, save accidentally [i.e. non-essentially], connected with any given place or time.'[126] Licona also notes the nearly universal consensus of modern scholarship that 'there were *no* dying and rising gods that preceded Christianity. They all post-dated the first century.'[127] Habermas concurs: 'there is no case of a mythical deity in the mystery religions for which we have both clear and early evidence that a resurrection was taught prior to the late second century A.D. Thus, it is certainly a plausible theory that the mystery religions borrowed this aspect from Christianity, not the reverse.'[128]

Swedish scholar T.N.D. Mettinger takes what he admits is the minority position that there are three to five myths about dying and rising gods that do predate Christianity, but he nevertheless concludes that none of these serve as parallels to Jesus, let alone as causal factors in the Christian understanding of Jesus: 'There is, as far as I am aware, no *prima facie* evidence that the death and resurrection of Jesus is a mythological construct . . . The death and resurrection of Jesus retains its unique character in the history of religions.'[129] Moreover, those who accept Mettinger's minority report should reckon with Lewis's belief that:

> The heart of Christianity is a myth which is also a fact. The old myth of the Dying God, *without ceasing to be myth*, comes down from the heaven of legend and imagination to the earth of history. It *happens* – at a particular date, in a particular place, followed by definable historical consequences. We pass from a [mythological figure], dying nobody knows when or where, to a historical Person crucified (it is all in order) *under Pontius Pilate*. By becoming fact it does not cease to be myth: that is the miracle . . . To be truly Christian we must both assent to the historical fact and also receive the myth (fact though it has become) with the same imaginative embrace which we accord to all myths . . . God is more than a god, not less . . . If God chooses to be mythopoeic . . . shall we refuse to be *mythopathic*? For this is the marriage of heaven and earth: Perfect Myth and Perfect Fact: claiming not only our love and our obedience, but also our wonder and delight, addressed to the savage, the child, and the poet in each one of us no less than to the moralist, the scholar, and the philosopher.[130]

Lee Strobel summarizes the case against the 'history of religions' school:

> First, 'copycat' proponents often illogically assume that just because two things exist side by side, one of them must have caused the other. Second, many alleged similarities are exaggerated or fabricated. Writers frequently use language borrowed from Christianity to describe pagan rituals, then marvel at the 'parallels' they've discovered. Third, the chronology is wrong. Writers cite beliefs and practices that postdate the first century in an attempt to argue that they influenced the first-century formation of Christianity. Just because a cult had a belief or practice in the third or fourth century AD doesn't mean it had the same belief or

practice in the first century. Fourth, Paul would never have consciously borrowed from pagan religions; in fact, he warned against this very thing. Fifth, early Christianity was exclusivistic; any hint of syncretism in the New Testament would have caused immediate controversy. Sixth, unlike the mystery religions, Christianity is grounded in actual historical events. And seventh, what few parallels remain could reflect a Christian influence on pagan beliefs and practices. Pagan attempts to counter the influence of Christianity by imitating it are clearly apparent.[131]

Hence Ronald H. Nash reports that 'the tide of scholarly opinion has turned dramatically against attempts to make early Christianity dependent on the so-called dying and rising gods of Hellenistic paganism.'[132] Today's quest for the historical Jesus is firmly grounded in the realization that 'pagan mythology is simply the wrong interpretative context for understanding Jesus of Nazareth . . . Jesus and his disciples were first-century Palestinian Jews, and it is against that background that they must be understood.'[133]

The Ring of Truth

On 27 April 1926 Lewis records in his diary:

> Weldon came in. This meant whiskey and talk till 12:30, greatly to my disappointment. We somehow got on the historical truth of the Gospels, and agreed that there was a lot that could not be explained away. He believes in the Hegelian doctrine of the Trinity and said the whole thing fitted in: in fact he is a Christian 'of a sort'. I should never have suspected it.[134]

As George Sayer explains: 'T.D. ("Harry") Weldon was the tutor and college lecturer in Greats at Magdalen College. He was a cynic who scoffed at all creeds and almost all positive assertions, a man, Jack once wrote, who "believes that he has seen through everything and lives at rock bottom".'[135] This may be the same incident reported by Lewis in his autobiography, where he recalls:

Early in 1926 the hardest boiled of all the atheists I ever knew sat in my room on the other side of the fire and remarked that the evidence of the historicity of the Gospels was really surprisingly good. 'Rum thing,' he went on. 'All that stuff of Frazer's about the Dying God. Rum thing. It almost looks as if it had really happened once.' To understand the shattering impact of it, you would need to know the man (who has certainly never since shown any interest in Christianity). If he, the cynic of cynics, the toughest of toughs, were not – as I would still have put it – 'safe', where could I turn? Was there then no escape?[136]

According to Sayer (who knew Lewis personally): 'The effect on Jack was shattering. He examined the evidence on his own and had to agree that it was surprisingly good. From this time onward, he felt under pressure to believe.'[137]

C.S. Lewis's approach could be viewed as part of the 'second quest' for the historical Jesus inasmuch as he offered trenchant criticism of Bultmann's scepticism about the historical reliability of the canonical gospels. In 1959, during an invited lecture at Westcott House, Cambridge, Lewis famously rebuffed the views of scholars who held that the gospels were legends or myths:

Whatever these men may be as Biblical critics, I distrust them as critics. They seem to me to lack literary judgement . . . A man who has spent his youth and manhood in the minute study of the New Testament texts and of other people's studies of them, whose literary experience of those texts lacks any standard of comparison such as can only grow from a wide and deep and genial experience of literature in general, is, I should think, very likely to miss the obvious things about them. If he tells me that something in the Gospel is legend or romance, I want to know how many legends and romances he has read, how well his palate is trained in detecting them by the flavour; not how many years he has spent on that Gospel . . . turn to *John*. Read the dialogues: that with the Samaritan woman at the well, or that which follows the healing of the man born blind. Look at the pictures: Jesus (if I may use the word) doodling with his finger in the dust . . . I have been reading poems, romances, vision-literature, legends, myths all my life. I know what they are like. I know that not one of them is like this.[138]

In an unrelated context, A.C. Grayling acknowledges the import-ance of making informed judgements concerning the reliability of historical testimony, noting that 'one gets a sense of when such descriptions ring true.'[139] Lewis concluded: 'as a literary historian, I am perfectly convinced that whatever else the Gospels are they are not legends. I have read a great deal of legend and I am quite clear that they are not the same sort of thing.'[140]

Myth Become Fact

Lewis recalls:

> I was by now too experienced in literary criticism to regard the Gospels as myths. They had not the mythical taste . . . If ever a myth had become fact, had been incarnated, it would be just like this. And nothing else in all literature was just like this. Myths were like it in one way. Histories were like it in another. But nothing was simply like it. And no person was like the Person it depicted; as real, as recognisable, through all that depth of time, as Plato's Socrates or Boswell's Johnson . . . yet also numinous, lit by a fire from beyond the world, a god. But if a god – we are no longer polytheists – then not a god, but God.[141]

The historical, biographical character of the New Testament testimony about Jesus contradicts the idea that he is a mytho-logical figure. As atheist Kai Nielson acknowledges: 'it wasn't a myth that the Christian community tried to purvey, rather they were recording what they actually believed happened.'[142] None of the pagan myths make a pretence of historicity; where-as the Christian revelation claim stands or falls by the historic-ity of certain specific events in a specific socio-political histori-cal context, one radically opposed to being influenced by pagan mythology. 'This is difficult,' observed Lewis, 'because [Jesus'] followers were all Jews; that is, they belonged to that Nation which of all others was most convinced that there was only one God – that there could not possibly be another.'[143] Michael Green elaborates:

The Jews had really learnt one lesson by the first century AD. That there is only one God, and no runners up. They believed this so strongly that they would allow no images of the divine to decorate their synagogue . . . So jealously did they stick to the Second Commandment that the Jews fought to the death rather than allow the Roman military standards, with their imperial medallions, to enter the Holy City. So seriously did Jews take their monotheism that they would not take the sacred name of God (Yahweh) upon their lips . . . In other words, if you had looked the whole world over for more stony and improbable soil in which to plant the idea of an incarnation you could not have done better than light upon Israel! Indeed, the Jews were unique. The Romans never could understand them, though they gave them a grudging kind of admiration. These people were different from all other races on earth; since they made no image of the deity they must be 'atheists', and such they called them. It was in this background, no other, that the conviction arose that God had incarnated himself in human flesh.[144]

As Bauckham observes, the first Christians:

include Jesus in the unique divine identity as Jewish monotheism understood it. The writers do this deliberately and comprehensively by using precisely those characteristics of the divine identity on which Jewish monotheism focused in characterizing God as unique. They included Jesus in the unique divine sovereignty over all things, they included him in the unique divine creation of all things, they identified him by the divine name which names the unique divine identity, and they portray him as accorded the worship which, for Jewish monotheists, is recognition of the divine identity.[145]

The conundrum produced by admitting that Jesus' disciples claimed Jesus correctly claimed to be divine while denying that Jesus claimed any such thing is both obvious and very great. As Craig A. Evans comments:

To assert that Jesus did not regard himself as in some sense God's son makes the historian wonder why others did. From the earliest time Jesus was regarded by Christians as the son of God. Why not regard him as the great Prophet, if that is all that he had claimed or accepted? Why not regard him as the great Teacher, if that had been all that he had ever pretended to be? Earliest Christianity regarded Jesus as Messiah and as Son of God, I think, because that is how his disciples understood him and how Jesus permitted them to understand him.[146]

Peter Kreeft argues:

> if the historical Jesus never claimed divinity . . . then this myth was invented by Jesus' apostles themselves, not by later generations or the early Christian community. But why would the apostles lie? What would motivate such a massive conspiracy of deceit? Liars always lie for selfish reasons. If they lied, what was their motive, what did they get out of it? What they got out of it was misunderstanding, rejection, persecution, torture, and martyrdom. Hardly a list of perks! And if they lied, why did not one of the liars ever confess this, even under torture? Martyrdom does not prove truth, but it certainly proves sincerity.[147]

Hence, having admitted the sincerity of the gospel writers, Michel Onfray is driven to accuse them of 'intellectual self-intoxication, ontological blindness.'[148] However, such a theologically radical misunderstanding, *by such people and despite the lack of sufficient prompting in this direction from Jesus himself*, is highly unlikely. As Lewis wrote: 'The idea that any man . . . should be opaque to those who lived in the same culture, spoke the same language, shared the same habitual imagery and unconscious assumptions, and yet be transparent to [modern critics] who have none of these advantages, is in my opinion preposterous.'[149]

Thus we have excellent grounds for agreeing with J.P. Moreland that 'a high Christology goes back to Jesus himself',[150] just as the New Testament reports. The trilemma argument as applied to the original Christian witness to Jesus therefore drives us to grapple with Jesus' divine self-understanding, for as N.T. Wright argues: 'Jesus was aware of a call, a vocation, to do and be what, according to the scriptures, only Israel's God gets to do and be.'[151] Carsten Peter Thiede likewise concludes: 'There is no room for doubt. Jesus claimed to be the Messiah, the Son of God and God himself.'[152] Richard Bauckham concurs: 'The only Jesus we can plausibly find in the sources is a Jesus who . . . speaks and acts for God in a way that far surpassed the authority of a prophet in the Jewish tradition. His opponents recognized this.'[153] That's why they crucified Jesus as a blasphemer. And either he was the liar they believed, or else a lunatic, or else the divine 'Son of Man' he claimed to be. The very fact that the new atheists fail to consistently grasp either non-Christian nettle, but instead spend their time fruitlessly trying to evade the issue by clinging to imaginary alternatives or long-discredited historical theories, only goes to reinforce Lewis's point.

Conclusion

Thus Lewis came to answer his own question: 'The question is, I suppose, whether any hypothesis covers the facts so well as the Christian hypothesis . . . The alternative hypothesis is not legend, nor exaggeration, nor [with reference to Jesus' resurrection] the apparitions of a ghost. It is either lunacy or lies. Unless one can take the second alternative (and I can't) one turns to the Christian theory.'[154]

Having examined the gospel's testimony to the historical Jesus, and having wrestled with the paradox of Jesus' claims and character, Lewis wrote to a friend in October 1931: 'I have just passed on from believing in God to definitely believing in Christ – in Christianity.'[155] Lewis recalls:

> As I drew near the conclusion, I felt a resistance almost as strong as my previous resistance to Theism. As strong, but shorter-lived, for I understood it better. Every step I had taken, from the Absolute to 'Spirit' and from 'Spirit' to 'God' . . . one had less chance 'to call one's soul one's own'. To accept the Incarnation was a further step in the same direction. It brings God nearer, or near in a new way. And this, I found, was something I had not wanted. But to recognise the ground for my evasion was of course to recognise both its shame and its futility.[156]

* * *

Recommended Resources

By C.S. Lewis:
Mere Christianity (London: Fount, 1997)
Miracles (London: Fount, 2002)
'What Are We to Make of Jesus Christ?' and 'Fern-Seed and Elephants', in *C.S. Lewis Essay Collection* (ed. Lesley Walmsley; London: HarperCollins, 2002)

Websites

Bethinking
  www.bethinking.org.
Biblical Archaeological Review
  www.bib-arch.org/.
William Lane Craig: Reasonable Faith
  www.reasonablefaith.org.
Gary R. Habermas
  www.garyhabermas.com.
Last Seminary – NT Biblical Studies Articles
  www.lastseminary.com/nt-biblical-studies-articles/.
Library of Historical Apologetics
  http://historicalapologetics.org/.
Michael Licona
  www.risenjesus.com.
Lee Strobel
  www.leestrobel.com.

Video

Clark, Greg. 'The Conversion of C.S. Lewis'
  https://publicchristianity.org/library/the-conversion-of-c.s.-lewis.
Licona, Michael. 'Did Christianity Borrow from Pagan Religions?'
  www.leestrobel.com/videoserver/video.php?clip=strobelT1085.
McGrew, Timothy. 'The Gospels and Acts as History'
  www.youtube.com/watch?v=JAPG3eECaxw.

Strobel, Lee. *The Case for Christ*
www.youtube.com/watch?v=2Fpr6ULGpik&feature=
related.

Williams, Peter S. 'Did Jesus Rise from the Dead?'
www.damaris.org/cm/podcasts/135 & http://idpluspeter-
swilliams.blogspot.com/2008/10/blog-post.html.

Wright, N.T. *Resurrection: Did It Happen? What Could It Mean?*
(Blakeway-IVP-Channel 4, 2004).

Audio

Craig, William Lane. 'The Historicity of the Resurrection of Jesus'
www.rfmedia.org/RF_audio_video/Other_clips/William
_Lane_Craig-Evidence_for_resurrection-2004-06-08-Liszt-
1030.mp3.

— 'Who Does Jesus Think He Was?'
www.rfmedia.org/RF_audio_video/Other_clips/National_
Faculty_Leadership_Conf_2008/Who_Jesus_Think_He_Was.
mp3.

— 'The Work of Bart Ehrman'
www.rfmedia.org/av/audio/gracepoint-the-work-of-bart-ehrman.

— vs John Dominic Crossan. 'Will the Real Jesus Please Stand Up?'
www.bringyou.to/CraigCrossanDebate.mp3.

— vs Gerd Ludemann. 'Jesus' Resurrection: Fact or Figment?'
www.bringyou.to/CraigLudemannResurrectionDebate.mp3.

Garthcole, Simon. 'Differences between Canonical and Noncanonical
Gospels.' http://tapesfromscotland.org/ToF/ToF_Session3.mp3.

Jongkind, Dirk. 'Why the Greek Text Is True'
http://tapesfromscotland.org/ToF/ToF_Session2.mp3.

Moreland, J.P. 'How Do We Know Christianity Is Right out of All
the Religions?'
www.bethinking.org/bible-jesus/how-do-we-know-christian-
ity-is-right-out-of-all.htm.

— 'The Search for the Historical Jesus', Parts 1–7 www.youtube
.com/watch?v=HA2d5jOpsH0&feature=PlayList&p=5C3ED0
50A38A301B&index=0.

Swinburne, Richard. 'Historical Evidence for the Resurrection'
www.blackhawkmedia.org/MP3/Swinburne3.mp3.

Williams, Peter J. 'Can We Trust the Gospels as History?'
http://tapesfromscotland.org/ToF/ToF_Session1.mp3.

Williams, Peter S. 'Archaeological Evidence for the Reliability of the New Testament'
www.damaris.org/cm/podcasts/637.
— 'The Gospels: Do We Have Now What They Wrote Then?'
www.damaris.org/cm/podcasts/590.
— 'The Gospels: Who Wrote What When?'
www.damaris.org/cm/podcasts/589.
— 'Understanding Jesus: An Overview'
www.damaris.org/cm/podcasts/591.
— 'Who Did Jesus Think He Was?'
www.damaris.org/cm/podcasts/631.
— 'Did Jesus Exist?' www.damaris.org/cm/podcasts/751.

Online papers

Barnett, Paul. 'Did Jesus Exist? Early Non-Christian References'
www.lastseminary.com/sources-outside-the-new-testam/.
Bayne, Tim and Greg Restall. 'A Participatory Model of the Atonement'
www.consequently.org/papers/pa.pdf.
Corduan, Winfried. 'Miracles: Liability and Asset'
www.ukapologetics.net/07/miraclesla.htm.
Craig, William Lane. 'Contemporary Scholarship and the Historical Evidence for the Resurrection of Jesus'
www.reasonablefaith.org/site/News2?page=NewsArticle&id=5214.
— 'Jesus the Son of God'
www.reasonablefaith.org/site/News2?page=NewsArticle&id=6247.
— 'The Problem of Miracles: A Historical and Philosophical Perspective'
www.reasonablefaith.org/site/News2?page=NewsArticle&id=5212.
— vs Bart Ehrman. 'Is There Historical Evidence for the Resurrection of Jesus?'
www.bringyou.to/apologetics/p96.htm.
Davis, Stephen T. 'The Mad/Bad/God Trilemma: A Reply to Daniel Howard Snyder'
www.lastseminary.com/trilemma/The%20Mad-Bad-God%20Trilemma%20-%20A%20Reply%20to%-20Daniel%20Howard-Snyder.pdf.

Geisler, Norman L. 'The Dating of the New Testament' www.bethinking.org/bible-jesus/advanced/the-dating-of-the-new-testament.htm.

Habermas, Gary R. 'The Lost Tomb of Jesus: A Response' www.garyhabermas.com/articles/The_Lost_Tomb_of_Jesus/losttombofjesus_response.htm.

— 'Recent Perspectives on the Historical Reliability of the Gospels' www.bethinking.org/bible-jesus/intermediate/recent-perspectives-on-the-reliability-of-the-gospels.htm.

— 'A Summary Critique: Questioning the Existence of Jesus' www.garyhabermas.com/articles/crj_summarycritique/-crj_summarycritique.htm.

— 'Why I Believe the New Testament Is Historically Reliable' www.apologetics.com/index.php?catid=39:historical-apologetics&id=165:why-i-believe-the-new-testament-is-historically-reliable&Itemid=54&option=com_content&view=article.

Kreeft, Peter. 'The Divinity of Christ' www.peterkreeft.com/topics/christ-divinity.htm.

Lennox, John. 'The Question of Miracles: The Contemporary Influence of David Hume' www.bethinking.org/resource.php?ID=59.

Lucas, J.R. 'Reflections on the Atonement' http://users.ox.ac.uk/~jrlucas/theology/atone.html.

McGrew, Linda. 'Historical Inquiry: Epistemology, Miracles, and the God Who Speaks' www.lydiamcgrew.com/Wholepaperdraft.pdf.

McGrew, Timothy and Linda McGrew. 'The Argument from Miracles: A Cumulative Case for the Resurrection of Jesus of Nazareth' www.lydiamcgrew.com/Resurrectionarticlesinglefile.pdf.

Moreland, J.P. 'The Historicity of the New Testament' www.bethinking.org/bible-jesus/advanced/the-historicity-of-the-new-testament.htm.

Rea, Michael. 'Philosophy and Christian Theology' http://plato.stanford.edu/entries/christiantheology-philosophy/.

Reichenbach, Bruce R. 'Inclusivism and the Atonement' www.faithandphilosophy.com/article_atonement.php.

Reppert, Victor. 'Hume on Miracles, Frequencies and Prior Probabilities' www.infidels.org/library/modern/victor_reppert/miracles-.html.

Roberts, Mark D. 'Did Jesus Even Exist?'
www.markdroberts.typepad.com/markdroberts/2007/11/-did-jesus-even-.html.

Williams, Peter S. 'Archaeology and the Historical Reliability of the New Testament'
www.bethinking.org/bible-jesus/advanced/archaeology-and-the-historical-reliability-of-the-new-testament.htm.

— 'The Impossible Planet and the Satin Pit'
www.damaris.org/content/content.php?type=5&id=492.

Books

Baggett, David, ed. *Did the Resurrection Happen? A Conversation with Gary Habermas and Antony Flew* (Downers Grove, IL: IVP, 2009).

Barnett, Paul. *Is the New Testament Reliable?* (Downers Grove, IL: IVP, rev. edn, 2003).

— *Messiah: Jesus – the Evidence of History* (Nottingham: IVP, 2009).

Bauckham, Richard. *Jesus and the Eyewitnesses: The Gospels as Eyewitness Testimony* (Grand Rapids, MI: Eerdmans, 2006).

— *Jesus: A Very Short Introduction* (Oxford University Press, 2011).

Blomberg, Craig L. *The Historical Reliability of the Gospels* (Nottingham: Apollos, 2nd edn, 2007).

Bock, Darrell L. and Daniel B. Wallace. *Dethroning Jesus: Exposing Popular Culture's Quest to Unseat the Biblical Christ* (Nashville: Thomas Nelson, 2007).

Boyd, Gregory A. and Paul Rhodes Eddy. *Lord or Legend? Wrestling with the Jesus Dilemma* (Grand Rapids, MI: Baker, 2007).

Comfort, Philip W. and Jason Driesbach. *The Many Gospels of Jesus: Sorting Out the Story of the Life of Jesus* (Carol Stream, IL: Tyndale House, 2008).

Copan, Paul, ed. *Will the Real Jesus Please Stand Up? A Debate between William Lane Craig and John Dominic Crossan* (Grand Rapids, MI: Baker, 1998).

— and Ronald K. Tacelli, eds. *Jesus' Resurrection: Fact or Figment? A Debate between William Lane Craig and Gerd Ludemann* (Downers Grove, IL: IVP, 2000).

Craig, William Lane. *On Guard: Defending Your Faith with Reason and Precision* (Paris, Ontario: David C. Cook, 2010).

— *Reasonable Faith: Christian Truth and Apologetics* (Wheaton, IL: Crossway, 3rd edn, 2008).

Davis, Stephen T. *Risen Indeed: Making Sense of the Resurrection* (London: SPCK, 1993).

Earman, John. *Hume's Abject Failure: The Argument against Miracles* (Oxford University Press, 2000).

Evans, Craig A. *Fabricating Jesus: How Modern Scholars Distort the Gospels* (Downers Grove, IL: IVP, 2006).

Evans, C. Stephen. *Why Believe? Reason and Mystery as Pointers to God* (Downers Grove, IL: IVP, 1996).

Geivett, R. Douglas and Gary R. Habermas. *In Defence of Miracles: A Comprehensive Case for God's Action in History* (Leicester: Apollos, 1997).

Green, Joel B. and Mark D. Baker. *Recovering the Scandal of the Cross: Atonement in New Testament and Contemporary Contexts* (Carlisle: Paternoster, 2000).

Green, Michael. *The Books the Church Suppressed: What the Da Vinci Code Doesn't Tell You* (Oxford: Monarch, 2006).

Habermas, Gary R. *The Historical Jesus: Ancient Evidence for the Life of Christ* (Joplin, MO: College Press, 1996).

— *The Verdict of History: Conclusive Evidence from Beyond the Bible for the Life of Jesus* (Eastbourne: Monarch, 1990).

—, Antony G.N. Flew and Terry L. Miethe. *Did Jesus Rise from the Dead? The Resurrection Debate* (Eugene, OR: Wipf & Stock, 1987).

Hill, C.E. *Who Chose the Gospels? Probing the Great Gospel Conspiracy* (Oxford University Press, 2010).

Hurtado, Larry W. *How on Earth Did Jesus Become a God? Historical Questions about Earliest Devotion to Jesus* (Grand Rapids, MI: Eerdmans, 2005).

Horner, David A. 'Aut Deus aut Malus Homo: A Defense of C.S. Lewis's "Shocking Alternative".' Pages 68–84 in *C.S. Lewis as Philosopher: Truth, Goodness and Beauty* (ed. David Baggett, Gary R. Habermas and Jerry L. Walls; Downers Grove, IL: IVP Academic, 2008).

Jones, Timothy Paul. *Misquoting Truth: A Guide to the Fallacies of Bart Ehrman's Misquoting Jesus* (Downers Grove, IL: IVP, 2007).

Komoszewski, J. Ed, M. James Sawyer and Daniel B. Wallace. *Reinventing Jesus: How Contemporary Skeptics Miss the Real Jesus and Mislead Popular Culture* (Grand Rapids, MI: Kregel, 2006).

Kreeft, Peter. *Between Heaven and Hell* (Downers Grove, IL: IVP, 2008).

— 'Why I Believe Jesus Is the Messiah and Son of God.' Pages 239–52 in *Why I Am a Christian* (ed. Norman L. Geisler and Paul K. Hoffman; Grand Rapids, MI: Baker, rev. edn, 2006).

Licona, Michael R. *The Resurrection of Jesus: A New Historiographical Approach* (Nottingham: Apollos, 2010).

McDowell, Sean and Jonathan Morrow. *Is God Just a Human Invention? And Seventeen Other Questions Raised by the New Atheists* (Grand Rapids, MI: Kregel, 2010).

McGrew, Timothy and Linda McGrew. 'The Argument from Miracles.' Pages 593–662 in *The Blackwell Companion to Natural Theology* (ed. William Lane Craig and J.P. Moreland; Oxford: Wiley-Blackwell, 2009). Available online at www.lydiamcgrew.com/Resurrectionarticlesinglefile.pdf.

Molnar, Michael R. *The Star of Bethlehem: The Legacy of the Magi* (Rutgers University Press, 2000).

Moreland, J.P. *The God Question: An Invitation to a Life of Meaning* (Eugene, OR: Harvest House, 2009).

Nash, Ronald H. *Christianity and the Hellenistic World* (Dallas, TX: Zondervan/Probe, 1984).

— *The Gospel and the Greeks* (New Jersey: Phillipsburg, 2nd edn, 2003).

Orr-Ewing, Amy. *Why Trust the Bible? Answers to 10 Tough Questions* (Nottingham: IVP, 2005).

Overman, Dean L. *A Case for the Divinity of Jesus: Examining the Earliest Evidence* (Plymouth: Rowman & Littlefield, 2009).

Owen, Huw Parri. *Christian Theism: A Study in Its Basic Principles* (Edinburgh: T&T Clark, 1984).

Sanders, John. *No Other Name: Can Only Christians Be Saved?* (London: SPCK, 1994).

Stanton, Graham. *The Gospels and Jesus* (Oxford University Press, 2nd edn, 2002).

Stewart, Robert B. and Gary R. Habermas, eds. *Memoirs of Jesus: A Critical Appraisal of James D.G. Dunn's Jesus Remembered* (Nashville, TN: B&H Academic, 2010).

Strobel, Lee. *The Case for the Real Jesus* (Grand Rapids, MI: Zondervan, 2007).

Swinburne, Richard. *Responsibility and Atonement* (Oxford: Clarendon Press, 1989).

— *The Resurrection of God Incarnate* (Oxford: Clarendon Press, 2003).

— *Was Jesus God?* (Oxford University Press, 2008).

Taylor, James E. *Introducing Apologetics: Cultivating Christian Commitment* (Grand Rapids, MI: Baker Academic, 2006).

Thiede, Carsten Peter. *Jesus: Life or Legend?* (Oxford: Lion, 1997).

Ward, Keith. *What the Bible Really Teaches: A Challenge for Fundamentalists* (London: SPCK, 2004).

Wilkins, Michael J. and J.P. Moreland. *Jesus under Fire: Modern Scholarship Reinvents the Historical Jesus* (Grand Rapids, MI: Zondervan, 1995).

Williams, Peter S. *Understanding Jesus: Five Ways to Spiritual Enlightenment* (Milton Keynes: Paternoster, 2011).

Witherington III, Ben. *The Gospel Code: Novel Claims about Jesus, Mary Magdalene and Da Vinci* (Downers Grove, IL: IVP, 2004).

— *The Jesus Quest: The Third Search for the Jew from Nazareth* (Downers Grove, IL: IVP, 1997).

Wright, N.T. *The Resurrection of the Son of God* (London: SPCK, 2003).

Conclusion: First Things First

I gave up Christianity at about fourteen. Came back to it
when getting on for thirty. Not an emotional conversion:
almost purely philosophical.
C.S. Lewis

According to A.C. Grayling:

These are the reasons why it is difficult to assess a famous person's
legacy until sufficient time has passed. Most fame is of the
moment; most of the stars, the politicians, the cynosures of fashion
and public interest whom the paparazzi once pursued, sink into
oblivion under history's weight. Those whose memory survives
either were truly outstanding in their generation, or did something that had real effects on what came after them.[1]

C.S. Lewis was both outstanding in his generation and had a real
influence upon subsequent generations because he didn't treat
ideas as fashionable or unfashionable, but only as true or false:
'The great difficulty is to get modern audiences to realise that you
are preaching Christianity soley and simply because you happen
to think it true; they always suppose you are preaching it because
you like it or think it good for society or something of that sort.'[2]
Lewis recalls that Owen Barfield:

made short work of what I have called my 'chronological snob-
bery,' the uncritical acceptance of the intellectual climate common
to our own age and the assumption that whatever has gone out of
date is on that account discredited. You must find why it went out

of date. Was it ever refuted (and if so by whom, where, and how conclusively) or did it merely die away as fashions do? If the latter, this tells us nothing about its truth or falsehood. From seeing this, one passes to the realization that our own age is also 'a period,' and certainly has, like all periods, its own characteristic illusions.[3]

While Lewis-the-atheist shared many illusions characteristic of today's 'new atheists', he never shared their scientistic theory of knowledge, and he never bought into 'logical positivism' or 'verificationism'. This refusal to kowtow to contemporary intellectual fashion left Lewis free to seriously consider metaphysical arguments for theism (such as the argument from desire, the argument from reason and the moral argument), and this intellectual freedom undoubtedly contributed to the fact that Lewis's fame has been far from 'of the moment' in nature. Since the mid twentieth-century death of logical positivism, several generations of scholars have looked to Lewis as an example of robust engagement with the big questions.

It remains to be seen how posterity treats what Paul Copan calls the 'angry, sarcastic, and sloppily argued attacks'[4] of the new atheists; but the process of writing this book has led me to believe that there's more than a hint of truth to theologian David Bentley Hart's judgement:

> atheism that consists entirely of vacuous arguments afloat on oceans of historical ignorance, made turbulent by storms of strident self-righteousness, is as contemptible as any other form of dreary fundamentalism . . . The sorts of 'scientific,' 'moral,' or 'rational' objections [made by the new atheists] are not really scientific, moral, or rational in any but a purely rhetorical sense . . . These are attitudes masquerading as ideas, emotional commitments disguised as intellectual honesty. However sincere the current evangelists of unbelief may be, they are doing nothing more than producing rationales – ballasted by a formidable collection of conceptual and historical errors – for convictions that are rooted not in reason but in a greater cultural will, of which their arguments are only reflexes . . . The reason that today's cultured despisers of religion tend to employ such extraordinarily bad arguments for their prejudices, without realizing how bad those arguments are, is that they are

driven by the pre-critical and irrational impulses of the purest kind of fideism . . . Materialism is not a fact of experience or a deduction of logic; it is a metaphysical prejudice, nothing more, and one that is arguably more irrational than almost any other.[5]

On the whole, the new atheists simply don't contemplate the arguments that made C.S. Lewis change his mind about God, despite the fact that they mention Lewis frequently enough that one would have thought they owed him some serious intellectual dialogue. But then, failing to take their critics seriously is a serial flaw of the new-atheist movement.[6] Consider, for example, A.C. Grayling's dismissive response to an invitation to debate God's existence with William Lane Craig:

> I am not interested in debating Professor Craig, though if he would like to co-opt me for the publicity for his tour – I would be happy to debate him on the question of the existence of fairies and water nymphs. But as for the very uninteresting matter of whether there is just one god or goddess and that it can be debated despite the claim that it is transcendently ineffable and unknowable – that is an empty prospect, hence my declining the invitation.[7]

Professor Craig no doubt subscribes to the traditional theistic view that humans cannot have a *comprehensive* (as opposed to a partial) knowledge of God; but it's hardly tenable to suppose that he wanted to debate the existence of a being of whom it was, by definition, impossible to have any knowledge at all (especially given that Craig is a leading contemporary advocate of theistic arguments)! Nor, in light of the robust state of the God debate within contemporary philosophy, is it tenable to suggest that belief in God is comparable to belief in 'fairies and water nymphs'. As Oxford philosopher (and atheist) Dr Daniel Came comments: 'Professor Grayling's attitude towards the status of the question of the existence of God – essentially that there is nothing to talk about – is hard to justify philosophically. Even though it might not be clear what the solution is, it is plainly a genuine philosophical problem, and there are few, if any, that are more profound or of greater interest to the general public.'[8]

Unfortunately, as Terry Eagleton observes:

Card-carrying rationalists like Dawkins [and his fellow 'new atheists'] . . . are in one sense the least well-equipped to understand what they castigate, since they don't believe there is anything there to be understood, or at least anything worth understanding. This is why they invariably come up with vulgar caricatures of religious faith that would make a first-year theology student wince. The more they detest religion, the more ill-informed their criticisms of it tend to be.[9]

C.S. Lewis would have sympathized with the sort of visceral aversion to God displayed by Christopher Hitchens:

I should not conceal the fact that I am not so much an atheist as an *anti*-theist. I am, in other words, not one of those unbelievers who wishes that they had faith, or that they could believe. I am, rather, someone who is delighted that there is absolutely no persuasive evidence for the existence of any of mankind's thousands of past and present deities. It is to me an appalling thought that anyone could wish for a supreme and absolute and unalterable ruler, whose reign was eternal and unchallengeable, who required incessant propitiation, and who kept us all under continual surveillance . . . Such an aweful system would mean that words like 'freedom' and terms like 'free will' were devoid of all meaning.[10]

After all, Lewis himself once felt that:

Christianity placed at the centre of what then seemed to me a transcendental Interferer. If its picture was true . . . There was no region even in the innermost depth of one's soul . . . which one could surround with a barbed wire fence and guard with a notice No Admittance. And that was what I wanted; some area, however small, of which I could say to all other beings, 'This is my business and mine alone.'[11]

However, Lewis prioritized truth over personal comfort:

Which of the religions of the world gives to its followers the greatest happiness? While it lasts, the religion of worshipping oneself is the best . . . I didn't go to religion to make me happy. I always knew a bottle of port would do that. If you want a religion to make you feel really comfortable, I certainly don't recommend Christianity. I am certain there must be a patent American article on the market which will suit you far better, but I can't give any advice on it.[12]

As we've seen, Hitchens doesn't engage with the argument from desire or the argument from rationality. He circles the moral argument, trailing red herrings about not needing to believe in God in order to behave decently; but he doesn't have the decency to grapple with the ontological issues at the heart of the moral argument. Hitchens squirms on the horns of the trilemma concerning Jesus' claims in the context of his character (one argument with which he deals directly) and seeks refuge in the arms of a highly implausible scepticism concerning the historical Jesus. In sum, when Hitchens says that there's 'absolutely no persuasive evidence' for the existence of God, *one is witnessing an example of precisely the sort of blind faith that neo-atheists like to accuse believers of embracing.*

In a September 2008 debate on the existence of God hosted by the 'United Secular Alliance' at Virginia Commonwealth University, Christopher Hitchens stated that 'there is no form of persuasion that would make me assent to this proposition' (i.e. that God exists),[13] and he described the theistic arguments articulated by Dr Frank Turek (including the arguments from reason and morality) as 'the mere equivalence of white noise.'[14] Perhaps Hitchens' self-professed immunity to reason explains why his response to the moral argument presented by Dr Turek was a typical neo-atheist red herring about moral motivation, despite the fact that philosopher Jay Richards had very clearly highlighted the fallacious nature of Hitchens' response to the moral argument in their January 2008 debate at Stanford University.[15] Like Richards before him, Turek tried to call Hitchens back to task:

> Christopher talked about atrocities, but again, on the atheistic worldview, here's the main point: how do you define what an atrocity is? Who defines it? Who has the authority to define what an atrocity is? The carbon atom? The benzene molecule? I'm not saying you have to believe in God to be moral. I'm not saying that

only religious people are moral. I'm not saying atheists can't be moral. I'm not saying atheists don't know morality. I'm saying there's no way to justify what is right and what is wrong unless there's some authority that provides it. What is the authority? In a materialistic worldview there is no authority. The carbon atom has no moral authority over you. And it seems that Christopher goes on and on about how he does not want to be under some kind of divine totalitarianism. That is a *moral rejection* of God. Where does he come up with this 'immoral totalitarianism'? His worldview does not afford immorality because his worldview does not afford morality. He has to borrow from the Christian worldview in order to argue against it. In fact he has to sit in God's lap to slap his face. Where does he get morality from?[16]

Astonishingly, during the debate's cross-examination period, Hitchens asked Turek how he could 'dare to say that without a belief in religion I would have no source for ethical or moral views'.[17] 'That's not what I'm saying,' replied Turek. 'I'm not saying you don't know morality, Christopher, I'm saying that you can't justify morality without a being outside of yourself.'[18] Turek tried several times to get Hitchens to address the ontological question at the heart of the moral argument, but Hitchens consistently responded with red herrings that evinced both his ignorance of Christian beliefs about moral *epistemology* and his disingenuous failure to grapple with the question of moral *ontology*. That failure was starkly highlighted when Hitchens dismissed Turek's restated question 'Where does evil come from?' with the quick-draw reply 'Religion.' This joke, which turns upon *and thus acknowledges* the ambiguity between the answer in terms of proximate causation given by Hitchens and the question of ultimate ontological grounding repeatedly posed by Turek, revealed an intellectual evasiveness surely better met by the aggrieved rending of garments than by the laughter and applause it actually garnered from the audience.[19] Hitchens continued to drown out Turek's questions about the ontological nature and grounding of moral values in a sea of red herrings about moral epistemology and the evils of totalitarian dictators until Turek was out of cross-examination time. As Turek commented after the debate: 'Hitchens was his usual charming and witty self (I really like him and said as much), but he did not answer any of the eight arguments that I presented for the existence of God. And as many in the audience acknowledged, he dodged nearly all of my questions.'[20]

Although he clearly didn't realize it, Hitchens 'gave the store away' on the issue of moral ontology towards the end of his debate with Dr Turek. Responding to an audience question about empathy, Turek returned to the moral argument: 'The question is: "What makes something right?" In a materialist worldview there's nothing that can make something right or wrong. As David Hume says, you can't get an ought from an is.' Christopher Hitchens immediately commented: 'Well, I'm happy to agree with that. I think that's true.'[21]

What goes for Hitchens in particular goes for the new atheists in general. For example, Richard Dawkins was clearly unfamiliar with the argument from reason put to him by philosopher Paul Copan, and his confused response took the simple expediency of changing the subject. As atheist Geoff Crocker complains: 'Dawkins . . . has become a campaigner rather than a thinker.'[22] Sad to say, the new atheists appear to be collectively recycling the mistakes frankly admitted by Aldous Huxley in his 1937 book *Ends and Means*:

> like so many of my contemporaries, I took it for granted that there was no meaning. This was partly due to the fact that I shared the common belief that the scientific picture of an abstraction from reality was a true picture of reality as a whole; partly also to other, non-intellectual reasons. I had motives for not wanting the world to have meaning; consequently assumed that it had none, and was able without any difficulty to find satisfying reasons for this assumption. Most ignorance is vincible ignorance. We don't know because we don't want to know. It is our will that decides how and upon what subjects we shall use our intelligence. Those who detect no meaning in the world generally do so because, for one reason or another, it suits their books that the world should be meaningless.[23]

C.S. Lewis would be the first to point out that it is illegitimate to *substitute* psychoanalysis for philosophical analysis. However, our philosophical review of the new-atheist's response to natural theology naturally raises the subsidiary psychological question of why their response is so shallow. The new atheists so contrive to ignore, misunderstand, evade and beg the question against the arguments for God and the evidence for Jesus that they call to mind the figure C.S. Lewis once described as 'deliberately trying not to know whether Christianity is true or false, because he foresees endless trouble if it should turn out to be true. He is like the man who deliberately "forgets" to look at the notice board because if he did, he might find his name down for some unpleasant duty.'[24] As Thomas Chalmers warned:

> Man is not to blame, if an atheist, because of the want of proof. But he is to blame, if an atheist, because he has shut his eyes. He is not to blame that the evidence for a God has not been seen by him, if no such evidence there were within the field of his observation. But he is to blame, if the evidence have not been seen, because he turned away his attention from it.[25]

In the tradition of Aldous Huxley, contemporary atheist Thomas Nagel candidly acknowledges:

> I want atheism to be true and am made uneasy by the fact that some of the most intelligent and well-informed people I know are religious believers. It isn't just that I don't believe in God and, naturally, hope that I'm right in my belief. It's that I hope there is no God! I don't want there to be a God; I don't want the universe to be like that. My guess is that this cosmic authority problem is not a rare condition and that it is responsible for much of the scientism and reductionism of our time.[26]

Perhaps this very traditional 'cosmic authority problem' explains why 'new' atheist engagement with natural theology ranges from practically non-existent (e.g. Daniel Dennett) to piecemeal and sophomoric (e.g. Richard Dawkins). As noted in chapter three, the sort of serious, sustained, in-depth consideration of the nature of ultimate reality that gradually moved C.S. Lewis to reject naturalism and to embrace theism simply isn't on the new-atheists' agenda.

It was through just such a pilgrimage of reason that Lewis came to see that, although the self-worshipping part of him feared 'a supreme and absolute and unalterable ruler, whose reign was eternal and unchallengeable' (not despite, but precisely *because* this divine ruler was also wholly good and loving), yet the existence of this Being was the corollary of his lifelong desire for that transcendent, numinous 'something more' half-glimpsed in so many aspects of life. Indeed, Lewis gradually became convinced that God was a necessary precondition of our ability to truthfully judge anything as being objectively good or bad (beautiful or ugly); a precondition of our ability to believe anything on the basis of good reasons rather than because of mindless causes; a precondition of the very freedom of the will (a freedom excluded by the materialistic hypothesis) to either welcome or reject relationship with the divine truth, goodness and beauty revealed in the paradox of Jesus Christ. Drawing upon his own expertise in history and mythological literature Lewis rejected the 'no quest' scepticism of Bultmann and concluded that the story of Jesus was that of a 'myth become fact'.

Émile Cammaerts remarked that 'when people stop believing in God, they don't believe in nothing – they believe in anything.'[27] This certainly seems to be the case with the new atheists. Rather than believe in God they believe that our transcendent longings should be satisfied by the very objects that occasion them, rejecting out of hand the link between an innate desire and its corresponding object of desire and thereby embracing a literally absurd worldview. Rather than believe in God they believe that mind is nothing but matter in a certain arrangement that just happens to have the (naturalistically inexplicable) qualities of consciousness and intentionality, as well as the capacity to be either true or false. Rather than believe in God they believe that their beliefs give them a true insight into the nature of reality despite being products of a mindless process that moulds behavioural 'black boxes' subject only to the pragmatic requirements of survival. Rather than believe in God they believe that no one is free to rationally investigate the God question (because no one has free will), while simultaneously blaming supernaturalists for supposedly failing to live up to intellectual obligations that can't exist if naturalism is true. Rather than believe in God they believe that there are no objective moral values (while simultaneously condemning the evils of religion); or else they believe that God isn't needed to ground objective value because (*contra* Hume, Moore, Russell, etc.) the fact that some empirically observable states of affairs are good or bad means that good and bad are nothing but empirically observable states of affairs (thereby confusing the 'is' of predication with the 'is' of identity). As Lewis complained: 'We badly need to revive formal logic.'[28] Rather than believe that Jesus is God incarnate, they believe that Jesus probably never existed (despite all the evidence being to the contrary). Rather than believe that Jesus is God incarnate, they believe that all that 'Son of God who rose from the dead' business was made up by Christians far removed from historical ground zero under the influence of pagan mythology (despite all the evidence to the contrary). Rather than believe that Jesus is God incarnate, they believe that even if early Christian beliefs about Jesus did reflect Jesus' own claims, a first-century Jew who sincerely claims to be the divine 'Son of Man' might simply be making an honest mistake!

Having swallowed all this (and far more besides) in order to avoid believing in God, the new atheists have the chutzpah to inform us that theism is, *as a matter of definition*, an irrational 'delusion' held in the teeth of contrary evidence! It's very tempting to regard this assertion (which is itself made in the teeth of evidence to the contrary) as a classic example of psychological 'projection'. It is certainly 'a bit rich' coming from a naturalistic movement busy sawing through the branch of reason upon which it so proudly professes to perch; for as Aldous Huxley (like Lewis) came to see:

> All men of science, whatever their views, consistently act *as though* they believed in the ability of the human intellect, using the method of logic, to make true judgements about the nature of the world. Such is the behaviour even of the Behaviourist. But, according to his own theory, the Behaviourist (like the other disparagers of mind) has no right to behave in this way. If mind is merely an epiphenomenon of matter, if consciousness is completely determined by physical motions, if the intellect is only a machine for securing food and sexual pleasure, then there is absolutely no reason for supposing that any theory produced by this instrument can have universal value. If Behaviourism, for example, is correct,

there is no reason for supposing that the mind can make any kind of valid judgement about the world. But among judgements about the world figures the theory of Behaviourism. Therefore, if Behaviourism is correct, there is no reason for attaching the slightest importance to the opinions, among others, of Behaviourists . . . All who advance theories of mind containing the words 'nothing but,' tend to involve themselves in this kind of contradiction.[29]

C.S. Lewis knew from personal experience that it takes guts to re-evaluate one's worldview and that it takes time to move from one position to another. He wouldn't expect anyone to change their metaphysical outlook on the strength of a single conversation or reading a single book (not even one he'd written himself). However, he would point out the importance of recognizing one's philosophical presuppositions (so as not to beg the question at the outset) and then doggedly heeding the Socratic Club's call to 'follow the argument, wherever it leads':

> Here is a door, behind which, according to some people, the secret of the universe is waiting for you. Either that's true, or it isn't. And if it isn't, then what the door really conceals is simply the greatest fraud, the most colossal 'sell' on record. Isn't it obviously the job of every man . . . to try to find out which, and then to devote his full energies either to serving this tremendous secret or to exposing and destroying this gigantic humbug?[30]

The new atheists give every appearance of being a movement dedicated to 'destroying this gigantic humbug' *despite refusing to give due diligence to the primary task of discovering whether or not it is true.* Instead, as Roy Abraham Varghese observes, they begin with assumptions inimitable to theism and proceed from there:

> In the first place, they refuse to engage the real issues involved in the question of God's existence . . . (Dennett spends seven pages on the arguments for God's existence, Harris none.) They fail to address the issue of the origins of the rationality embedded in the fabric of the universe, of life understood as autonomous agency, and of consciousness, conceptual thought, and the self . . . Second, they show no awareness of the fallacies and muddles that led to

the rise and fall of logical positivism. Those who ignore the mistakes of history will have to repeat them at some point . . . At the foundation of the 'new atheism' is the belief that there is no God . . . This is the key belief that needs to be established for most of the other arguments to work. It is my contention . . . that the 'new atheists' . . . not only fail to make a case for this belief, but ignore the very phenomena that are particularly relevant to the question of whether God exists.[31]

Even more so than in Lewis's day, God is a being whose existence 'many reputable philosophers think they can establish.'[32] I concur with Keith Ward that 'the God conclusion stands firm, and that it is the best intellectual defence of the intelligibility of the cosmos, of the objective importance of our moral ideals, of an affirmation of the goodness, the joy and the beauty of life, and of the authenticity of those intimations of transcendence that provide some of the most sublime and transformative human experiences.'[33] We have examined just those arguments that had the greatest impact upon Lewis, and we've seen that the new atheists generally evince their culpable ignorance of these arguments, or else they fail to respond to the arguments, or they change the subject when confronted with the arguments, or respond to 'straw man' misrepresentations of the arguments, or (despite repeated correction from those who defend these arguments) they make logically fallacious objections to the arguments. Little wonder Alvin Plantinga castigates the new atheists for 'their close-mindedness, their reluctance to consider evidence, and their resort to ridicule, mockery, and misrepresentation in the place of serious argument . . .'[34]

Lewis knew from personal experience that the God question wasn't a merely intellectual pursuit, but a quest that touches upon and is thus affected by every part of one's being:

To believe that God – at least this God – exists is to believe that you as a person now stand in the presence of God as a Person. What would, a moment before, have been variations in opinion, now become variations in your personal attitude to a Person. You are no longer faced with an argument which demands your assent, but with a Person who demands your confidence.[35]

There are certainly motives that pull people towards belief in God (and perhaps these motives reflect our creation in his image), just as there are motives for pushing God away; but debating motives is no substitute for the primary task of doing one's best to 'follow the argument, wherever it leads', as the Socratic Club enjoined. For as Lewis wrote:

> One of the things that distinguishes man from the other animals is that he wants to know things, wants to find out what reality is like, simply for the sake of knowing. When that desire is completely quenched in anyone, I think he has become something less than human . . . Christianity claims to give you an account of the facts – to tell you what the real universe is like. Its account of the universe may be true, or it may not, and once the question is really before you, then your natural inquisitiveness must make you want to know the answer . . . Honest rejection of Christ, however mistaken, will be forgiven and healed – 'Whosoever shall speak a word against the Son of Man, it shall be forgiven him' (Luke 12:10). But to *evade* the Son of Man, to look the other way, to pretend you haven't noticed, to leave the receiver off the telephone because it might be He who is ringing up, to leave unopened certain letters in a strange handwriting because they might be from Him – this is a different matter. You may not be certain yet whether you ought to be a Christian; but you do know you ought to be a man, not an ostrich, hiding its head in the sands.[36]

* * *

Recommended Resources

By C.S. Lewis:
'Man or Rabbit?', in *C.S. Lewis Essay Collection: Faith, Christianity and the Church* (ed. Lesley Walmsley; London: HarperCollins, 2002)
www.merelewis.org/CSL.gitd.1-12.ManOrRabbit.htm.

Selected Resources

A young man who wishes to remain a sound Atheist cannot
be too careful of his reading.

C.S. Lewis

By C.S. Lewis

The Abolition of Man (Grand Rapids, MI: Zondervan, 2001)
www.columbia.edu/cu/augustine/arch/lewis/abolition1. htm#1.
Christian Reflections (ed. Walter Hooper; London: Fount, 1991).
The Chronicles of Narnia (London: HarperCollins, 2002).
The Complete C.S. Lewis Signature Classics (Grand Rapids, MI:
Zondervan, 2007) – contains 'Mere Christianity', 'The
Screwtape Letters', 'The Great Divorce', 'The Problem of Pain',
'Miracles', 'A Grief Observed' and 'The Abolition of Man'.
The Cosmic Trilogy (New York: Tor, 1990).
C.S. Lewis Essay Collection: Faith, Christianity and the Church (ed.
Lesley Walmsley; London: HarperCollins, 2002).
*The Discarded Image: An Introduction to Medieval and Renaissance
Literature* (Cambridge University Press/Canto, 1994).
The Four Loves (London: HarperCollins, 2012).
The Great Divorce (London: HarperCollins, 2012).
Mere Christianity (London: HarperCollins, 2011).
Miracles (London: HarperCollins, 1998).
The Pilgrim's Regress (London: Fount, 1998).
The Problem of Pain (London: HarperCollins, 2012).
Reflections on the Psalms (London: Fount, 1993).
The Screwtape Letters (London: HarperCollins, 2002).
Studies in Words (Cambridge University Press/Canto, 2000).
Surprised by Joy (London: HarperCollins, 2012).

C.S. Lewis Online

Video
'Peter Kreeft on C.S. Lewis'
 www.youtube.com/watch?v=u9-rMbYCOr4&feature=related.
'The Narnian Heavens'
 www.youtube.com/user/thenarnianheavens?feature=watch.

Audio
Kreeft, Peter. 'C.S. Lewis on Truth, Goodness and Beauty'
 www.peterkreeft.com/audio.htm.
— 'Mere Christianity'
 www.peterkreeft.com/audio/14_cslewis-mere-christi
 anity.htm.
— 'The Problem of Pain'
 www.peterkreeft.com/audio/15_cslewis-problem-of-
 pain.htm.
Lewis, C.S. BBC audio clip from 'Beyond Personality'
 www.youtube.com/watch?v=JHxs3gdtV8A.
— 2nd BBC audio clip from 'Beyond Personality'
 www.youtube.com/watch?v=xYoU5_MQOU0&feature=
 related.
— *Mere Christianity*
 www.philvaz.com/CSLewisMereChristianityCOMPLETE
 .mp3.
— *The Problem of Pain*
 www.philvaz.com/CSLewisProblemOfPainCOMPLETE.mp3.
Ward, Michael. 'Planet Narnia'
 http://sptc.htb.org.uk/files/sptc/michael-ward. mp3.
Williams, Peter S., 'C.S. Lewis vs the New Atheists' (Hungry,
 2012).
 www.damaris.org/cm/podcasts/716.
— 'Interview on C.S. Lewis and the New Atheists' (Hungry, 2012)
 www.damaris.org/cm/podcasts/717.
— 'C.S. Lewis vs the New Atheists' (L'abri, 2012)
 www.damaris.org/cm/podcasts/732.

Websites
The C.S. Lewis Foundation
   www.cslewis.org/.
The C.S. Lewis Review
   www.cslewisreview.org/?vm=r.
The C.S. Lewis Society of California
   www.lewissociety.org/index.php.
Into the Wardrobe
   http://cslewis.drzeus.net/.
Steven Lovell. Philosophical Themes from C.S. Lewis
   http://myweb.tiscali.co.uk/annotations/phd_thesis.html.
The New York C.S. Lewis Society
   www.nycslsociety.com.
Oxford C.S. Lewis Society
   http://sites.google.com/site/lewisinoxford/home.
Planet Narnia
   www.planetnarnia.com.
The Question of God
   www.pbs.org/wgbh/questionofgod/.

Books about C.S. Lewis

Baggett, David, Gary R. Habermas and Jerry L. Walls, eds. *C.S. Lewis as Philosopher: Truth, Goodness and Beauty* (Downers Grove, IL: IVP Academic, 2008).

Barkman, Adam. *C.S. Lewis and Philosophy as a Way of Life: A Comprehensive Historical Examination of His Philosophical Thoughts* (Allentown, PA: Zossima, 2009).

Burson, Scott R. and Jerry L. Walls. *C.S. Lewis and Francis Schaeffer: Lessons for a New Century from the Most Influential Apologists of Our Time* (Downers Grove, IL: IVP, 1998).

Carnell, Corbin Scott. *Bright Shadow of Reality: Spiritual Longing in C.S. Lewis* (Cambridge: Eerdmans, 1999).

Carpenter, Humphrey. *The Inklings: C.S. Lewis, J.R.R. Tolkien, Charles Williams and Their Friends* (London: HarperCollins, 2006).

Christensen, Michael. *C.S. Lewis on Scripture* (London: Hodder & Stoughton, 1979).

Downing, David C. *The Most Reluctant Convert: C.S. Lewis's Journey to Faith* (Downers Grove, IL: IVP, 2002).

Heck, Joel D. *Irrigating Deserts: C.S. Lewis on Education* (St Louis: Concordia Academic Press, 2005).

Kreeft, Peter. *Between Heaven and Hell: A Dialog Somewhere beyond Death with John F. Kennedy, C.S. Lewis and Aldous Huxley* (Downers Grove, IL: IVP, 2008).

— *C.S. Lewis for the Third Millennium* (San Francisco: Ignatius, 1990).

MacSwain, Robert, ed. *The Cambridge Companion to C.S. Lewis* (Cambridge University Press, 2010).

Nicholi Jr, Armand M. *The Question of God: C.S. Lewis and Sigmund Freud Debate God, Love, Sex, and the Meaning of Life* (New York: The Free Press, 2002).

Purtill, Richard. *C.S. Lewis' Case for the Christian Faith* (San Francisco: Ignatius, 2004).

Reppert, Victor. *C.S. Lewis's Dangerous Idea: In Defense of the Argument from Reason* (Downers Grove, IL: IVP, 2003).

Vander Elst, Philip. *C.S. Lewis: An Introduction* (London: Continuum, 1996).

Walker, Andrew and James Patrick. *Rumours of Heaven: Essays in Celebration of C.S. Lewis* (Guildford: Eagle, 1998).

Ward, Michael. *The Narnia Code: C.S. Lewis and the Secret of the Seven Heavens* (Milton Keynes, Paternoster, 2010).

— *Planet Narnia: The Seven Heavens in the Imagination of C.S. Lewis* (Oxford University Press, 2008).

West, John G. ed. *The Magician's Twin: C.S. Lewis on Science, Scientism, and Society* (Seattle: Discovery Institute Press, 2012).

Some Old Books Worth Reading

> After reading a book, never . . . allow yourself another new
> one till you have read an old one inbetween.
> C.S. Lewis, 'On the Reading of Old Books'

Alexander, Samuel. *Space, Time and Deity* (1924).

Ayer, A.J. *Language, Truth and Logic* (London: Penguin, 1990).

Balfour, Arthur J. *Theism and Humanism* (Seattle: Inkling Books, 2000).

Caldecott, Alfred and H.R. Mackintosh. *Selections from the Literature of Theism* (New York: T&T Clark, 3rd edn, 1931).

Chesterton, G.K. *Autobiography* (London: House of Stratus, 2001).

— *Eugenics and Other Evils: An Argument against the Scientifically Organized Society* (ed. Michael W. Perry; Seattle: Inkling Books, 2000).

— *The Everlasting Man* (San Francisco: Ignatius, 1993) www.cse.dmu.ac.uk/~mward/gkc/books/everlasting_man.html.

— *Orthodoxy* (Thirsk: House of Stratus, 2001) www.ccel.org/ccel/chesterton/orthodoxy.html.

Clark, R.E.D. *Scientific Rationalism and Christian Faith* (London: InterVarsity Fellowship, 1945).

Copleston, Frederick. *Contemporary Philosophy* (London: Burns & Oates, 1956).

Farrer, Austin. *Love Almighty and Ills Unlimited* (Wm Collins Sons & Co, 1962).

Grahame, Kenneth. *The Wind in the Willows* (Everyman's Library Children's Classics, 1993).

Greenleaf, Simon. *The Testimony of the Evangelists: The Gospels Examined by the Rules of Evidence* (Grand Rapids, MI: Kregel, 1995).

Hammond, T.C. *Reasoning Faith: An Introduction to Christian Apologetics* (London: IVP, 1943).

Hick, John, ed. *The Existence of God* (London: Macmillan, 1964).

Huxley, Aldous. *Ends and Means* (London: Chatto & Windus, 1940).

Joad, C.E.M. *Guide to Modern Thought* (London: Faber, 1933).

— *Guide to Philosophy* (London: Victor Gollancz, 1946).

— *The Recovery of Belief* (London: Faber, 1952).

— *Return to Philosophy* (London: Faber, 1935).

Lewis, H.D. *Philosophy of Religion* (London: The English Universities Press, 1965).

MacDonald, George. *Phantastes: The Annotated 150th Anniversary Edition* (Milton Keynes: Paternoster, 2008).

Maritain, Jacques. *An Introduction to Philosophy* (New York: Continuum, 2005).

Mascall, E.L. *He Who Is: A Study in Traditional Theism* (London: Longmans, Green & Co, 1943).

Morison, Frank. *Who Moved the Stone?* (London: Faber, 1930).

Otto, Rudolf. *The Idea of the Holy* (Oxford University Press, 1968).

Ross, W.D. *The Right and the Good* (Oxford University Press, 1930).

Russell, Bertrand. *The Problems of Philosophy* (Oxford University Press, 1980).

— *Why I Am Not a Christian* (London: Routledge, 1996).

Sorley, W.R. *Moral Values and the Idea of God* (Cambridge University Press, 1921).

Taylor, A.E. *Does God Exist?* (London: Macmillan, 1945).

Tolkien, J.R.R. *The Hobbit/The Lord of the Rings Box Set* (London: HarperCollins, 2010).

Waterhouse, Eric S. *The Philosophical Approach to Religion* (London: The Epworth Press, 1933).

Debates with Neo-Atheists

Craig, William Lane vs Peter Atkins. 'What Is the Evidence for/against the Existence of God?' www.rfmedia.org/av/video/evidence-for-against-the-existence-of-god-craig-vs-atkins/.

— vs A.C. Grayling. 'The Problem of Evil and the Existence of God' www.reasonablefaith.org/site/News2?page=NewsArticle&id=9031.

— vs Sam Harris. 'Is the Foundation for Morality Natural or Supernatural?' www.rfmedia.org/av/video/craig-vs-harris-foundation-of-morality/.

— vs Christopher Hitchens. 'Does God Exist?' www.youtube.com/watch?v=4KBx4vvlbZ8&feature=player_embedded.

— vs Lawrence Krauss. 'Is There Evidence for God?' www.rfmedia.org/av/video/craig-vs-krauss-is-there-evidence-for-god/.

Lennox, John vs Peter Atkins. 'Duelling Professors' www.bigquestions.com/bonus-interviews.

— vs Richard Dawkins. 'Has Science Buried God?' http://cdn.cloudfiles.mosso.com/c114612/audio/2009/LennoxDawkinsOxfordMuseum.mp3.

McGrath, Alister vs Daniel Dennett. 'God and Religion' http://bit.ly/djOCdH.

Plantinga, Alvin vs Daniel Dennett. 'Science and Religion: Are They Compatible?' www.apologetics315.com/2009/02/alvin-plantinga-daniel-dennett-debate.html.

Richards, Jay vs Christopher Hitchens. 'Atheism, Theism and Scientific Evidence of Intelligent Design' (Audio) www.brianauten.com/Apologetics/debate-richards-hitchens.mp3 and (Video) www.youtube.com/watch?v=HnAETv5Ujcc.

Ridley, Matt, Michael Shermer and Richard Dawkins vs David Wolpe, William Lane Craig and Douglas Geivett. 'Does the Universe Have a Purpose?' www.youtube.com/watch?v=p6tIee8FwX8.

Turek, Frank vs Christopher Hitchens. 'Does God Exist?' (Audio) www.philvaz.com/HitchensTurekDebate.mp3.

Books Responding to Neo-Atheism

Copan, Paul and William Lane Craig, eds. *Contending with Christianity's Critics: Answering New Atheists and Other Objectors* (Nashville, TN: B&H Academic, 2009).

Craig, William Lane and Chad Meister, eds. *God Is Good, God Is Great: Why Believing in God Is Reasonable and Responsible* (Downers Grove, IL: IVP, 2009).

Ganssle, Gregory E. *A Reasonable God: Engaging the New Face of Atheism* (Baylor University Press, 2009).

Hart, David Bentley. *Atheist Delusions: The Christian Revolution and Its Fashionable Enemies* (Yale University Press, 2009).

Lennox, John. *Gunning for God: Why the New Atheists are Missing the Target* (Oxford: Lion, 2011).

Marshall, David. *The Truth behind the New Atheism: Responding to the Emerging Challenges to God and Christianity* (Eugene, OR: Harvest House, 2007).

McDowell, Sean and Jonathan Morrow. *Is God Just a Human Invention? And Seventeen Other Questions Raised by the New Atheists* (Grand Rapids, MI: Kregel, 2010).

McGrath, Alister. *Why God Won't Go Away: Engaging with the New Atheism* (London: SPCK, 2011).

Plantinga, Alvin. *Where the Conflict Really Lies: Science, Religion, and Naturalism* (Oxford University Press, 2011).

Ward, Keith. *Why There Almost Certainly Is a God: Doubting Dawkins* (Oxford: Lion, 2008).

Williams, Peter S. *A Sceptic's Guide to Atheism: God Is Not Dead* (Milton Keynes: Paternoster, 2009).

Books on the Philosophy of Religion

Craig, William Lane, ed. *Philosophy of Religion: A Reader and Guide* (Edinburgh University Press, 2002).

Davies, Brian. *An Introduction to the Philosophy of Religion* (Oxford University Press, 3rd edn, 2003).

— *Philosophy of Religion: A Guide and Anthology* (O.U.P., 2000).

Evans, C. Stephen. *Philosophy of Religion: Thinking about Faith* (Downers Grove, IL: IVP, 1982).

Geisler, Norman L. and Winfried Corduan. *Philosophy of Religion* (Eugene, OR: Wipf & Stock, 2003).

Meister, Chad. *Introducing Philosophy of Religion* (London: Routledge, 2009).

Murray, Michael J. and Michael Rea. *An Introduction to the Philosophy of Religion* (Cambridge University Press, 2008).

Taliaferro, Charles. *Contemporary Philosophy of Religion* (Oxford: Blackwell, 2001).

— *Philosophy of Religion* (Oxford: OneWorld, 2009).

Yandell, Keith E. *Philosophy of Religion: A Contemporary Introduction* (London: Routledge, 1999).

Books on God

Alston, William P. *Perceiving God: The Epistemology of Religious Experience* (Ithaca: Cornell University Press, 1991).

Beckwith, Francis J., William Lane Craig and J.P. Moreland, eds. *To Everyone an Answer: A Case for the Christian Worldview* (Downers Grove, IL: IVP, 2004).

Copan, Paul and Paul K. Moser, eds. *The Rationality of Theism* (London: Routledge, 2003).

Craig, William Lane and J.P. Moreland, eds. *The Blackwell Companion to Natural Theology* (Oxford: Wiley-Blackwell, 2009).

— *Naturalism: A Critical Analysis* (London: Routledge, 2000).

Flew, Antony with Roy Abraham Varghese. *There Is a God: How the World's Most Notorious Atheist Changed His Mind* (New York: HarperOne, 2007).

Moreland, J.P. *The Recalcitrant Imago Dei: Human Persons and the Failure of Naturalism* (London: SCM Press, 2009).

— *Scaling the Secular City* (Grand Rapids, MI: Baker, 1987).

— and Kai Nielson. *Does God Exist? The Debate between Theists and Atheists* (New York: Prometheus, 1993).

Nagasawa, Yujin. *The Existence of God: A Philosophical Introduction* (London: Routledge, 2011).

Sennett, James F. and Douglas Groothuis, eds. *In Defense of Natural Theology: A Post-Humean Assessment* (Downers Grove, IL: IVP, 2005).

Books on Jesus

Bauckham, Richard. *Jesus and the Eyewitnesses: The Gospels as Eyewitness Testimony* (Grand Rapids, MI: Eerdmans, 2006).

— *Jesus: A Very Short Introduction* (Oxford University Press, 2011).

Barnett, Paul. *Is the New Testament Reliable?* (Downers Grove, IL: IVP, 2nd edn, 2003).

— *Messiah: Jesus – the Evidence of History* (Nottingham: IVP, 2009).

Beckwith, Francis J., William Lane Craig and J.P. Moreland, eds. *To Everyone an Answer: A Case for the Christian Worldview* (Downers Grove, IL: IVP, 2004).

Blomberg, Craig L. *The Historical Reliability of the Gospels* (Nottingham: Apollos, 2nd edn, 2007).

Davis, Stephen T. *Risen Indeed: Making Sense of the Resurrection* (London: SPCK, 1993).

Evans, Craig A. *Fabricating Jesus: How Modern Scholars Distort the Gospels* (Downers Grove, IL: IVP, 2006).

Geivett, R. Douglas and Gary R. Habermas, eds. *In Defense of Miracles: A Comprehensive Case for God's Action in History* (Leicester: Apollos, 1997).

Habermas, Gary R. *The Historical Jesus: Ancient Evidence for the Life of Christ* (Joplin, MO: College Press, 1996).

—, Antony G.N. Flew and Terry L. Miethe. *Did Jesus Rise from the Dead? The Resurrection Debate* (Eugene, OR: Wipf & Stock, 1987).

Hill, C.E. *Who Chose the Gospels? Probing the Great Gospel Conspiracy* (Oxford University Press, 2010).

Hurtado, Larry W. *How on Earth Did Jesus Become a God? Historical Questions about Earliest Devotion to Jesus* (Grand Rapids, MI: Eerdmans, 2005).

Komoszewski, J. Ed, M. James Sawyer and Daniel B. Wallace. *Reinventing Jesus: How Contemporary Skeptics Miss the Real Jesus and Mislead Popular Culture* (Grand Rapids, MI: Kregel, 2006).

Licona, Michael R. *The Resurrection of Jesus: A New Historiographical Approach* (Nottingham: Apollos, 2010).

Moreland, J.P. *The God Question: An Invitation to a Life of Meaning* (Eugene, OR: Harvest House, 2009).

Overman, Dean L. *A Case for the Divinity of Jesus: Examining the Earliest Evidence* (Plymouth: Rowman & Littlefield, 2009).

Roberts, Mark D. *Can We Trust the Gospels? Investigating the Reliability of Matthew, Mark, Luke, and John* (Wheaton, IL: Crossway, 2007).

Strobel, Lee. *The Case for the Real Jesus* (Grand Rapids, MI: Zondervan, 2007).

Swinburne, Richard. *The Resurrection of God Incarnate* (Oxford: Clarendon Press, 2003).

— *Was Jesus God?* (Oxford University Press, 2008).

Wilkins, Michael J. and J.P. Moreland. *Jesus under Fire: Modern Scholarship Reinvents the Historical Jesus* (Grand Rapids, MI: Zondervan, 1995).

Willard, Dallas. *Knowing Christ Today: Why We Can Trust Spiritual Knowledge* (New York: HarperOne, 2009).

Williams, Peter S. *Understanding Jesus: Five Ways to Spiritual Enlightenment* (Milton Keynes: Paternoster, 2011).

Wright, N.T. *The Resurrection of the Son of God* (London: SPCK, 2003).

Peter S. Williams

Online

Evangelical Philosophical Society Profile
  http://epsociety.org/library/authors.asp?mode=profile&
  pid=37.
ID.Plus Blog
  http://idpluspeterswilliams.blogspot.com/.
Peter S. Williams' Podcast Channel
  www.damaris.org/cm/podcasts/category/peterswilliams.

Books

The Case for God (Crowborough: Monarch, 1999).
The Case for Angels (Carlisle: Paternoster, 2002).
I Wish I Could Believe in Meaning: A Response to Nihilism
  (Southampton: Authentic/Damaris, 2004).
A Sceptic's Guide to Atheism: God Is Not Dead (Milton Keynes,
  Paternoster, 2009).
Understanding Jesus: Five Ways to Spiritual Enlightenment (Milton
  Keynes, Paternoster, 2011).
*A Faithful Guide to Philosophy: A Christian Introduction to the Love of
  Wisdom* (Milton Keynes, Paternoster, 2013).

Notes

Chapter 1: Old-Time Atheism

[1] Frank Skinner, 'The NS Interview', *New Statesman*, 21 March 2011, p. 32.

[2] 'Obituary', *The Economist*, 23 December 1999, cf. www.econo-mist.com/node/347578?Story_ID=347578&CFID=168562596&CFTO KEN=60221445.

[3] John Micklethwait and Adrian Wooldridge, *God Is Back: How the Global Rise of Faith Is Changing the World* (London: Allen Lane, 2009), p. 194.

[4] Dinesh D'Souza, *What's So Great about Christianity* (Washington: Regnery, 2007), p. 1.

[5] Timothy J. Keller, 'Reason for God', in *A Place for Truth: Leading Thinkers Explore Life's Hardest Questions* (ed. Dallas Willard; Downers Grove, IL: IVP, 2010), p. 56.

[6] 'Leader: Keepers of the Faith', *New Statesman*, 15 July 2010, p. 5.

[7] Alister McGrath, 'The Spell of the Meme' www.st-edmunds.cam.ac.uk/faraday/issues/McGrath%20RSA%20Lecture%2013-03-06.pdf.

[8] David Fergusson, *Faith and Its Critics: A Conversation* (OUP, 2011), p. 7.

[9] A.C. Grayling, 'Science and Faith before Darwin', in *The Form of Things: Essays on Life, Ideas and Liberty in the 21st Century* (London: Weidenfeld & Nicolson, 2006), p. 132.

[10] Michel Onfray, *In Defence of Atheism: The Case against Christianity, Judaism and Islam* (London: Serpent's Tail, 2007), p. 37.

[11] D'Souza, *What's So Great about Christianity*, p. 21.

[12] Gary Wolf, 'The Church of the Non-Believers', *Wired* magazine, November 2006, p. 184 www.wired.com/wired/archive/14.11/athe-ism.html.

[13] C.S. Lewis, *Surprised by Joy* (London: Fount, 1998), p. 82.

14 Alister McGrath, *Why God Won't Go Away: Engaging with the New Atheism* (London: SPCK, 2011), p. 3.

15 Keith Ward, *Is Religion Irrational?* (Oxford: Lion, 2011), p. 6. On the question of whether Christmas is merely a myth, cf. Charles Foster, *The Christmas Mystery: What on Earth Happened at Bethlehem?* (Milton Keynes: Authentic Media, 2007); Mark Kidger, *The Star of Bethlehem: An Astroomer's View* (Princeton University Press, 1999); Peter May, 'The Star of Bethlehem' www.bethinking.org/bible-jesus/beginner/the-star-of-bethlehem.htm; Michael R. Molnar, *The Star of Bethlehem: The Legacy of the Magi* (Rutgers University Press, 2000); John Redford, *Born of a Virgin: Proving the Miracle from the Gospels* (London: St Pauls, 2007); Peter S. Williams, 'The Nativity and the Star' www.damaris.org /cm/podcasts/757.

16 C.S. Lewis, 'The Decline of Religion', in *C.S. Lewis Essay Collection: Faith, Christianity and the Church* (ed. Lesley Walmsley; London: HarperCollins, 2002), pp. 182–3.

17 Christopher Jervis, *Philosophy, Science and the God Debate* (The Nationwide Christian Trust, 2011).

18 'Rethinking Failure' http://oxfordstudent.com/2010/11/25/rethinking-failure-2/.

19 Christopher Hitchens, *The Quotable Hitchens* (ed. Windsor Mann; Cambridge, MA: Da Capo, 2011), p. 211.

20 Keith Ward, *Why There Almost Certainly Is a God: Doubting Dawkins* (Oxford: Lion, 2008), p. 8.

21 That is, R.M. Dawkins, Professor of Byzantine and Modern Greek, who was part of the 'Coalbiter' society formed by J.R.R. Tolkien in 1926 to promote the reading of Old Icelandic sagas and myths. C.S. Lewis was likewise a member.

22 cf. Clive Hamilton, *Spirits in Bondage* www.fullbooks.com/Spirits-in-Bondage.html.

23 Lewis, *Surprised by Joy*, p. 4.

24 Quoted by David C. Downing, *The Most Reluctant Convert: C.S. Lewis's Journey to Faith* (Downers Grove, IL: IVP, 2002), p. 49.

25 Quoted by Downing, *Reluctant Convert*, p. 23.

26 cf. Downing, *Reluctant Convert*, p. 21.

27 Quoted by Downing, *Reluctant Convert*, p. 40.

28 C.S. Lewis, *The Pilgrim's Regress* (London: Fount, 1977), p. 30.

29 Lewis, *Surprised by Joy*, pp. 13, 15.

30 ibid., p. 15.

31 ibid., p. 46.

32 ibid., pp. 46–7.

33 C.S. Lewis, *Letters* (London: Fount, 1988), p. 136.

34 Philip Vander Elst, *C.S. Lewis: A Short Introduction* (London: Continuum, 1996), p. 5.

35 Lewis, *Surprised by Joy*, pp. 105, 107.

36 C.S. Lewis, quoted by Downing, *Reluctant Convert*, p. 11.

37 Downing, *Reluctant Convert*, pp. 49–50.

38 Lewis, *Surprised by Joy*, p. 49.

39 C.S. Lewis, letter to Arthur Greeves, 12 October 1916, *Letters* (London: Fount, 1988), p. 52.

40 Lewis, letter to Arthur Greeves, 12 October 1916, *Letters*, p. 52.

41 Lewis, *Surprised by Joy*, p. 159.

42 Quoted by Downing, *Reluctant Convert*, p. 11.

43 ibid., p. 58.

44 C.S. Lewis, *All My Road before Me: The Diary of C.S. Lewis* (ed. Walter Hooper; London: Harvest, 1991), p. 332.

45 Lewis, *Surprised by Joy*, p. 134.

46 Lewis, *All My Road*, pp. 345–6, my italics.

47 Richard Dawkins, 'The Ultraviolet Garden', Royal Institution Christmas Lecture no. 4, 1991.

48 Lewis, *All My Road*, p. 361.

49 Lewis, letter to Arthur Greeves, 12 October 1916, *Letters*, p. 52.

50 Lewis, *Surprised by Joy*, p. 47.

51 Richard Norman, 'Holy Communion', *New Humanist*, November-December 2007, pp. 16–17.

52 Rabbi Moshe Averick, *Nonsense of a High Order: The Confused and Illusory World of the Atheist* (Chicago: Tradition & Reason, 2010), p. 5.

53 Kenneth D. Boa and Robert M. Bowman Jr, *Faith Has Its Reasons: An Integrative Approach to Defending Christianity* (Milton Keynes: Paternoster, 2006), p. 54.

54 cf. Michael Ward, *The Narnia Code: C.S. Lewis and the Secret of the Seven Heavens* (Milton Keynes: Paternoster, 2010).

55 David Van Biema, 'Religion: Beyond the Wardrobe', *Time* magazine, 30 October 2005.

56 A.N. Wilson, *C.S. Lewis: A Biography* (London: Flamingo, 1991), p. 191.

57 Richard Dawkins, *The God Delusion* (London: Black Swan, 2007), p. 13.

58 Mortimer J. Adler, 'A Philosopher's Religious Faith', in *Philosophers Who Believe: The Spiritual Journeys of 11 Leading Thinkers* (ed. Kelly James Clark; Downers Grove, IL: IVP, 1993).

[59] Charles Colson interview www.youtube.com/watch?v=S-FlqZ8-EhGc.

[60] Interview with Francis S. Collins www.youtube.com/watch?v=Ml0-FqyFYfrU&feature=related.

[61] William Lane Craig's testimony www.bethinking.org/resources/william-lane-craigs-testimony.htm.

[62] cf. C.E.M. Joad, *The Recovery of Belief* (London: Faber, 1952).

[63] Peter Hitchens, *The Rage against God* (London: Continuum, 2010).

[64] cf. Peter Van Invagen, 'Quam Dilecta', in *God and the Philosophers: The Reconciliation of Faith and Reason* (ed. Thomas V. Morris; OUP, 1994).

[65] Alister McGrath and Richard Dawkins www.philvaz.com/McGrathDawkinsGod.mp3.

[66] Anne Rice on her return to faith in Christ www.youtube.com/watch?v=qAMOlSpKTmo&feature=related. See also ABC News Interview www.youtube.com/watch?v=l5Wb5CnYrmA.

[67] cf. Lee Strobel, 'Testimony' www.leestrobel.com/videoserver/video.php?clip=strobelT1026.

[68] 'Profile: Fay Weldon', *Christianity*, January 2012 www.christianity-magazine.co.uk/Browse%20By%20Category/features/ProfileFayWeldon.aspx.

[69] A.N. Wilson, 'Why I Believe Again', *The New Statesman*, 2 April 2009 www.newstatesman.com/religion/2009/04/conversion-experience-atheism; A.N. Wilson, 'Religion of Hatred: Why We Should No Longer Be Cowed by the Chattering Classes Ruling Britain Who Sneer at Christianity', *Daily Mail*, 11 April 2009 www.dailymail.co.uk/news/article-1169145/Religion-hatred-Why-longer-cowed-secular-zealots.html.

[70] Richard Dawkins, *The God Delusion* (London: Bantam, 2006), pp. 5–6.

[71] ibid., p. 6.

[72] Richard Dawkins www.philvaz.com/McGrathDawkinsGod.mp3.

[73] C.S. Lewis, *The Cosmic Trilogy* (London: Pan, 1989), p. 403.

[74] Sam Harris, 'The Strange Case of Francis Collins' www.project-reason.org/archive/item/the_strange_case_of_francis_collins2/.

[75] Henry F. Schaefer, *Science and Christianity: Conflict or Coherence?* (Athens, GA: The University of Georgia, 2003), p. 34.

[76] William D. Phillips, back cover endorsement, Francis Collins, *The Language of God* (New York: Free Press, 2006).

[77] Sam Harris, *The Moral Landscape: How Science Can Determine Human Values* (London: Bantam, 2011), p. 160.

[78] Sam Harris, 'War on Weak-Tea Christians', *New Statesman*, 18 April 2011, p. 37.

79 Francis Collins, *The Language of God: A Scientist Presents Evidence for Belief* (New York: Free Press, 2006), p. 21.

80 Harris, *Moral Landscape*, p. 162.

81 Collins, *Language of God*, p. 21.

82 ibid.

83 ibid.

84 Victor J. Stenger, *The New Atheism: Taking a Stand for Science and Reason* (New York: Prometheus, 2009), p. 77.

85 ibid.

86 Downing, *Reluctant Convert*, p. 124.

87 Joel D. Heck, *Irrigating Deserts* (St Louis: Concordia Academic Press, 2005), p. 84.

88 Basil Mitchell, 'Reflections on C.S. Lewis', in *Rumours of Heaven: Essays in Celebration of C.S. Lewis* (ed. Andrew Walker and James Patrick; Guildford: Eagle, 1998), p. 14.

89 Roger Lancelyn Green and Walter Hooper, *C.S. Lewis: A Biography* (London: HarperCollins, rev. edn, 2003), p. 76.

90 Stenger, *New Atheism*, p. 77.

91 Tom Morris, Foreword, *C.S. Lewis as Philosopher: Truth, Goodness and Beauty* (ed. David Baggett, Gary R. Habermas and Jerry L. Walls; Downers Grove, IL: IVP Academic, 2008), p. 9.

92 C. Stephen Layman, 'Faith Has Its Reasons', in *God and the Philosophers* (ed. Morris), p. 89.

93 Norman L. Geisler, *Baker Encyclopedia of Christian Apologetics* (Grand Rapids, MI: Baker, 1999), p. 420.

94 ibid.

95 Mitchell, 'Reflections on C.S. Lewis', p. 14.

96 Victor Reppert, *C.S. Lewis's Dangerous Idea: In Defense of the Argument from Reason* (Downers Grove, IL: IVP, 2003), p. 12.

97 Adam Barkman, *C.S. Lewis and Philosophy as a Way of Life: A Comprehensive Historical Examination of His Philosophical Thoughts* (Allentown, PA: Zossima, 2009), p. 532.

98 Robert MacSwain, Introduction, *The Cambridge Companion to C.S. Lewis* (CUP, 2010), p. 2.

99 C.S. Lewis, 'Answers to Questions on Christianity', in *C.S. Lewis Essay Collection*, p. 327.

100 Richard Harris, *C.S. Lewis: The Man and His God* (London: Fount, 1987), p. 11.

101 Richard Purtill, *C.S. Lewis' Case for the Christian Faith* (San Francisco: Ignatius, 2004), p. 10.

[102] Van Invagen, 'Quam Dilecta', p. 33.

[103] Mary Midgely www.lewisiana.nl/marymidgley/.

[104] ibid.

[105] C.E.M. Joad, *The Recovery of Belief* (London: Faber, 1952), p. 81.

[106] 'National Review's 100 Best Non-Fiction Books of the Century', www.librarything.com/bookaward/National+Review's+100+Best+Nonfiction+Books+of+the+Century.

[107] Terry L. Miethe, *C.S. Lewis' Miracles* (Nashville, TN: Broadman & Holman, 2000), p. 9.

[108] Miethe, *C.S. Lewis' Miracles*, p. 9.

[109] Jerry L. Walls, Introduction, *C.S. Lewis as Philosopher* (ed. Baggett, Habermas and Walls), p. 17.

[110] Craig J. Hazen, 'My Pilgrimage from Atheism to Theism: An Exclusive Interview with Former British Atheist Professor Antony Flew' www.biola.edu/antonyflew/flew-interview.pdf.

[111] Antony Flew, *God and Philosophy* (London: Hutchinson, 1974), p. 47 (see also p. 55).

[112] Flew in 'My Pilgrimage from Atheism to Theism'.

[113] Antony Flew, *There Is a God* (New York: HarperOne, 2007), p. 23.

[114] ibid., pp. 22–3.

[115] ibid., p. 23.

[116] Walls, Introduction, *C.S. Lewis as Philosopher*, p. 15.

[117] Flew, *There Is a God*, p. 25.

[118] Antony Flew, 'From Atheism to Deism', in *C.S. Lewis as Philosopher* (ed. Baggett, Habermas and Walls), p. 38.

[119] Flew, *There Is a God*, p. 24.

[120] Thomas D. Williams, *Greater Than You Think: A Theologian Answers the Atheists about God* (New York: Faith Words, 2008), p. xii.

[121] Christopher Hitchens, *God Is Not Great: The Case against Religion* (London: Atlantic Books, 2007), p. 119.

[122] Mary Midgely www.lewisiana.nl/marymidgley/.

[123] C.S. Lewis, Preface to the third edition, *The Pilgrim's Regress* (London: Fount, 3rd edn, 1977).

[124] Vander Elst, *C.S. Lewis: A Short Introduction*, p. 14.

Chapter 2: The Positively Blunt Sword of Scientism

[1] H.D. Lewis, *Philosophy of Religion* (London: English Universities Press, 1965), p. 70.

[2] C.S. Lewis, 'Is Theology Poetry?', in *C.S. Lewis Essay Collection: Faith, Christianity and the Church* (ed. Lesley Walmsley; London: HarperCollins, 2002), p. 13.

[3] C.S. Lewis, *All My Road before Me: The Diary of C.S. Lewis* (ed. Walter Hooper; London: Harvest, 1991), p. 281.

[4] Bertrand Russell, 'A Free Man's Worship' www.philosophicalsociety.com/Archives/A%20Free%20Man's%20Worship.htm.

[5] C.S. Lewis, 'De Futilitate', in *Christian Reflections* (ed. Walter Hooper; London: Fount, 1991), p. 82.

[6] W.B. Provine, 'Darwinism: Science or Naturalistic Philosophy?', *Origins Research* 16:1 (1994): p. 9.

[7] Peter Atkins, *On Being* (OUP, 2011), p. 100.

[8] Richard John Neuhaus, 'Is There Life after Truth?', in *A Place for Truth: Leading Thinkers Explore Life's Hardest Questions* (ed. Dallas Willard; Downers Grove, IL: IVP, 2010), p. 34.

[9] Steven Weinberg, *The First Three Minutes*, quoted by Frank Miele, 'Darwin's Dangerous Disciple: An Interview with Richard Dawkins', *Skeptic* 3:4, 1995.

[10] Richard Dawkins in Frank Miele, 'Darwin's Dangerous Disciple: An Interview with Richard Dawkins', ibid.

[11] ibid.

[12] A.C. Grayling, 'The Meaning of Life: What Is It?', in *Thinking of Answers: Questions in the Philosophy of Everyday Life* (London: Bloomsbury, 2011), p. 325.

[13] Terry Eagleton, *The Meaning of Life: A Very Short Introduction* (OUP, 2008), p. 76.

[14] André Comte-Sponville, *The Book of Atheist Spirituality* (London: Bantam, 2008), p. 51.

[15] Richard Dawkins, 'Is Science a Religion?', *The Humanist*, January-February 1997, p. 27.

[16] Richard Dawkins, 'Science and God: A Warming Trend?', *Science* 277 (1997): p. 892.

[17] C.S. Lewis, *The Personal Heresy: A Controversy* (London: OUP, 1965), pp. 29–30.

[18] C.S. Lewis, *Surprised by Joy* (London: Fount, 1998), p. 132.

[19] Jacques Maritain, *Scholasticism and Politics* (New York: Image, 1960), p. 46.

[20] Edgar Andrews, *Who Made God? Searching for a Theory of Everything* (Carlisle: EP, 2009), p. 9.

[21] William Lane Craig, 'Theism Defended', in *The Nature of Nature: Examining the Role of Naturalism in Science* (ed. Bruce L. Gordon and William A. Dembski; Wilmington, DE: ISI, 2011), p. 901.

[22] A.J. Ayer, *Language, Truth and Logic* (London: Victor Gollancz, 1946), p. 115.

[23] F.C. Copleston, *Contemporary Philosophy* (London: Burns & Oates, 1957), p. 9.

[24] Peter Hitchens, *The Rage against God* (London: Continuum, 2010), pp. 11, 12, 31–2.

[25] H.D. Lewis, *Philosophy of Religion*, p. 131.

[26] Richard Dawkins, *The God Delusion* (London: Bantam, 2006), pp. 46, 48.

[27] ibid., p. 361.

[28] See Peter S. Williams, 'Design and the Humean Touchstone' www.arn.org/docs/williams/pw_humeantouchstone.htm.

[29] Dawkins, *God Delusion*, p. 59.

[30] William Lane Craig, 'Naturalism and Intelligent Design', in *Intelligent Design: William A. Dembski and Michael Ruse in Dialogue* (ed. Robert B. Stewart; Minneapolis, MN: Fortress, 2007), pp. 70–71.

[31] Copleston, *Contemporary Philosophy*, p. 9.

[32] ibid., p. 175.

[33] Victor Reppert, *C.S. Lewis's Dangerous Idea* (Downers Grove, IL: IVP, 2003), p. 20.

[34] Craig, 'Theism Defended', p. 902.

[35] Kai Nielsen, 'Naturalistic Explanations of Theistic Belief', in *A Companion to the Philosophy of Religion* (Oxford: Blackwell, 1999), p. 402.

[36] Luke Muehlhauser, 'The Renaissance of Christian Philosophy' http://commonsenseatheism.com/?p=6448.

[37] Antony Flew, 'Theology and Falsification', in *The Existence of God* (ed. John Hick; London: Collier, 1964), pp. 226–7.

[38] Antony Flew with Roy Abraham Varghese, *There Is a God* (New York: HarperOne, 2007), pp. 44–5.

[39] ibid.

[40] ibid., pp. 45–6.

41 ibid., p. 43.

42 ibid.

43 Flew, 'Theology and Falsification', p. 226.

44 John Hick, 'Theology and Verification', in *The Philosophy of Religion* (ed. Basil Mitchell; OUP, 1971), p. 71.

45 ibid., p. 69.

46 Basil Mitchell, 'Reflections on C.S. Lewis, Apologetics, and the Moral Tradition: Basil Mitchell in Conversation with Andrew Walker', in *Rumours of Heaven: Essays in Celebration of C.S. Lewis* (ed. Andrew Walker and James Patrick; Guildford: Eagle, 1998), p. 19.

47 William Lane Craig, *Philosophy of Religion: A Reader and Guide* (Edinburgh University Press, 2002), p. 1.

48 Alvin Plantinga, *God and Other Minds* (Cornell University Press, 1967), p. 271.

49 cf. Alvin Plantinga, 'The Ontological Argument' www.lastseminary .com/ontological-argument/Plantinga%20-%20The%20 Ontological%20Argument.pdf; Peter S. Williams 'The Ontological Argument', www.damaris.org/cm/podcasts/231.

50 Roger Scruton, *An Intelligent Person's Guide to Philosophy* (London: Duckworth, 1997), p. 93.

51 R. Douglas Geivett, 'The Evidential Value of Religious Experience', in *The Rationality of Theism* (ed. Paul Copan and Paul K. Moser; London: Routledge, 2003), p. 175.

52 Craig, 'Theism Defended', p. 902.

53 William P. Alston, 'Religious Language and Verificationism', in *Rationality of Theism* (ed. Copan and Moser), p. 21.

54 A.J. Ayer, quoted by Keith Ward, *The Turn of the Tide* (London: BBC Publications, 1986), p. 59.

55 A.J. Ayer, *The Central Questions of Philosophy* (London: Penguin, 1973), p. 34.

56 A.J. Ayer in *Great Thinkers on Great Questions* (ed. Roy Abraham Varghese; Oxford: Oneworld, 2009), p. 49.

57 Hugh J. McCann, 'The Case for Free Will', in *Analytic Philosophy without Naturalism* (ed. Antonella Corrandini, Sergio Galvan and E. Jonathan Lowe; London: Routledge, 2010), p. 240.

58 Craig, 'Theism Defended', p. 902.

59 Hilary Spurling, 'The Wickedest Man in Oxford' www.nytimes.com/ books/00/12/24/reviews/001224.24spurlit.html.

60 C.S. Lewis, *The Problem of Pain* (London: Fount, 2002), p. 134.

[61] C.S. Lewis, *The Collected Letters of C.S. Lewis*, vol. III (HarperCollins, 2007), p. 540, quoted by Adam Barkman, *C.S. Lewis and Philosophy as a Way of Life* (Allentown, PA: Zossima, 2009), p. 204.

[62] C.S. Lewis, *Miracles* (London: Fount, 1998), p. 75.

[63] C.S. Lewis, 'The Language of Religion', in *C.S. Lewis Essay Collection: Faith, Christianity and the Church* (ed. Lesley Walmsley; London: HarperCollins, 2002), p. 266.

[64] ibid., p. 255.

[65] ibid.

[66] ibid., p. 265.

[67] ibid., p. 256.

[68] Lewis, *Miracles*, pp. 74–5.

[69] ibid., p. 81.

[70] Humphrey Carpenter, *The Inklings* (London: HarperCollins, 2006), pp. 41–2.

[71] Lewis, 'Language of Religion', p. 255.

[72] ibid., p. 262.

[73] ibid., p. 263.

[74] ibid.

[75] ibid.

[76] ibid., pp. 260–61.

[77] Lewis, 'Is Theology Poetry?', p. 18.

[78] Stephen Hawking and Leonard Mlodinow, *The Grand Design: New Answers to the Ultimate Questions of Life* (London: Bantam, 2010), p. 5.

[79] Lewis, 'De Futilitate', p. 85.

[80] William Lane Craig www.reasonablefaith.org/site/News2?page=NewsArticle&id=5352.

[81] Bruce Sheiman, *An Atheist Defends Religion: Why Humanity Is Better Off With Religion Than Without It* (New York: Alpha, 2009), p. 154.

[82] Michael Novak, 'Lonely Atheists of the Global Village' www.aei.org/article/society-and-culture/religion/lonely-atheists-of-the-global-village/.

[83] Randy Everist, 'Can Science Explain Everything?' http://randy-everist.blogspot.com/2011/04/can-science-explain-everything.html.

[84] Lawrence Krauss, debate with William Lane Craig 2011, cf. http://winteryknight.wordpress.com/2011/03/30/audio-and-video-from-the-debate-between-william-lane-craig-and-lawrence-krauss/.

[85] William Lane Craig, debate with Lawrence Krauss, 2011, cf. http://winteryknight.wordpress.com/2011/03/30/audio-and-video-from-the-debate-between-william-lane-craig-and-lawrence-krauss/.

[86] William Lane Craig, *Reasonable Faith Podcast*, 12 June 2011.

[87] Francis Collins, *The Language of God* (New York: Free Press, 2006), p. 229.

[88] cf. 'Modernizing the Case for God', *Time* magazine www.time.com/time/magazine/article/0,9171,921990,00.html.

[89] J.P. Moreland, *Love God with All Your Mind: The Role of Reason in the Life of the Soul* (Colorado Springs: NavPress, 1997), pp. 144–5.

[90] Victor J. Stenger, *The New Atheism: Taking a Stand for Science and Reason* (New York: Prometheus, 2009), pp. 238–9.

[91] Harry Kroto, *The Times*, 7 April 2011, p. 10, my italics.

[92] Peter Atkins www.ideacenter.org/contentmgr/showdetails.php/id/1461.

[93] Atkins, *On Being*, p. xiii, my italics.

[94] Stephen Hawking and Leonard Mlodinow, *The Grand Design: New Answers To The Ultimate Questions of Life* (London: Bantam, 2010), p. 5.

[95] Richard Dawkins, *A Devil's Chaplain* (London: Weidenfeld & Nicolson, 2003), p. 242.

[96] ibid.

[97] ibid.

[98] Richard Dawkins, *Conversations on Religion* (ed. Mike Gordon and Chris Wilkinson; London: Continuum, 2008), p. 120.

[99] Richard Dawkins, *The Magic of Reality: How We Know What's Really True* (London: Bantam, 2011), pp. 16, 19.

[100] Dawkins, *Conversations on Religion*, p. 120.

[101] Dawkins, *Devil's Chaplain*, p. 248.

[102] Richard Dawkins, *Daily Telegraph*, 31 August 1993.

[103] Stenger, *New Atheism*, p. 21.

[104] ibid., pp. 15, 45.

[105] Moreland, *Love God*, pp. 146–8.

[106] Del Ratzsch, 'Science and Design' www.galilean-library.org/ratzsch.html.

[107] Robert C. Koons, 'Science and Theism: Concord, Not Conflict', in *Rationality of Theism* (ed. Copan and Moser), pp. 76–7.

[108] Sam Harris, *Letter to a Christian Nation* (London: Bantam, 2007), p. 33.

[109] ibid.

[110] ibid., p. 67.

[111] G.K. Chesterton, 'A Plea for Popular Philosophy', in *Prophet of Orthodoxy: The Wisdom of G.K. Chesterton* (ed. Russell Sparkes; London: Fount, 1997), p. 128.

[112] C.S. Lewis, 'Why I Am Not a Pacifist', in *C.S. Lewis Essay Collection*, p. 282.

[113] Sam Harris, *The Moral Landscape: How Science Can Determine Human Values* (London: Bantam, 2011), p. 37.

[114] J.P. Moreland, *Christianity and the Nature of Science* (Grand Rapids, MI: Baker, 1998), p. 107.

[115] Andrews, *Who Made God?*, p. 9.

[116] Augustine, *Concerning Faith in Things Not Seen*, quoted by Sean McDowell and Jonathan Morrow, *Is God Just a Human Invention? And Seventeen Other Questions Raised by the New Atheists* (Grand Rapids, MI: Kregel, 2010), p. 23.

[117] John Lennox, *Gunning for God: Why the New Atheists Are Missing the Target* (Oxford: Lion, 2011), p. 56.

[118] Stenger, *New Atheism*, pp. 15, 45.

[119] Christopher Hitchens, *Hitchens vs Blair: Is Religion a Force for Good in the World?* (ed. Rudyard Griffiths; London: Black Swan, 2011), p. 25.

[120] Grayling, *Conversations on Religion* (ed. Gordon and Wilkinson), p. 3.

[121] Daniel Dennett, 'Is Religion a Threat to Rationality and Science?' http://richarddawkins.net/article,2498,Is-religion-a-threat-to-rationality-and-science,Dan-Dennett-Lord-Winston.

[122] Richard Dawkins, *The Selfish Gene* (Oxford Paperbacks, 1989), p. 198.

[123] Dawkins, *God Delusion*, pp. 286, 308, my italics.

[124] Richard Norman, 'Holy Communion', *New Humanist*, November-December 2007, p. 17.

[125] Richard Dawkins, quoted by Norman, 'Holy Communion', p. 17.

[126] C.S. Lewis, *An Experiment in Criticism* (CUP/Canto, 2000), p. 19.

[127] A.C. Grayling, 'Aiming for the Good', in *The Form of Things: Essays of Life, Ideas and Liberty in the 21st Century* (London: Weidenfeld & Nicolson, 2006), p. 6.

[128] Sam Harris, *The End of Faith: Religion, Terror, and the Future of Reason* (London: Free Press, 2006), p. 64.

[129] Harris, *End of Faith*, p. 64.

[130] C.S. Lewis, *Studies in Words* (CUP/Canto, 2000), pp. 5, 11.

[131] Harris, *End of Faith*, p. 65.

[132] A.C. Grayling, 'Humanism and Religion', in *The Form of Things*, p. 123.

[133] A.C. Grayling, 'Science and Rationality', in *Thinking of Answers*, p. 112.

[134] cf. Michael R. Licona, *The Resurrection of Jesus: A New Historiographical Approach* (Nottingham: IVP/Apollos, 2010); Timothy McGrew and Lydia McGrew, 'The Argument from Miracles: A Cumulative Case for the Resurrection of Jesus of Nazareth' www.lydiamcgrew.com /Resurrectionarticlesinglefile.pdf; Richard Swinburne, *The Resurrection of God Incarnate* (Oxford: Clarendon, 2003); N.T. Wright, *The Resurrection of the Son of God* (London: SPCK, 2003).

[135] Roger Steer, *Letter to an Influential Atheist* (Carlisle: Authentic Lifestyle/Paternoster, 2003), pp. 137–8.

[136] My italics in all biblical quotations above.

[137] Alister McGrath, *Dawkins' God* (Oxford: Blackwell, 2005), pp. 91, 99.

[138] Alister McGrath, *Why God Won't Go Away: Engaging with the New Atheism* (London: SPCK, 2011), p. 26.

[139] Keith M. Parsons, 'Atheism: Twilight or Dawn?', in *The Future of Atheism: Alister McGrath and Daniel Dennett in Dialogue* (ed. Robert B. Stewart; London: SPCK, 2008), p. 61.

[140] Norman, 'Holy Communion', p. 18.

[141] J.P. Moreland, *The Kingdom Triangle* (Grand Rapids, MI: Zondervan, 2007), pp. 130–31.

[142] J.P. Moreland, 'Living Smart', in *Passionate Conviction* (ed. Paul Copan and William Lane Craig; Nashville, TN: B&H Academic, 2007), p. 22.

[143] C.S. Lewis, 'Is Theism Important?', in *C.S. Lewis Essay Collection*, p. 54.

[144] ibid., p. 55.

[145] ibid.

[146] C.S. Lewis, 'Religion: Reality or Substitute?', in *C.S. Lewis Essay Collection*, p. 135.

[147] ibid., pp. 121–2.

[148] ibid., pp. 123–4.

[149] ibid. pp. 136–7.

[150] Lewis, 'Is Theism Important?', p. 55.

[151] Sean McDowell and Jonathan Morrow, *Is God Just a Human Invention? And Seventeen Other Questions Raised by the New Atheists* (Grand Rapids, MI: Kregel, 2010), p. 21.

[152] Lewis, 'Is Theism Important?', p. 57.

Chapter 3: A Desire for Divinity?

1 A.C. Grayling, *The Good Book: A Secular Bible*, Genesis 13:2 (London: Bloomsbury, 2011).

2 Augustine, *Confessions* (Oxford Paperbacks, 1998), pp. 22–3.

3 ibid., p. 201.

4 http://en.wikiquote.org/wiki/Augustine_of_Hippo.

5 John Haldane, *Atheism and Theism* (Oxford: Blackwell, 2nd edn, 2003), pp. 247–8.

6 Peter Kreeft, *Heaven: The Heart's Deepest Longing* (San Francisco: Ignatius, 1989), p. 201.

7 Phil Fernandes, 'The Absurdity of Life without God', in *The Big Argument: Does God Exist?* (ed. John Ashton and Michael Westacott; Green Forest, AZ: Master Books, 2006), p. 385.

8 C.S. Lewis, *The Problem of Pain* (London: Fount, 1977), p. 118.

9 J.R.R. Tolkien, *The Return of the King* (New York: Ballantine Books, 1965), p. 244.

10 Kenneth Grahame, *The Wind in the Willows* (London: Everyman's Library Children's Classics, 1993), pp. 126–7.

11 C.S. Lewis, 'The Weight of Glory', in *C.S. Lewis Essay Collection* (London: Harper Collins, 2002), pp. 98–9.

12 C.E.M. Joad, *Guide to Philosophy* (London: Victor Gollancz, 1946), p. 354.

13 ibid.

14 cf. Kreeft, *Heaven*, p. 201.

15 C.S. Lewis, *Surprised by Joy* (London: Fount, 1998), p. 12.

16 ibid., p. 130.

17 Simone Weil, *Waiting for God* (trans. Emma Crawford; New York: Putnam's, 1951), p. 165.

18 Lewis, *Surprised by Joy*, p. 137.

19 ibid., p. 185.

20 G.K. Chesterton, *The Everlasting Man* (London: Hodder & Stoughton, 1927), p. 106.

21 C.S. Lewis, Preface, *The Pilgrim's Regress* (London: Fount, 1977).

22 ibid.

23 ibid.

24 ibid.

25 ibid.

26 Richard Dawkins, *The God Delusion* (London: Bantam, 2006), p. 347.

27 ibid, p. 347.

[28] Lewis, *Pilgrim's Regress*, p. 15.

[29] Grayling, *Good Book*, p. 9.

[30] Kreeft, *Heaven*, p. 209.

[31] Albert Camus, *The Myth of Sisyphus* (trans. Justin O'Brien; London: Penguin, 1975).

[32] Stephen T. Davis, *God, Reason and Theistic Proofs* (Edinburgh University Press, 1997), p. 177.

[33] Thomas Chalmers, *On Natural Theology*, Book II, p. 233, quoted by T.C. Hammond, *Reasoning Faith: An Introduction to Christian Apologetics* (London: IVP, 1943), p. 56.

[34] C.S. Lewis, *Mere Christianity* (London: Fount, 1997), p. 111; cf. Gary R. Habermas and J.P. Moreland, *Beyond Death: Exploring the Evidence for Immortality* (Wheaton, IL: Crossway, 1998); Peter Kreeft, *Heaven: The Heart's Deepest Longing* (San Francisco: Ignatius, 1989); Jerry L. Walls, *Heaven: The Logic of Eternal Joy* (OUP, 2002).

[35] ibid., p. 112.

[36] ibid.

[37] ibid.

[38] Blaise Pascal, *Pensées and Other Writings* (trans. Honor Levi; OUP, 1995), p. 181.

[39] Lewis, *Mere Christianity*, p. 112.

[40] Dawkins, *God Delusion*, p. 347.

[41] Lewis, *Mere Christianity*, pp. 112–13.

[42] ibid., p. 113.

[43] ibid.

[44] Chalmers, *Natural Theology*, Book II, p. 230, quoted by Hammond, *Reasoning Faith*, p. 56.

[45] C. Stephen Evans, *Why Believe? Reason and Mystery as Pointers to God* (Downers Grove, IL: IVP, 1996), pp. 57–8.

[46] Charles Darwin, quoted in *Now Panic and Freak Out* (Chichester: Summersdale, 2010).

[47] Dawkins, *God Delusion*, p. 347.

[48] James E. Taylor, 'The New Atheists', in *Internet Encyclopedia of Philosophy* www.iep.utm.edu/n-atheis/.

[49] Alvin Plantinga, *Where the Conflict Really Lies: Science, Religion, and Naturalism* (OUP, 2011), p. 49.

[50] Daniel Dennett, 'Review of Richard Dawkins' *The God Delusion* for *Free Inquiry*, October 10, 2006' www.philvaz.com/apologetics/DawkinsGodDelusionReviewFreeInquiry.pdf.

51 Jeremy Pierce commenting on 'Dawkins Review' http://prosblogion.ektopos.com/archives/2006/10/dawkins-review.html.

52 James Hannam, 'The God Delusion by Richard Dawkins' www.bede.org.uk/goddelusion.htm.

53 Daniel Dennett, 'Review of Richard Dawkins' *The God Delusion* for *Free Inquiry*, October 10, 2006' www.philvaz.com/apologetics/DawkinsGodDelusionReviewFreeInquiry.pdf.

54 Dennett, 'Review of Richard Dawkins' *The God Delusion* for *Free Inquiry*, October 10, 2006' www.philvaz.com/apologetics/ Dawkins-GodDelusionReviewFreeInquiry.pdf.

55 cf. Last Seminary, 'Philosophy of Religion Articles' www.lastseminary.com/philosophy-of-religion-article/.

56 Peter Kreeft and Ronald Tacelli, 'Twenty Arguments for the Existence of God' www.peterkreeft.com/topics-more/20_arguments-gods-existence.htm.

57 Alvin Plantinga, 'Two Dozen or so Theistic Arguments' www.calvin.edu/academic/philosophy/virtual_library/articles/pl antinga_alvin/two_dozen_or_so_theistic_arguments.pdf.

58 P.Z. Myers, 'Bad Religion' http://richarddawkins.net/article,211, Bad-Religion,PZ-Myers--Seed-Magazine.

59 Richard Dawkins, *The God Delusion* (London: Black Swan, 2007), p. 131.

60 Alvin Plantinga, 'The Dawkins Confusion', *Books and Culture*, March-April 2007 www.christianitytoday.com/bc/2007/002/1.21.html.

61 Barney Zwartz, 'The God Delusion' http://richarddawkins.net/articles/366-the-god-delusion-review.

62 Michael Ruse, 'The God Delusion', Isis (December 2007).

63 Thomas Nagel, 'Fear of Religion', *The New Republic* www.tnr.com/article/the-fear-religion.

64 Jay Tolson, 'The New Unbelievers' www.templeton-cambridge.org fellows/tolson/publications/2006.11.05/the_new_unbelievers/.

65 Quentin Smith, cover endorsement.

66 cf. William Lane Craig and James D. Sinclair, 'The Kalam Cosmological Argument' http://commonsenseatheism.com/wp-content/uploads/2009/05/craig-and-sinclair-the-kalam-cosmological-argument.pdf.

67 cf. Mark D. Lindville, 'The Moral Argument' http://commonsenseatheism.com/wp-content/uploads/2009/11/Linville-The-Moral-Argument.pdf.

68 cf. Timothy McGrew and Lydia McGrew, 'The Argument from Miracles: A Cumulative Case for the Resurrection of Jesus of Nazareth' www.lydiamcgrew.com/Resurrectionarticlesinglefile.pdf.

69 Paul Copan, 'Interview with Paul Copan: Is Yahweh a Moral Monster?' www.epsociety.org/blog/2008/04/interview-with-paul-copan-is-yahweh.asp.

70 Peter Atkins, *On Being: A Scientist's Exploration of the Great Questions of Existence* (OUP, 2011), p. xi.

71 Kreeft, *Heaven*, p. 202.

72 ibid., pp. 202–3.

73 Richard Purtill, *C.S. Lewis' Case for the Christian Faith* (San Francisco: Ignatius, 2004), pp. 38–9.

74 Steve Lovell, 'Philosophical Themes from C.S. Lewis' http://myweb.tiscali.co.uk/annotations/phd_thesis.html.

75 John Beversluis, *C.S. Lewis and the Search for Rational Religion* (Grand Rapids, MI: Eerdmans, 1985), p. 19.

76 cf. 'The Argument from Desire' http://proofofgod.org/index.php/arguments-fo-the-existence-of-god/argument-from-desire.

77 Edward M. Cook, 'Does Joy Lead to God? Lewis, Beversluis, and the Argument from Desire' www.lastseminary.com/argument-from-desire/Does%20Joy%20Lead%20to%20God%20-%20Lewis%20Beversluis%20and%20the%20Argument%20from%20Desire.pdf.

78 C.S. Lewis, *The Personal Heresy: A Controversy* (OUP, 1965), pp. 29–30.

79 Beversluis, *Search for Rational Religion*, quoted by Kreeft, *Heaven*, p. 229.

80 Jacques Maritain, *Approaches to God* (New York: Harper & Brothers, 1954), p. 112.

81 C.S. Lewis, 'The Weight of Glory', in *C.S. Lewis Essay Collection*, p. 99.

82 Lewis, *Surprised by Joy*, p. 178.

83 ibid.

84 Beversluis, *Search for Rational Religion*, quoted by Kreeft, *Heaven*, p. 230.

85 ibid.

86 Adam Barkman, *C.S. Lewis and Philosophy as a Way of Life* (Allentown, PA: Zossima, 2009), p. 97.

87 Kreeft, *Heaven*, p. 230.

88 ibid.

89 Lewis, *Mere Christianity*, p. 112.

[90] ibid., p. 225.

[91] Albert Camus, *The Fall* (New York: Random House, 1956), p. 133.

[92] Friedrich Nietzsche, *The Portable Nietzsche* (ed. Walter Kaufmann; New York: Doubleday, 1954), p. 441.

[93] Jean-Paul Sartre, *The Words* (trans. B. Frenchman; New York: George Braziller, 1964), pp. 97, 102.

[94] Arthur F. Holmes, *All Truth Is God's Truth* (Leicester: IVP, 1979).

[95] Jean-Paul Sartre, quoted by Norman L. Geisler and Winfried Corduan, *Philosophy of Religion* (Grand Rapids, MI: Baker, 2nd edn, 1988), p. 72.

[96] Bruce Sheiman, *An Atheist Defends Religion: Why Humanity Is Better Off With Religion Than Without It* (New York: Alpha, 2009), p. ix.

[97] H.G. Wells, quoted by C.E.M. Joad, *Guide to Philosophy* (London: Victor Gollancz, 1946), p. 33.

[98] Bertrand Russell, 'A Free Man's Worship', in *Why I Am Not a Christian and Other Essays* (London: Routledge, 1979).

[99] Peter Kreeft and Ronald Tacelli, *Handbook of Christian Apologetics* (Crowborough: Monarch, 1995), p. 249.

[100] Bertrand Russell, *The Autobiography of Bertrand Russell* (Boston: Little Brown, 1968), pp. 125–6.

[101] Bertrand Russell, quoted by Philip Yancey, *Disappointment with God* (Grand Rapids, MI: Zondervan, 2003), p. 253.

[102] Kreeft and Tacelli, *Handbook of Christian Apologetics*, p. 80.

[103] Clark H. Pinnock, *Reason Enough: A Case for the Christian Faith* (Exeter: Paternoster, 1980), pp. 35–6.

[104] ibid., p. 37.

[105] Stephen D. Schwarz, 'Philosophy: Introduction', in *The Intellectuals Speak Out about God* (ed. Roy Abraham Varghese; Chicago: Regner Gateway, 1984), pp. 98, 121–2.

[106] Lewis, *Pilgrim's Regress*, p. 15.

Chapter 4: The Argument from Reason

[1] C.S. Lewis, 'Evil and God', in *C.S. Lewis Essay Collection: Faith, Christianity and the Church* (ed. Lesley Walmsley; London: HarperCollins, 2002), p. 93.

[2] C.S. Lewis, *All My Road before Me: The Diary of C.S. Lewis* (ed. Walter Hooper; London: Harvest, 1991), p. 281.

3 Bertrand Russell, 'A Free Man's Worship' www.philosophicalsociety.com/Archives/A%20Free%20Man's%20Worship.htm.

4 Bertrand Russell, 'What I Believe', in *Why I Am Not a Christian* (London: Routledge, 1996), pp. 42, 47.

5 Lewis, *All My Road*, p. 281.

6 ibid.

7 'Lewis himself encountered the Argument from Reason in conversations with Owen Barfield, became persuaded that the argument was a good one, and in consequence rejected the naturalistic realism he had hitherto accepted . . .' – Victor Reppert, 'Some Supernatural Reasons Why My Critics Are Wrong', *Philosophia Christi* 3:1 (2003): p. 77.

8 C.S. Lewis, *Surprised by Joy* (London: Fount, 1998), pp. 161–2.

9 C.E.M. Joad, *Guide to Modern Thought* (London: Faber, 1933), pp. 58–9.

10 Henry F. Schaefer, *Science and Christianity: Conflict or Coherence?* (Athens, GA: University of Georgia, 2003), p. 136.

11 Richard Dawkins, 'Is Science Killing the Soul?' www.edge.org/documents/archive/edge53.html.

12 Peter Atkins, *On Being: A Scientist's Exploration of the Great Questions of Existence* (OUP, 2011), p. 89.

13 ibid.

14 Sam Harris, *The End of Faith: Religion, Terror, and the Future of Religion* (London: Free Press, 2006), pp. 208–9.

15 ibid., p. 207.

16 J.P. Moreland, 'The Argument from Consciousness', in *The Rationality of Theism* (ed. Paul Copan and Paul K. Moser; London: Routledge, 2003), p. 211.

17 Atkins, *On Being*, p. 89.

18 Susan Blackmore, *Conversations on Consciousness* (OUP, 2005), pp. 3–4.

19 Ned Block, 'Consciousness', in *A Companion to Philosophy of Mind* (ed. Samuel Guttenplan; Oxford: Blackwell, 1994), p. 211.

20 Francis Crick in Blackmore, *Conversations on Consciousness*, p. 68.

21 Richard Dawkins, 'Is Science Killing the Soul?' www.edge.org/documents/archive/edge53.html.

22 Jerry Fodor, 'The Big Idea: Can There Be a Science of Mind?', *Times Literary Supplement*, 3 July 1992, p. 5.

23 A.C. Grayling, 'Consciousness', in *The Mystery of Things: Life, and What It Means* (London: Phoenix, 2007), p. 194.

24 A.C. Grayling, 'Body and Soul', in *Thinking of Answers* (London: Bloomsbury, 2011), p. 36.

[25] Stuart Hameroff and Roger Penrose, 'Conscious Events as Orchestrated Space-Time Selections', in *The Nature of Nature: Examining the Role of Naturalism in Science* (ed. Bruce L. Gordon and William A. Dembski; Wilmington, DE: ISI, 2011), p. 790.

[26] Sam Harris, *The Moral Landscape: How Science Can Determine Human Values* (London: Bantam, 2011), p. 158.

[27] Steven Pinker, 'The Mystery of Consciousness', *Time* magazine, 19 January 2007. www.time.com/time/magazine/article/0,9171,1580394-1,00.html.

[28] Victor J. Stenger, *The New Atheism: Taking a Stand for Science and Reason* (New York: Prometheus, 2009), pp. 184, 187.

[29] James Le Fanu, *Why Us? How Science Rediscovered the Mystery of Ourselves* (London: Harper, 2009), p. 177; cf. 'Matter and the Mind' http://intelligentdesign.podomatic.com/player/web/2009-06-22T14_42_40-07_00.

[30] ibid.

[31] ibid.

[32] Dawkins, 'Is Science Killing the Soul?' www.edge.org/documents/archive/edge53.html.

[33] David Chalmers in Blackmore, *Conversations on Consciousness*, pp. 38, 42.

[34] ibid., p. 23.

[35] Anthony O'Hear, *Philosophy* (London: Continuum, 2001), p. 13.

[36] Robert C. Koons and George Bealer, *The Waning of Materialism* (OUP, 2010), pp. ix, xvii, xx.

[37] Moreland, *Consciousness and the Existence of God*, p. viii.

[38] David Chalmers http://fragments.consc.net/djc/2005/09/jaegwon_kim_com.html, my italics.

[39] William Hasker, 'Persons as Emergent Substances', in *Soul, Body and Survival* (ed. Kevin Corcoran; Ithaca: Cornell University Press, 2001), p. 107.

[40] C. Stephen Evans, 'Separable Souls: Dualism, Selfhood, and the Possibility of Life after Death' www.lastseminary.com/dualism/Separable%20Souls%20-%20Dualism%20Selfhood%20and%20the%20Possibility%20of%20Life%20after%20Death.pdf.

[41] Edward Feser, *Philosophy of Mind: A Short Introduction* (Oxford: OneWorld, 2005), p. x.

[42] Kevin Corcoran, *Introduction, Soul, Body and Survival* (ed. Kevin Corcoran; Ithaca: Cornell University Press, 2001), p. 2.

[43] John Heil, *Philosophy of Mind: A Contemporary Introduction* (London: Routledge, 1998), p. 53.

[44] 'Nick Pollard Talks to Dr Richard Dawkins' www.damaris.org/content/content.php?type=5&id=102.

[45] Richard Dawkins, *The Blind Watchmaker* (London: Penguin, 1988), p. 13.

[46] Dawkins, 'Is Science Killing the Soul?' www.edge.org/documents/archive/edge53.html.

[47] William Hasker, 'How Not to Be a Reductivist', PCID 2.3.5 (October 2003) www.iscid.org/papers/Hasker_NonReductivism_103103.pdf.

[48] ibid.

[49] Dawkins, *Blind Watchmaker,* p. 151, my italics.

[50] Richard Dawkins, 'Genes and Determinism', in *What Philosophers Think* (ed. Julian Baggini and Jeremy Stangroom; London: Continuum, 2003), p. 51.

[51] B.F. Skinner, *Beyond Freedom and Dignity* (Cambridge: Hackett, 2002), pp. 200–01.

[52] Mary Midgely, 'Against Humanism', *New Humanist* 125 (November/December 2010). http://newhumanist.org.uk/2419/against-humanism.

[53] C. S. Lewis, 'The Empty Universe', *Present Concerns* (London: Fount, 1991), p. 81.

[54] ibid., p. 81.

[55] ibid., p. 83.

[56] ibid., p. 85.

[57] Richard Purtill, *Thinking about Religion: A Philosophical Introduction to Religion* (Harlow: Longman, 1978), p. 6.

[58] ibid., p. 10.

[59] Victor Reppert, 'The Argument from Reason', in *The Blackwell Companion to Natural Theology* (ed. William Lane Craig and J.P. Moreland; Oxford: Wiley-Blackwell, 2009), p. 388.

[60] Victor Reppert, *C.S. Lewis's Dangerous Idea* (Downers Grove, IL: IVP, 2003), p. 51.

[61] Paul M. Churchland, *Matter and Consciousness* (MIT Press, 1988), p. 21.

[62] John C. Lennox, *God's Undertaker: Has Science Buried God?* (Oxford: Lion, 2009), p. 57.

[63] C.S. Lewis, *Miracles* (London: Fount, 1998), p. 11.

[64] ibid., p. 14.

[65] Thomas V. Morris, *Francis Schaeffer's Apologetics: A Critique* (Chicago: Moody Press, 1976), p. 42.

[66] Lewis, *Miracles*, p. 14.

[67] ibid.

[68] ibid., p. 15.

[69] ibid. According to Arthur J. Balfour: 'The business of philosophy is to deal with the grounds, not the causes of belief. There is no distinction which has to be kept more steadily in view than this between the causes or antecedents which produce a belief, and the grounds or reasons which justify one.' – *A Defence of Philosophic Doubt: Being an Essay on the Foundations of Belief* (London: Macmillan, 1879), p. 5.

[70] Thomas Nagel, *The Last Word* (New York: OUP, 1997), p. 129.

[71] Lewis, *Miracles*, p. 15.

[72] ibid., pp. 15–20.

[73] Henry Melvill Gwatkin, *The Knowledge of God and Its Historical Development* (Edinburgh: T&T Clark, 3rd edn, 1918), p. 65.

[74] A.E. Taylor, *Does God Exist?* (London: Fontana, 1945), p. 41.

[75] William Hasker, *The Emergent Self* (Ithaca: Cornell University Press, 1999), p. 71.

[76] C. S. Lewis, 'Religion without Dogma?', *Timeless at Heart* (London: Fount, 1991), p. 92.

[77] Hasker, *Emergent Self*, pp. 67–8.

[78] Thanks to Professor Angus J. Menuge for correspondence on this issue.

[79] Karl Popper, *Objective Knowledge: An Evolutionary Approach* (OUP, 1972), p. 223.

[80] Daniel Dennett, *Science and Religion: Are They Compatible?* (ed. James P. Sterba; OUP, 2011), p. 35.

[81] Alvin Plantinga, *Science and Religion: Are They Compatible?* (ed. James P. Sterba; OUP, 2011), p. 43.

[82] Victor Reppert, 'Several Formulations of the Argument from Reason', *Philosophia Christi* 5:1 (2003): p. 24.

[83] John Searle, *Minds, Brains, and Science* (Cambridge, MA: Harvard University Press, 1984), pp. 32–3.

[84] John Searle, 'Do Brains Make Minds?', on *Closer to Truth*, quoted by Lee Strobel, *The Case for a Creator* (Grand Rapids, MI; Zondervan, 2004), p. 248.

[85] Mark Baker, 'Brains and Souls; Grammar and Speaking', in *The Soul Hypothesis: Investigations into the Existence of the Soul* (ed.

Mark C. Baker and Stewart Goetz; London: Continuum, 2011), p. 92.

86 Matt Lawrence, *Like a Splinter in Your Mind: The Philosophy Behind the 'Matrix' Trilogy* (Oxford: Blackwell, 2004), p. 51.

87 Angus Menuge, personal correspondence, January 2007.

88 John Searle in Blackmore, *Conversations on Consciousness*, p. 210.

89 Dennett, *Science and Religion*, p. 35.

90 Aristotle, quoted by Mortimer J. Adler, *Aristotle for Everybody* (New York: Simon & Schuster, 1997), pp. 183–4.

91 Lewis, 'Religion without Dogma?', p. 93.

92 C.S. Lewis, 'Answers to Questions about Christianity', in *C.S. Lewis Essay Collection*, p. 321.

93 C.S. Lewis, 'De Futilitate', in *Christian Reflections* (ed. Walter Hooper; London: Fount, 1991), pp. 88–9.

94 Richard Taylor, *Metaphysics* (Englewood Cliffs, NJ: Prentice Hall, 1974), p. 115.

95 ibid. At the very least, one would be assuming the existence of a supervising intelligence that would have acted to ensure that the words spelt out by the stones were truthful if whatever natural forces were involved in their formation didn't produce such a result on their own. Of course, as an instance of 'specified complexity', it is more plausible to attribute the arrangement of stones to the actions of an intelligent designer.

96 ibid., pp. 118–19.

97 Paul Copan, 'My Recent Interaction with Richard Dawkins' www.reclaimingthemind.org/blog/2011/03/my-recent-interaction-with-richard-dawkins/.

98 ibid., audio clip.

99 ibid.

100 ibid.

101 ibid.

102 ibid.

103 ibid. One wonders if that hesitation in Dawkins' answer marks a switch from saying something on-topic like 'why scientific rationalism is rational' to the off-topic 'why scientific rationalism is true'?

104 Copan, 'My Recent Interaction with Richard Dawkins' www.reclaimingthemind.org/blog/2011/03/my-recent-interaction-with-richard-dawkins/.

[105] E. Jonathan Lowe, 'Rational Selves and Freedom of Action', in *Analytic Philosophy without Naturalism* (ed. Antonella Corrandini, Sergio Galvan and E. Jonathan Lowe; London: Routledge, 2010), p. 177.

[106] Raymond Tallis, *Aping Mankind: Neuromania, Darwinitis and the Misrepresentation of Humanity* (Durham: Acumen, 2011), p. 339.

[107] Richard Dawkins, *Sunday Telegraph*, 18 October 1998.

[108] Richard Dawkins, *The God Delusion* (London: Bantam, 2006), p. 368.

[109] Leslie D. Weatherhead, *The Christian Agnostic* (London: Hodder & Stoughton, 1965), p. 47.

[110] Arthur J. Balfour, *Theism and Humanism* (Seattle: Inkling Books, 2000), pp. 147–8.

[111] G.K. Chesterton, *Orthodoxy* (Thirsk: House of Stratus, 2001), pp. 20–21.

[112] Chesterton, *Orthodoxy*, p. 21.

[113] Richard Rorty, 'Untruth and Consequences', *The New Republic*, 31 July 1995, p. 36.

[114] John Gray, *Straw Gods: Thoughts on Humans and Other Animals* (London: Granta, 2002), pp. 20, 26, 27.

[115] Patricia Churchland, quoted by Alvin Plantinga, *Where the Conflict Really Lies: Science, Religion, and Naturalism* (OUP, 2011), p. 315.

[116] John F. Haught, *God and the New Atheism: A Critical Response to Dawkins, Harris, and Hitchens* (London: WJK, 2008), p. 49.

[117] Stenger, *New Atheism*, p. 72.

[118] André Comte-Sponville, *The Book of Atheist Spirituality: An Elegant Argument for Spirituality without God* (London: Bantam, 2008), p. 82.

[119] Harris, *Moral Landscape*, p. 66.

[120] Alvin Plantinga, 'Evolution versus Naturalism', in *The Nature of Nature* (ed. Gordon and Dembski), p. 139.

[121] ibid., p. 146.

[122] Charles Darwin, letter to William Graham, 3 July 1881, in *The Life and Letters of Charles Darwin* (ed. Francis Darwin; University Press of the Pacific, 2001).

[123] Stephen Stitch, 'Evolution and Rationality', in *The Fragmentation of Reason* (Cambridge, MA: MIT Press, 1990), p. 56.

[124] Dennett, *Science and Religion*, p. 35.

[125] Plantinga, *Science and Religion*, pp. 67–8.

[126] ibid., pp. 69–70.

[127] Plantinga, 'Evolution versus Naturalism', p. 148.

128 Hasker, *Emergent Self*, p. 76.
129 ibid., p. 79.
130 Lewis, *Miracles*, pp. 18, 20–21.
131 Geoffrey Madell, *Mind and Materialism* (Edinburgh University Press, 1988), p. 11.
132 H.W.B. Joseph, *Some Problems in Ethics* (OUP, 1931), pp. 14–15.
133 C.E.M. Joad, *Guide to Philosophy* (London: Victor Gollancz, 1946), pp. 535–6.
134 Lewis, *Miracles*, p. 16.
135 ibid.
136 Lewis, 'De Futilitate', pp. 87–8.
137 C.S. Lewis, *The Discarded Image* (CUP, 1964), pp. 165–6.
138 Howard Robinson, *Matter and Sense* (CUP, 2009), p. 3.
139 Tallis, *Aping Mankind*, p. 359.
140 Dallas Willard, 'Knowledge and Naturalism', in *Naturalism: A Critical Analysis* (ed. William Lane Craig and J.P. Moreland; London: Routledge, 2001), p. 39.
141 John Searle, *The Rediscovery of the Mind* (Cambridge, MA: MIT Press, 1992), p. 51.
142 J.P. Moreland, *Scaling the Secular City* (Grand Rapids, MI: Baker, 1987), p. 96.
143 Willard, 'Knowledge and Naturalism', p. 44.
144 Peter Geach, *The Virtues* (CUP, 1977), p. 52.
145 Lewis, *Miracles*, p. 18.
146 Hasker, 'How Not to Be a Reductivist', *PCID* 2.3.5 (October 2003) www.iscid.org/papers/Hasker_NonReductivism_103103.pdf.
147 Reppert, *Dangerous Idea*, pp. 87, 101.
148 Stuart C. Hackett, *The Reconstruction of the Christian Revelation Claim* (Grand Rapids, MI: Baker, 1984), p. 111.
149 Lewis, *Miracles*, p. 28.
150 ibid.
151 ibid., p. 29.
152 Keith Ward, *Is Religion Irrational?* (Oxford: Lion, 2011), p. 61.
153 Nagel, *Last Word*, p. 140.
154 ibid., p. 130.
155 Anthony O'Hear, *Philosophy* (London: New Century, 2001), p. 125.
156 Peter Cave, *Humanism* (Oxford: OneWorld, 2009), p. 29.
157 ibid.

158 Angus J. Menuge, *Agents under Fire* (New York: Rowman & Littlefield, 2004), p. 84.
159 Moreland, *Scaling the Secular City*, p. 103.
160 C.S. Lewis, 'The Moral Good: Its Place among the Values', p. 18, quoted by Adam Barkman, *C.S. Lewis and Philosophy as a Way of Life* (Allentown, PA: Zossima, 2009), p. 219.
161 Bertrand Russell, 'What I Believe', in *Why I Am Not a Christian* (London: Routledge, 1996), pp. 42, 47.
162 Lewis, 'Moral Good', pp. 23, 25.
163 ibid., p. 43.
164 Lewis, 'Religion without Dogma?', p. 95.

Chapter 5: The Problem of Goodness

1 Christopher Hitchens, *God Is Not Great: The Case against Religion* (London: Atlantic, 2007), p. 256.
2 Christopher W. Mitchell, Foreword to Douglas Gresham, *Jack's Life: The Life Story of C.S. Lewis* (Nashville, TN: Broadman & Holman, 2005).
3 Douglas Gresham, *Jack's Life: The Life Story of C.S. Lewis* (Nashville, TN: Broadman & Holman, 2005), p. 44.
4 C.S. Lewis, *Surprised by Joy* (London: Fount, 1998), p. 151.
5 Lewis, *Surprised by Joy*, pp. 151–2.
6 ibid., p. 151.
7 Gresham, *Jack's Life*, p. 46.
8 ibid., p. 49.
9 C.S. Lewis, *The Abolition of Man* (London: Fount, 1999), p. 13.
10 Thomas L. Carson and Paul K. Moser, Introduction, *Moral Relativism: A Reader* (OUP, 2001), p. 2
11 C.S. Lewis, 'De Futilitate', in *Christian Reflections* (ed. Walter Hooper; London: Fount, 1991), p. 85.
12 The book in question is Alex King and Martin Ketley's *The Control of Language*. Lewis calls it 'the Green book', and its cover was indeed light green. The authors were influenced by the writings of A.J. Ayer and I.A. Richards; cf. Joel D. Heck, *Irrigating Deserts: C.S. Lewis on Education* (Wheaton, IL: Concordia Academic Press, 2005), Appendix III, p. 107.
13 In the Romantic era, 'sublime' replaced 'beautiful' as the pre-eminent aesthetic term of praise.

14 C.S. Lewis, *The Abolition of Man* (London: Fount, 1999), p. 7.

15 Quoted, ibid.

16 Quoted, ibid., p. 8.

17 Lewis, *Abolition of Man*, p. 8.

18 ibid.

19 W.D. Ross, *The Right and the Good* (OUP, 1930), p. 128.

20 Russ Shafer-Landau, *Whatever Happened to Good and Evil?* (OUP, 2003), p. 35.

21 Lewis, *Abolition of Man*, p. 14.

22 ibid.

23 ibid, p. 16.

24 Roger Scruton, *Beauty* (OUP, 2009), pp. x, 6, 32.

25 Lewis, 'De Futilitate', p. 94.

26 ibid., p. 85.

27 Arthur F. Holmes, *Ethics: Approaching Moral Decisions* (Nottingham: IVP, 2nd edn, 2007), p. 32.

28 C.S. Lewis, *Mere Christianity* (London: Fount, 1997), p. 16.

29 Lewis, *Surprised by Joy*, p. 49.

30 C.S. Lewis, *The Problem of Pain* (London: Fount, 1977), pp. 11–12.

31 Lewis, 'De Futilitate', p. 90.

32 Lewis, *Mere Christianity*, pp. 31–2.

33 C.S. Lewis, *All My Road Before Me: The Diary of C.S. Lewis* (ed. Walter Hooper; London: Harvest, 1991), p. 281.

34 C.S. Lewis, 'On Living in the Atomic Age', in *C.S. Lewis Essay Collection: Faith, Christianity and the Church* (ed. Lesley Walmsley; London: HarperCollins, 2002), pp. 364–5.

35 Lewis, 'De Futilitate', in *Christian Reflections*, p. 95.

36 On Thursday 10 January 1924 Lewis records: 'I . . . went to the Union and took out . . . Sorley's *Moral Values and the Idea of God* . . .' – C.S. Lewis, *All My Road Before Me*, p. 283; cf. Joel D. Heck, *Irrigating Deserts: C.S. Lewis on Education* (St Louis: Concordia, 2005), Appendix I, p. 150.

37 W.R. Sorley, *Moral Values and the Idea of God* (CUP, 3rd edn, 1919), in *Philosophy of Religion* (ed. George L. Abernathy and Thomas A. Langford; London: Macmillan, 2nd edn, 1968), p. 203.

38 ibid.

39 ibid., p. 204.

40 ibid.

41 ibid.

42 ibid., p. 202.

[43] Bruce Sheiman, *An Atheist Defends Religion: Why Humanity Is Better Off with Religion than without It* (New York: Alpha, 2009), p. xiv.

[44] William Lane Craig, *God? A Debate between a Christian and an Atheist* (OUP, 2004), p. 17.

[45] John Cottingham, 'Philosophers Are Finding Fresh Meanings in Truth, Goodness and Beauty', *The Times*, 17 June 2006.

[46] Peter Cave, *Humanism* (Oxford: OneWorld, 2009), p. 146.

[47] Sam Harris, *The End of Faith: Religion, Terror, and the Future of Reason* (London: Free Press, 2006), p. 183.

[48] C.S. Lewis, 'On Ethics', in *C.S. Lewis Essay Collection*, p. 304.

[49] Lewis, *Mere Christianity*, p. 5.

[50] Adolf Hitler, quoted by Francis J. Beckwith and Gregory Koukl, *Relativism: Feet Firmly Planted in Mid-Air* (Grand Rapids, MI: Baker, 1998), p. 155.

[51] Richard Swinburne, *The Existence of God* (OUP, 1991), p. 97.

[52] Shafer-Landau, *Whatever Happened to Good and Evil?*, pp. 16–17.

[53] Quoted by Charles Taliaferro, *Contemporary Philosophy of Religion* (Oxford: Blackwell, 2001), p. 199.

[54] Friedrich Nietzsche, *The Portable Nietzsche* (ed. Walter Kaufmann; New York: Doubleday, 1954).

[55] Margarita Rosa Levin, 'A Defence of Objectivity', in *Classics of Philosophy, vol III: The Twentieth Century* (ed. Louis J. Pojman; OUP, 2001), pp. 550, 558.

[56] C.S. Lewis, *Mere Christianity*, p. 20.

[57] Craig J. Hazen, 'Can We Be Good without God?' http://magazine.biola.edu/article/11-summer/can-we-be-good-without-god/.

[58] Paul Copan, *Is God a Moral Monster? Making Sense of the Old Testament God* (Grand Rapids, MI: Baker, 2011), p. 210.

[59] Harris, *End of Faith*, p. 171.

[60] Lewis, 'On Ethics', pp. 305–6.

[61] Peter Singer, ed., *A Companion to Ethics* (Oxford: Blackwell, 1991), pp. 553, 544.

[62] J.L. Mackie, *The Miracle of Theism* (OUP, 1982), p. 36.

[63] Harris, *End of Faith*, p. 172.

[64] ibid.

[65] ibid.

[66] A.C. Grayling, 'Where Are We in History?', in *To Set Prometheus Free: Essays on Religion, Reason and Humanity* (London: Oberon, 2009), p. 17.

67 Richard Dawkins, *The God Delusion* (London: Bantam, 2006), p. 211.

68 Dawkins, *God Delusion*, p. 226.

69 ibid., pp. 226–7.

70 A.C. Grayling, *Conversations on Religion* (ed. Mick Gordon and Chris Wilkinson; London: Continuum, 2008), p. 2.

71 Christopher Hitchens, *God Is Not Great* (New York: Twelve, 2007), p. 214.

72 C.S. Lewis, quoted in Adam Barkman, *C.S. Lewis and Philosophy as a Way of Life* (Allentown, PA: Zossima, 2009), p. 345.

73 Lewis, *Mere Christianity*, p. 76.

74 Sheiman, *Atheist Defends Religion*, p. 26.

75 J.P. Moreland and William Lane Craig, *Philosophical Foundations for a Christian Worldview* (Downers Grove, IL: IVP, 2003), p. 492.

76 Paul Copan, *True for You, but Not for Me* (Minneapolis, MN: Bethany House, 1998), p. 45.

77 Richard Dawkins, 'God's Utility Function', *Scientific American*, November 1995, p. 85, my italics.

78 F.C. Copleston, *Contemporary Philosophy: Studies of Logical Positivism and Existentialism* (London: Burns & Oates, 1956), p. 175.

79 Joel Marks, 'An Amoral Manifesto: Part I' www.philosophynow.org/issue80/An_Amoral_Manifesto_Part_I?vm=r.

80 Richard Dawkins, Afterword, in *What Is Your Dangerous Idea?* (ed. John Brockman; London: Pocket Books, 2006), p. 307.

81 Chistopher Hitchens, in *Is Christianity Good for the World? A Debate* (Moscow, ID: Canon Press, 2009), p. 36.

82 Chistopher Hitchens, in *Hitchens vs Blair: Is Religion a Force for Good in the World?* (ed. Richard Griffiths; London: Black Swan, 2011), p. 51.

83 Stephen Unwin, 'Dawkins Needs to Show Some Doubt', *Guardian Online* www.guardian.co.uk/commentisfree/2006/sep/29/comment.religion.

84 H.P. Owen, 'Why Morality Implies the Existence of God', edited extract from *The Moral Argument for Christian Theism* (George Allen and Unwin, 1965), in *Philosophy of Religion: A Guide and Anthology* (ed. Brian Davies; OUP, 2000), p. 648.

85 Albert Einstein, cited by John C. Lennox, *Gunning for God* (Oxford: Lion, 2011), p. 99.

86 Sam Harris, *The Moral Landscape: How Science Can Determine Human Values* (London: Bantam, 2010), p. 1.

87 Dawkins, *God Delusion*, p. 80.

88 'Richard Dawkins Answers Reddit Questions' http://richard-dawkins.net/videos/547385-richard-dawkins-answers-reddit-questions, my italics.

89 Richard Dawkins, *The Magic of Reality: How We Know What's Really True* (London: Bantam, 2011), p. 238.

90 ibid., pp. 233, 238.

91 'Richard Dawkins Answers Reddit Questions' http://richard-dawkins.net/videos/547385-richard-dawkins-answers-reddit-questions.

92 A.C. Grayling, 'Morality and Empathy', in *Thinking of Answers: Questions in the Philosophy of Everyday Life* (London: Bloomsbury, 2011), p. 7.

93 A.C. Grayling, 'The Moral and the Ethical', in *Thinking of Answers*, p. 15.

94 C.S. Lewis, 'The Moral Good: Its Place among the Values', p. 59, quoted by Barkman, *C.S. Lewis and Philosophy*, p. 332.

95 Lewis, *Problem of Pain*, p. 17.

96 Harris, *Moral Landscape*, p. 10.

97 Bertrand Russell, *The Problems of Philosophy* (OUP, 1980), pp. 42–3.

98 Kenan Malik, 'Test Tube Truths', *New Humanist*, May-June 2011, p. 28.

99 Sam Harris's Opening Speech, 'Are the Foundations of Objective Moral Values Natural or Supernatural?'.

100 Harris, *Moral Landscape*, p. 1.

101 Harris, *End of Faith*, p. 183.

102 Harris's Opening Speech, 'Are the Foundations of Objective Moral Values Natural or Supernatural?'.

103 Harris, *Moral Landscape*, p. 1.

104 Harris's Opening Speech, 'Are the Foundations of Objective Moral Values Natural or Supernatural?'.

105 ibid.

106 Lewis, *Mere Christianity*, p. 16.

107 Harris, *Moral Landscape*, p. 12.

108 Harris's Opening Speech, 'Are the Foundations of Objective Moral Values Natural or Supernatural?'.

109 Harris, *Moral Landscape*, p. 1.

110 ibid., p. 37, my italics.

111 ibid.

112 The reason that (as Harris observes) 'no one thinks that the failure of standard science to silence all possible dissent' (Harris, *Moral*

Landscape, p. 37) based upon disputed values 'has any significance whatsoever' (ibid.) as an argument against science is precisely the same reason we should (contra Harris) 'demand more of a science of morality' (ibid.) – namely, science isn't the same thing as meta-ethics.

113 A.E. Taylor, *Does God Exist?* (London: Fontana, 1961), p. 28.

114 William Lane Craig's Opening Speech, 'Are the Foundations of Objective Moral Values Natural or Supernatural?'.

115 Harris, *Moral Landscape*, p. 106.

116 Harris, *End of Faith*, p. 264.

117 Harris, *Moral Landscape*, p. 112.

118 Richard Dawkins, 'Let's All Stop Beating Basil's Car' http://edge.org/q2006/q06_9.html.

119 Craig's Opening Speech, 'Are the Foundations of Objective Moral Values Natural or Supernatural?'.

120 Harris, *Moral Landscape*, p. 10.

121 ibid.

122 Michael Licona, 'Answering Brian Flemmings' "The God Who Wasn't There"' http://risenjesus.com/the-god-who-wasnt-there.

123 Julian Baggini, *Atheism: A Very Short Introduction* (OUP, 2003), pp. 41–51.

124 Richard Dawkins, *River out of Eden* (New York: Basic Books, 1995), p. 133.

125 Paul Kurtz, *Forbidden Fruit* (Prometheus, 1988), p. 65.

126 cf. C.S. Lewis, *Letters* (London: Fount, 1991), p. 495.

127 Jean-Paul Sartre, *Existentialism Is a Humanism* (New Haven, CT: Yale University Press, 2007), p. 28 www.marxists.org/reference/archive/sartre/works/exist/sartre.htm.

128 Sheiman, *Atheist Defends Religion*, pp. 31, 40–41.

129 Keith E. Yandell, 'Theology, Philosophy, and Evil', in *For Faith and Clarity* (ed. James K. Beilby; Grand Rapids, MI: Baker, 2006), p. 240.

130 Harris, *End of Faith*, p. 170.

131 Plato, *Euthyphro*, 10a, Plato, *The Collected Dialogues of Plato* (trans. Lane Cooper; ed. Edith Hamilton and Huntingdon Cairns; Princeton University Press, 1961), p. 178.

132 Michael Peterson et al, *Reason and Religious Belief: An Introduction to the Philosophy of Religion* (OUP, 1992), p. 85.

133 Shafer-Landau, *Good and Evil?*, p. 79.

134 ibid., p. 78.

135 Beckwith and Koukl, *Relativism*, p. 232.

136 Shafer-Landau, *Good and Evil?*, p. 80.
137 ibid., p. 83.
138 C.S. Lewis, *The Collected Letters of C.S. Lewis*, vol. III, p. 1227, quoted by Barkman, *C.S. Lewis and Philosophy*, p. 353.
139 Taylor, *Does God Exist?*, p. 107.
140 Bruce Sheiman, *Atheist Defends Religion*, p. 31.
141 John Cottingham, *Why Believe?* (London: Continuum, 2009), pp. 26–7.
142 Cottingham, 'Philosophers Are Finding Fresh Meanings'.
143 Lewis, *Mere Christianity*, p. 21.
144 ibid., pp. 24–5.

Chapter 6: Jesus in the Dock

1 C.S. Lewis, 26 March 1940, *Letters* (London: Fount, 1991), p. 345.
2 C.S. Lewis, *All My Road Before Me: The Diary of C.S. Lewis* (ed. Walter Hooper; London: Harcourt, 1991), pp. 431–2.
3 C.S. Lewis, *Miracles* (London: Fount, 1998), p. 29.
4 C.S. Lewis, *Surprised by Joy* (London: Fount, 1998), pp. 162–3.
5 C.S. Lewis, *Mere Christianity* (London: Fount, 1997), pp. 31–2.
6 Lewis, *Mere Christianity*, p. 21.
7 Lewis, *Surprised by Joy*, p. 173.
8 C.S. Lewis, *The Pilgrim's Regress* (London: Fount, 1977), p. 9.
9 C.S. Lewis, 'Fern-Seed and Elephants', in *C.S. Lewis Essay Collection* (ed. Lesley Walmsley; London: HarperCollins, 2002), p. 251.
10 Lewis, *Letters*, p. 138.
11 Humphrey Carpenter, *The Inklings* (London: HarperCollins, 2006), pp. 39–40.
12 Lewis, *Surprised by Joy*, pp. 166–7.
13 C.S. Lewis, *The Collected Letters of C.S. Lewis*, vol. II, p. 145 [25 October 1934], quoted by Adam Barkman, *C.S. Lewis and Philosophy as a Way of Life* (Allentown, PA: Zossima, 2009), p. 22.
14 Lewis, *Surprised by Joy*, pp. 176–7.
15 ibid., p. 178.
16 C.S. Lewis, 'Cross-Examination', quoted by Barkman, *C.S. Lewis and Philosophy*, p. 53.
17 Lewis, *Surprised by Joy*, p. 183.
18 ibid., p. 179.
19 Lewis, *Mere Christianity*, p. 21.

[20] Lewis, *Surprised by Joy*, p. 133.

[21] C.S. Lewis, 'Fern-Seed and Elephants', in *C.S. Lewis Essay Collection*, p. 247.

[22] C.S. Lewis, *Miracles* (New York: Macmillan, 1960), p. 102.

[23] C.S. Lewis, *Studies in Words* (CUP/Canto, 2000), p. 64.

[24] Lewis, *Surprised by Joy*, pp. 173–4.

[25] Lewis, 'Is Theism Important?', in *C.S. Lewis Essay Collection*, p. 57.

[26] C.S. Lewis, *The Problem of Pain* (London: Fount, 1977), p. 14.

[27] ibid., p. 14.

[28] ibid., pp. 17–18.

[29] ibid., p. 18.

[30] ibid., pp. 18–19.

[31] Lewis, *Mere Christianity*, pp. 25–6.

[32] Lewis, *Problem of Pain*, p. 19.

[33] Christopher Hitchens, *God Is Not Great* (London: Atlantic, 2007), p. 209.

[34] C. Stephen Evans, *Why Believe? Reason and Mystery as Pointers to God* (Leicester: IVP, 1996), p. 131.

[35] Lewis, *Mere Christianity*, p. 44.

[36] Lewis, *Letters*, p. 288.

[37] Lewis, *Mere Christianity*, p. 46.

[38] Joel B. Green and Mark D. Baker, *Recovering the Scandal of the Cross: Atonement in New Testament and Contemporary Contexts* (Carlisle: Paternoster, 2000), p. 51.

[39] Keith Ward, *What the Bible Really Teaches: A Challenge for Fundamentalists* (London: SPCK, 2004), pp. 109–10.

[40] ibid., p. 49.

[41] Lewis, *Mere Christianity*, pp. 45–6.

[42] Evans, *Why Believe?*, pp. 130–31.

[43] Lewis, *Mere Christianity*, p. 45.

[44] Lewis, *Letters*, p. 288.

[45] Francis S. Collins, 'The Language of God', in *A Place for Truth* (ed. Dallas Willard; Downers Grove, IL: IVP, 2010), p. 97.

[46] C.S. Lewis, letter to Owen Barfield, April? 1932, *Letters* (London: Fount, 1991), p. 306.

[47] Peter Kreeft, *Between Heaven and Hell: A Dialog Somewhere beyond Death with John F. Kennedy, C.S. Lewis and Aldous Huxley* (Downers Grove, IL: IVP, 1982), pp. 38–9.

[48] John Duncan http://en.wikipedia.org/wiki/Lewis's_trilemma.

[49] G.K. Chesterton, *The Everlasting Man* (London: Hodder & Stoughton, 1927), pp. 229–230.

[50] Lewis, *Mere Christianity*, pp. 42–3.

[51] Quoted by Christopher Hitchens, 'In the Name of the Father, the Sons . . .', *New York Times*, 9 July 2010.

[52] Christopher Hitchens, 'In the Name of the Father, the Sons . . .', *New York Times*, 9 July 2010.

[53] ibid.

[54] ibid.

[55] Lewis, *Mere Christianity*, pp. 54–6.

[56] Hitchens, 'In the Name of the Father'.

[57] Hitchens, *God Is Not Great*, p. 119.

[58] ibid.

[59] ibid.

[60] Christopher Hitchens, 'Q&A: Christopher Hitchens', *The Walrus*, July 2009.

[61] Hitchens, *God Is Not Great*, p. 120.

[62] Hitchens, *God Is Not Great*, p. 118, my italics.

[63] Hitchens, 'Q&A: Christopher Hitchens', *The Walrus*, July 2009, my italics.

[64] Christopher Hitchens, *The Quotable Hitchens* (ed. Windsor Mann; Cambridge, MA: Da Capo, 2011), p. 187.

[65] Richard Dawkins, *The God Delusion* (London: Black Swan, 2007), p. 284.

[66] ibid., pp. 283–4.

[67] Richard Dawkins, 'Atheists for Jesus' www.richarddawkins.net/articles/20.

[68] ibid.

[69] Hitchens, *God Is Not Great*, p. 120.

[70] According to Mark D. Roberts, 'It's likely that this story is true, but that it was added to John well after the evangelist finished his task.' – *Can We Trust the Gospels?* (Wheaton, IL: Crossway, 2007), p. 35.

[71] C.S. Lewis, 'Fern-Seed and Elephants', in *Fern-Seed and Elephants: And Other Essays on Christianity* (ed. Walter Hooper; Glasgow: Fount, 1975), p. 108.

[72] Hitchens, *God Is Not Great*, p. 120.

[73] Lewis, *Letters*, letter to Owen Barfield, April? 1932, p. 306.

[74] Michel Onfray, *In Defence of Atheism: The Case against Christianity, Judaism and Islam* (London: Serpent's Tail, 2007), p. 125.

75 cf. 'Richard Dawkins on Studio 4 in Vancouver – Part 3 of 5' www.youtube.com/watch?v=XwWQamTzjA0&feature=related.

76 Dawkins, *God Delusion*, p. 117.

77 Stephen T. Davis, 'The Mad/Bad/God Trilemma: A Reply to Daniel Howard Snyder' www.lastseminary.com/trilemma/The%20Mad-Bad-God%20Trilemma%20-%20A%20Reply%20to%20-Daniel%20Howard-Snyder.pdf.

78 Nicky Gumbel, *Is God a Delusion?* (London: Alpha, 2008), p. 80.

79 Mike King, *The God Delusion Revisited* (Lulu, 2007), p. 63.

80 Richard Purtill, *Reason to Believe: Why Faith Makes Sense* (San Francisco: Ignatius, 2009), p. 138.

81 Paul Maier, 'Did Jesus Really Exist?', in *Evidence for God* (ed. William A. Dembski and Michael R. Licona; Grand Rapids, MI: Baker, 2010), p. 143.

82 Onfray, *Defence of Atheism*, p. 115.

83 Victor J. Stenger, *The New Atheism: Taking a Stand for Science and Reason* (New York: Prometheus, 2009), p. 58.

84 Hitchens, *God Is Not Great*, p. 114.

85 Christopher Hitchens, *Red Eye*, Fox News Channel, 5 December 2007.

86 Dawkins, *God Delusion*, p. 122.

87 ibid.; cf. Gary R. Habermas, 'A Summary Critique: Questioning the Existence of Jesus' www.garyhabermas.com/articles/crj_summary-critique/crj_summarycritique.htm.

88 'Bart Ehrman on the Existence of Jesus' http://1peter315.word-press.com/2011/07/23/bart-ehrman-on-the-existence-of-jesus/.

89 Michael Grant, *Jesus: An Historian's Review of the Gospels* (New York: Charles Scribner's Sons, 1977), pp. 199–200.

90 Michael Licona, 'Licona's Reply to Doherty' www.risenjesus.com/.

91 Gerd Ludemann, *The Resurrection of Christ: A Historical Inquiry* (New York: Prometheus, 2004), p. 50.

92 J.D. Crossan, *Jesus: A Revolutionary Biography* (San Francisco: HarperCollins, 1994).

93 Bart Ehrman, 'The Historical Jesus: Lecture Transcript and Course Guidebook', Part II (Chantilly, VA: The Teaching Company, 2000), p. 162, quoted by Michael R. Licona, *The Resurrection of Jesus: A New Historiographical Approach* (Nottingham: Apollos, 2010), p. 600.

94 Geza Vermes, *The Resurrection* (London: Penguin, 2008), p. 1.

95 Mark Allan Powell, *The Jesus Debate: Modern Historians Investigate the Life of Jesus* (Oxford: Lion, 1998), p. 180.

[96] Dawkins, *God Delusion*, pp. 118, 121, 122–3.

[97] Richard Dawkins, *The Magic of Reality* (London: Bantam, 2011), p. 262.

[98] N.T. Wright, *Judas and the Gospel of Jesus* (London: SPCK, 2006), p. 30.

[99] Richard Bauckham, *Jesus: A Very Short Introduction* (OUP, 2011), p. 15.

[100] Craig A. Evans, 'Textual Criticism and Textual Confidence: How Reliable Is Scripture?', in *The Reliability of the New Testament: Bart D. Ehrman and Daniel B. Wallace in Dialogue* (ed. Robert B. Stewart; Minneapolis, MN: Fortress, 2011), p. 171.

[101] Darrell L. Bock, *Studying the Historical Jesus: A Guide to Sources and Methods* (Grand Rapids, MI: Baker Academic, 2002), p. 147.

[102] ibid., pp. 147–8.

[103] Daniel B. Wallace, 'Opening Remarks', in *Reliability of the New Testament* (ed. Stewart), p. 34.

[104] Sam Harris, *The Moral Landscape* (London: Bantam, 2010), p. 168.

[105] Winfried Corduan, *No Doubt About It* (Nashville, TN: Broadman & Holman, 1997), p. 193.

[106] Darrell L. Bock and Daniel B. Wallace, *Dethroning Jesus: Exposing Popular Culture's Quest to Unseat the Biblical Christ* (Nashville, TN: Thomas Nelson, 2007), p. 48.

[107] Roberts, *Can We Trust the Gospels?*, p. 37.

[108] Bart Ehrman, *The New Testament: A Historical Introduction to the Early Christian Writings* (New York: OUP, 3rd edn, 2003), p. 481, quoted in *Reliability of The New Testament* (ed. Stewart), p. 31.

[109] Antony Flew in *Did Jesus Rise from the Dead? The Resurrection Debate* (ed. Terry L. Miethe; Eugene, OR: Wipf & Stock, 2003), p. 66.

[110] N.T. Wright, Foreword to F.F. Bruce, *The New Testament Documents: Are They Reliable?* (Grand Rapids, MI: Eerdmans, 2000), p. x.

[111] Harris, *End of Faith*, p. 204.

[112] J.P. Moreland, *Scaling the Secular City* (Grand Rapids, MI: Baker, 1987), p. 149.

[113] Richard Dawkins, *The God Delusion* (London: Black Swan, 2007), p. 119.

[114] A.C. Grayling, *Conversations on Religion* (ed. Mark Gordon and Chris Wilkinson; London: Continuum, 2008), p. 5.

[115] cf. John Dickson, 'The New Atheist's Questionable History' https://publicchristianity.org/library/the-new-atheists-questionable-history.

[116] A.C. Grayling, *The Form of Things: Essays on Life, Ideas and Liberty in the 21st Century* (London: Weidenfeld & Nicolson, 2006), p. 97, my italics.

[117] On the dating of Mark's gospel, cf. Peter S. Williams, *Understanding Jesus: Five Ways to Spiritual Enlightenment* (Milton Keynes: Paternoster, 2011).

[118] Bauckham, *Jesus: A Very Short Introduction*, p. 17.

[119] C.S. Lewis, letter to Arthur Greeves, 12 October 1916, *Letters* (London: Fount, 1988), p. 52.

[120] Gary R. Habermas, *The Verdict of History: Conclusive Evidence from beyond the Bible for the Life of Jesus* (Eastbourne: Monarch, 1990), p. 38.

[121] Michael Green, *Lies, Lies, Lies! Exposing Myths about the Real Jesus* (Nottingham: IVP, 2009), pp. 59–60.

[122] Edwin M. Yamauchi in Lee Strobel, *The Case for the Real Jesus* (Grand Rapids, MI: Zondervan, 2007), p. 165.

[123] Michael Green, 'Jesus in the New Testament', in *The Truth of God Incarnate* (ed. Michael Green; London: Hodder & Stoughton, 1977), pp. 36–8.

[124] Alister McGrath, 'Resurrection and Incarnation', in *Different Gospels: Christian Orthodoxy and Modern Theologies* (ed. Andrew Walker, London: SPCK, 1988), p. 30.

[125] Michael Licona in Lee Strobel, *The Case for the Real Jesus* (Grand Rapids, MI: Zondervan, 2007), p. 161.

[126] C.S. Lewis, *The Collected Letters of C.S. Lewis*, vol. III, p. 1619, quoted by Barkman, *C.S. Lewis and Philosophy*, p. 117.

[127] Licona in Strobel, *Case for the Real Jesus*, p. 160.

[128] Habermas, *Verdict of History*, p. 39.

[129] T.N.D. Mettinger, *The Riddle of Resurrection* (Stockholm; Almqvist & Wicksell, 2001), p. 221.

[130] C.S. Lewis, 'Myth Became Fact', in *God in the Dock* (London: Fount, 1979), pp. 43–5.

[131] Strobel, *Case for the Real Jesus*, p. 186.

[132] Ronald H. Nash, *The Gospel and the Greeks* (New Jersey: Phillipsburg, 2nd edn, 2003), p. 162.

[133] William Lane Craig, *Reasonable Faith: Christian Truth and Apologetics* (Wheaton, IL: Crossway, 2008), p. 391.

[134] Lewis, *All My Road*, p. 379.

[135] George Sayer, *Jack: A Life of C.S. Lewis* (Wheaton, IL: Crossway, 1994), p. 222.

[136] Lewis, *Surprised by Joy*, p. 174.

[137] Sayer, *Jack*, pp. 222–3.

[138] Lewis, 'Fern-Seed and Elephants', in *Fern-Seed and Elephants* (ed. Hooper), pp. 106–7, 108.

[139] A.C. Grayling, *Thinking of Answers: Questions in the Philosophy of Everyday Life* (London: Bloomsbury, 2011), p. 98.

[140] C.S. Lewis, 'What Are We to Make of Jesus Christ?', in *C.S. Lewis Essay Collection*, p. 40.

[141] Lewis, *Surprised by Joy*, pp. 183–4.

[142] Kai Nielson in *Does God Exist? The Debate between Theists and Atheists* (New York: Prometheus, 1993), p. 66.

[143] Lewis, 'What Are We to Make of Jesus Christ?', p. 40.

[144] Green, 'Jesus in the New Testament', p. 40.

[145] Richard Bauckham, *God Crucified: Monotheism and Christology in the New Testament* (Grand Rapids, MI: Eerdmans, 1999), p. 26.

[146] Craig A. Evans, 'The Jesus of History and the Christ of Faith', in *Who Was Jesus? A Jewish-Christian Dialogue* (ed. Paul Copan and Craig A. Evans; London: Westminster-John Knox, 2001) p. 66.

[147] Peter Kreeft, 'Why I Believe Jesus Is the Messiah and Son of God', in *Why I Am a Christian* (ed. Norman L. Geisler and Paul K. Hoffman; Grand Rapids, MI: Baker, rev. edn, 2006), p. 250.

[148] Onfray, *Defence of Atheism*, p. 126.

[149] C.S. Lewis, 'Fern-Seed and Elephants', in *C.S. Lewis Essay Collection*, p. 247.

[150] J.P. Moreland, *The God Question: An Invitation to a Life of Meaning* (Eugene, OR: Harvest House, 2009), p. 111.

[151] Tom Wright, *Simply Christian* (London: SPCK, 2006), p. 101.

[152] Carsten Peter Thiede, *Jesus, Man or Myth?* (Oxford: Lion, 2005), p. 136.

[153] Bauckham, *Jesus: A Very Short Introduction*, pp. 93–4.

[154] Lewis, 'What Are We to Make of Jesus Christ?', p. 41.

[155] C.S. Lewis, quoted by David C. Downing, *The Most Reluctant Convert: C.S. Lewis's Journey to Faith* (Downers Grove, IL: IVP, 2002), p. 46.

[156] Lewis, *Surprised by Joy*, p. 184.

Conclusion: First Things First

[1] A.C. Grayling, 'Celebrity', in *Thinking of Answers: Questions in the Philosophy of Everyday Life* (London: Bloomsbury, 2011), p. 48.

[2] C.S. Lewis, 'Christian Apologetics', in *C.S. Lewis Essay Collection: Faith, Christianity and the Church* (ed. Lesley Walmsley; London: HarperCollins, 2002), p. 148.

³ C.S. Lewis, *Surprised by Joy* (London: Fount, 1998), pp. 207–8.

⁴ Paul Copan, *Contending with Christianity's Critics: Answering New Atheists and Other Objectors* (ed. Paul Copan and William Lane Craig; Nashville, TN: B&H Academic, 2009), p. vii.

⁵ David Bentley Hart, *Atheist Delusions: The Christian Revolution and Its Fashionable Enemies* (London: Yale University Press, 2009), pp. 4, 19–20, 103.

⁶ cf. http://idpluspeterswilliams.blogspot.com/2011/06/william-lane-craig-richard-dawkins-and.html; http://idpluspeterswilliams.blogspot.com/2011/05/richard-dawkins-refuses-calls-to-debate.html; http://idpluspeterswilliams.blogspot.com/2011/09/british-human-ists-toynbee-dawkins.html.

⁷ A.C. Grayling, '"New Atheists" – Grayling and Dawkins – Run Shy of Debating God: "*Better to debate fairies*," says Grayling' (Reasonable Faith Tour 2011 Press Release); cf. 'British Humanists Take to the Bunkers' www.bethinking.org/what-is-apologetics/introductory/british-humanists-take-to-the-bunkers.htm.

⁸ Daniel Came, '"New Atheists" – Grayling and Dawkins – Run Shy of Debating God: "*Better to debate fairies*," says Grayling' (Reasonable Faith Tour 2011 Press Release).

⁹ Terry Eagleton, 'Lunging, Flailing, Mispunching', *London Review of Books* www.lrb.co.uk/v28/n20/terry-eagleton/lunging-flailing-mis-punching.

¹⁰ Christopher Hitchens in *Is Christianity Good for the World? A Debate* (Moscow, ID: Canon, 2009), p. 12.

¹¹ Lewis, *Surprised by Joy*, p. 133.

¹² C.S. Lewis, 'Answers to Questions on Christianity', in *C.S. Lewis Essay Collection*, p. 325.

¹³ Frank Turek and Christopher Hitchens, 'Does God Exist?' Hitchens' Opening Speech www.youtube.com/watch?v=C0NnINofER4&feature=related.
For video of the whole debate cf. www.youtube.com/watch?v=MR2wtrD8HnM.
For an audio recording of the whole debate cf. www.philvaz.com/HitchensTurekDebate.mp3.
For a transcript of the debate cf. http://hitchensdebates.blogspot.com/2010/11/hitchens-vs-turek-vcu.html.

¹⁴ ibid.

[15] cf. Christopher Hitchens and Jay Richards, 'Atheism, Theism and Scientific Evidence for Intelligent Design' www.brianauten.com/Apologetics/debate-richards-hitchens.mp3 (cf. www.youtube.com/watch?v=-nVIIuSG69k&feature=related and www.youtube.com/watch?v=bKbNE9mGDtw&feature=related).

[16] Turek and Hitchens, 'Does God Exist?' Turek's Rebuttal Speech www.youtube.com/watch?v=sqVrbp_9Wq4&feature=related.

[17] ibid., Cross-Questioning www.youtube.com/watch?NR=1&v =I4Jh 9b4Rt8g.

[18] ibid.

[19] ibid.

[20] Frank Turek, 'Turek-Hitchens Debate' www.crossexamined.org/ blog/?p=84.

[21] Hitchens, 'Does God Exist?' www.youtube.com/watch?NR=1&v =s8_kNW6hDI0.

[22] Geoff Crocker, *An Enlightened Philosophy: Can an Atheist Believe Anything?* (Ropley: Winchester Books, 2010), p. 13.

[23] Aldous Huxley, *Ends and Means* (London: Chatto & Windus, 1940), pp. 269–70.

[24] C.S. Lewis, 'Man or Rabbit?', in *C.S. Lewis Essay Collection*, p. 354.

[25] Thomas Chalmers, *On Natural Theology*, vol. I (Bibliolife [1850]), p. 72.

[26] Thomas Nagel, *The Last Word* (New York: OUP, 1997), p. 130.

[27] Émile Cammaerts, *The Laughing Prophet: The Seven Virtues and G.K. Chesterton* (London: Methuen & Co, 1937).

[28] C.S. Lewis, *The Collected Letters of C.S. Lewis*, vol. II (London: HarperCollins, 2007), p. 778 [5 June 1947].

[29] Huxley, *Ends and Means*, p. 257.

[30] Lewis, 'Man or Rabbit?', p. 355.

[31] Roy Abraham Varghese in Antony Flew, *There Is a God* (New York: HarperOne, 2007), pp. xvii–xviii, 161.

[32] Lewis, 'Is Theism Important?', p. 57.

[33] Keith Ward, *The God Conclusion: God and the Western Philosophical Tradition* (London: DLT, 2009), p. 147.

[34] Alvin Plantinga, back cover endorsement quote, John Lennox, *Gunning for God: Why the New Atheists Are Missing the Target* (Oxford: Lion, 2011).

[35] C.S. Lewis, 'On Obstinacy in Belief', in *C.S. Lewis Essay Collection*, pp. 213–14.

[36] Lewis, 'Man or Rabbit?', pp. 352, 354–5.